RURAL CREDIT IN DISARRAY
MONEYLENDER'S CREDIT OR GLOBALISATION'S DISCREDIT

RURAL CREDIT IN DISARRAY

Moneylender's Credit or Globalisation's Discredit

Dr. Gautam Purkayastha

GYAN PUBLISHING HOUSE
NEW DELHI-110002

Rural Credit in Disarray Moneylender's Credit or Globalisation's Discredit

ISBN: 978-81-212-1011-9

ICSSR Consultant : Prof. M.N. Buch

(The responsibility for the facts stated, conclusions reached and opinions expressed in this book is that of the author concerned and not of the ICSSR, which has extended financial support towards publications of the book)

Published in 2008 in India by
Gyan Publishing House
23, Ansari Road, Darya Ganj,
New Delhi-110002
Phones : 23282060, 23261060
Fax : 011-23285914
E-mail: books@gyanbooks.com
Website: www.gyanbooks.com

Lasser Type Setting by: Rudra Computer Graphics, Delhi
Printed at : G. Print Process, Delhi

Contents

Preface

The present book 'Rural Credit in Disarray Moneylender's Credit or Globalisation's Discredit' is the outcome of the author's Post-doctoral studies on 'Rural Indebtedness in Assam: A Cross-section Study', awarded by the University Grants Commission, New Delhi, for a period of three years, 2002-2005. Before the publication of the report, one new chapter on 'Poverty-free Assam through Micro Credit: Vision 2020' was added.

The incidence of poverty borne indebtedness and overall debt-incidence had been quite high in the NE-India over the years. Most unfortunately, all the NSSO Rounds have failed miserably to highlight this aspect of indebtedness in the region.

In the recent times, the Structural Adjustment Programmes have led to the withdrawal or cuts in the extension of certain loan schemes meant for the downtrodden. New schemes and strategies have replaced the old ones. However, since the region is lagging far behind in the sphere of major infrastructures, institutional credits to the underprivileged have substantially dried up under the new strategies adopted by the institutional agencies. In other words, financial sector reforms have led to the further fall in the Credit-Deposit ratio in the region on the one hand, and accentuated the problem of concentration of loans among the better off section, on the other. This has encouraged moneylenders to play a much larger exploitative role in the region. In the present study, an in-depth attempt has been made to explore the above aspects of indebtedness which have afflicted the rural credit scenario.

The first Chapter of the book contains the following main points: Introduction, objectives, review of the Literature and a comparative study of the rural debt scenario of India's North-East and the rest of India (1950-51 to 2002-03). Chapter II included a brief description of the sample region. Chapter III explains the incidence, extent and nature of indebtedness, while Chapter IV analyses in detail the purpose, source, repayment and overdue position of debt. Chapter V incorporated image of moneylenders in rural credit scenario, review of the literature, moneylender's position in Assam, NER and all-India. Chapter VI gives details about the status of the SHGs and KCCs in Assam compared to the all-India. Chapter VII makes a projection about the poverty-free Assam through micro credit: Vision 2020, while the concluding Chapter VIII incorporated summary of the report and policy implications.

Gautam Purkayastha

Acknowledgements

The present work is the fruit of continuous inspirational support of a large number of individuals and institutions. At the outset, I acknowledge my sincere gratitude to all those generous personalities (whose name could not be mentioned here) who have directly or indirectly lent me a helping hand in the preparation of this report.

I am grateful to the University Grants Commission, New Delhi for awarding me the Post-doctoral Research Project for the period of three years and also, for their valuable suggestions and intellectual inspiration at the time of Mid-term Review.

I am highly grateful to Prof. M. N. Buch, the ICSSR consultant, who has evaluated the report and the Indian Council of Social Science Research, New Delhi for awarding publication grants.

I take this opportunity to express my sincere thanks to the enlightened staff of the National Library, Kolkata; NSSO Library, Mahalanobis Bhavan, Kolkata; NABARD, Mumbai Head Office; Indian Council of Social Science Research, New Delhi; Dibrugarh University Library, Dibrugarh; Documentation Centre of the Economics Department of Dibrugarh University and Margherita College Library, Margherita for allowing me an easy access to these institutions/ extending me necessary 'support services'.

I am particularly grateful to Mr. H N Sharma Retd. Principal, Margherita College, Mr. Prodyut Bordoloi, Hon'ble Minister of State for Power and Forests and President of Margherita College Governing Body, for their intellectual support, advice and continuous inspiration.

I express my deep sense of gratitude to the Registrar (Dr K K Deka), Dibrugarh University; Prof. H. Goswami, Prof. J K Gogoi, Prof. K C Bora, Late Prof. Bhuban Barua and other esteemed faculty members of the Department of Economics for their kind cooperation and intellectual support. I am also thankful to the Section Officer, UGC Section, Dibrugarh University for assisting me in preparation of the expenditure statement.

During the field survey, I received full support and cooperation from Mr. B. Tanti Lecturer, Margherita College; Dr S. Ahmed, Principal, ADP College, Nagaon; Mr. D. Sharma, Assist. Registrar (Admn.), IIT, Guwahati; Mr. R Paul, Lecturer, Lanka College, Mr. Ashokananda Chakraborty, Lecturer, Digboi College; Dr Mrinmoy Deb (MBBS), Karimganj; Mr. Deepak Goswami; Mr. Santanu Roy, Mr. Nitul Gogoi, Powaimukh and above all, the very kind respondents, for which I remain grateful to them. Also, I owe thanks to Dr. B Gogoi, Principal, Margherita College, Mr P. Gogoi, Vice-Principal, my esteemed colleagues, students and office staff for extending me moral support.

I am thankful to Gyan Publishing House, New Delhi for publishing the book in record time.

My wife Sujaya and my mother-in-law deserve special thanks for their tremendous support and sacrifices during the project work. I will be failing in my duty if I do not acknowledge the priceless service received from the other members of my family who stood by me all throughout. My special thanks are due to my sisters Banya and Banani and brother Ashim for their valuable intellectual support.

Gautam Purkayastha
August 15, 2007

1

Introduction, Objectives, Methodology and Review of the Literature

Introduction

For long times, rural indebtedness and rural poverty were considered as synonyms. Almost all the official reports and academic studies till the late 1970s assumed that rural indebtedness is the most serious manifestation of rural poverty. It is also compared with lack of productive avenues for the borrowers which can put them above the subsistence level of living and growing inequalities in the society. Thus, 'Main Elements of the Problem' chapter in the "General Report on the All-India Rural Credit Survey – 1954" began with a quotation from an old French proverb: credit supports the farmer as the hangman's rope supports the hanged! But, even if credit is sometimes 'fatal', it is often indispensable to the cultivator.

During the pre-nationalisation of major Indian banks, the highly exploitative informal sources of credit constituted a lion's share in rural credit. The practice of usury loans was responsible for large scale alienation of (mortgaged) land from the marginalized farming community to the moneylenders. The chain of moneylenders was so strong that they could even influence the local administration in their favour, if and when muscle power had to be applied to recover usury loans.

The usury loan was partially responsible for continuation of subsistence living of the weaker section in the society. This was one of the reasons why bank was nationalized. One of the objectives of the (old) 20-point Economic Programme was liquidation of rural indebtedness step by step through institutional credit to farmers and artisans in rural areas to free them from the clutches of greedy moneylenders and middlemen. With the much faster growth of the primary sector in the 1970s and 1980s and the wide and extensive reach of the formal rural banking sector, the employment market was considerably diversified in selective pockets of the country. The familiarity with the capital intensive agriculture and subsequently, much faster growth of income were responsible for sharp increase in the volume of indebtedness in states like Punjab and Haryana. The composition of rural indebtedness has changed considerably since then and it was no longer perceived as a negative phenomenon. The institutional credit agencies have come up as agents of rural development. In other words, credit is being considered as an important input of development, since lack of entitlement to critical minimum financial resources was identified as the vital reason for high incidence of poverty among the landless and landed poor in the countryside. In recent times, it is observed, social activists, development economists and politicians try to define access to institutional credit as access to productive economic activities — sometimes as working capital, sometimes as seed capital and still sometimes as an input for expansion of the current economic operations.

With significant changes in the monetary and fiscal policies in the country over the last one and half decades, there was an urgent need to take a close look at the changing behaviour of the institutional credit agencies in the countryside. It is very important to look afresh the deviations of the credit institutions, if any, from playing their critical role in meeting the holistic developmental goals.

Most unfortunately, the growth of institutional credit in Assam is not at par with the rest of India. The incidence as well as volume of institutional credit was found very low in this region even after the substantial growth of the banking sector. In this region, the incidence of poverty was very high. Being predominantly rural, the problem of poverty has concentrated in rural areas. In fact, this was at the root of different forms of undesired manifestations in the region. Farm size distribution in Assam has become highly skewed towards marginal farms. Nearly four-fifths of the total farm holdings are constituted by the small farms. Higher percentage share of forest land, non-agricultural land, land under tea estate, etc. on one hand, and the alarming growth of population over the years, slow growth of the non-agricultural sectors, etc on the other, led to sharp fall in the per capita availability of land. In 1991, as against India's average farm size of 1.55 hectare, the state had 1.27 hectare which further decreased to 1.24 in 1995-96. Thus, the diversification of rural employment both in the agricultural and non-agricultural sectors is the need of the hour to get a hold of the increasing incidence of joblessness and poverty. This warrants increasing institutional support, both quantitatively and qualitatively.

The government has taken initiative to create productive employment opportunities in the region by launching different developmental schemes including directed loans to the youth. However, despite the governments' extra attention, the quantum of institutional loans in recent times has come down miserably thereby bringing the credit-deposit ratio down to 50 per cent of the national average. Recently, the Union Minister of Rural Development expressed his deep concern that rural development programmes in several areas of the region have failed because of the attitude of certain bank officials to deny loans to the needy people. 'While the well-to-do people are being offered loans by banks to buy houses, cars and other luxuries at interests between 6 and 7 per cent, the poor are being charged interests between 10 to 12 per cent on loans that could bring about development'. Despite high interest rates, some of the bank branches in the region have recorded zero finance.

In the above context, the study of incidence of indebtedness, its nature, size, purpose and source assumed special significance in modern times. Indebtedness is no longer looked as the sign of economic weakness of the borrower, especially after the tremendous growth of the institutional sources of credit. The faster growth in rural areas requires diversified agriculture driven healthy growth of cottage and small industries and services sector which can be achieved through wide and extensive reach of the formal rural credit system. The share of rural household borrowings from formal institutional sources increased from about 6 per cent in 1951, at the national level, to 66 per cent by 1991. The share of informal sources of credit in total credit remains high at 50 per cent in Assam, over the past three decades. Much higher percentage of the non-cultivator households, who constituted the large chunk of the rural poor, were dependent on informal sources of credit. Assetless as well as asset poor households received much lesser amount of institutional loans compared to the medium and big farmers. It is alleged that in the era of economic liberalization, the share of rural sector in institutional credit, the priority sector loans, the share of the weaker section in formal loans, share of productive loans in total advances, etc. have received a set back. There is no gainsaying that borrowed for productive purposes i.e., 'credit' as seed capital and/or, working capital can play the catalytic role in regeneration of the economy for the underprivileged and vice versa.

Objectives

- to explore the dynamics of rural indebtedness in Assam (on the basis of primary data) vis-à-vis all-India (secondary data) in the context of financial sector reforms.
- to look into the reasons behind the fall in the incidence of institutional loans in rural areas – size and composition wise – in the post-liberalisation period in particular.
- to explore the image of moneylenders in rural credit scenario. In the globalised world with financial sector reforms, moneylenders role in rural credit may increase further.
- effectiveness of SHGs and KCCs in meeting the credit need of the so far deprived lots will be looked into.
- There are some experts who believe that since there is no demand for loans/opportunities for lending in the state of Assam/NER, a continuous outflow of resources from the region to the relatively advanced states of the country are taking place over the years. One important objective of this project was to unearth the truth behind the present dismal rural debt scenario in the state.

Hypothesis

- In the era of globalisation and financial sector reforms, the provision of institutional credit support to the 'assetless and asset poor' may become scarce, and obviously dearer.
- SHGs and KCCs can serve the credit needs of the weaker section in a more appropriate manner, without putting much financial burden on the existing structure.

Methodology

The present study is primarily based on the primary data collected from four different districts spatially covering the state of Assam. For collecting the necessary data, a schedule specifically prepared for the purpose was canvassed among the sample households directly and personally.

To ensure spatial coverage of the state of Assam, 4 districts —— one each from upper, central and lower Assam (fall in the Brahmaputra valley) and Karimganj district in Barak valley —— were purposively selected for field investigation. The sample districts are: Kamrup (lower Assam), Nagaon (central Assam), Tinsukia (upper Assam) and Karimganj (Barak valley). Sample households were drawn both from the North bank (140 households) and South bank (240 households) of the Brahmaputra and the Barak Valley (120 households).

Altogether 16 villages were selected for field investigation. Two villages – one remote village and the other located near urban centers – from two different sub-divisions/blocks under each district were selected purposively. In the selection of the villages, advanced village (/agriculturally surplus village) as well as the backward ones; ST, SC, BC and general caste dominated villages; villages with/ without SGSY scheme (SHGs/KCCs), flood affected and unaffected villages, etc. were received due consideration.

The final selection of the households was made on the basis of stratified random sampling method.

Review of the relevant works done on Assam/NER

The rural credit scenario has experienced a continuous change since the Royal Commission reported in the early part of the twentieth century that the poor are born in debt, live in debt and bequeath debt passing on its burden to posterity. Although debt is not always considered as a negative phenomenon, the incidence of farmers falling in debt-trap has been reported across the nation even when the percentage share of productive loans (institutional loans) to total loans has increased substantially. The incidence of suicides committed by the farmers who were in debt-trap has not decreased at all.

Realising the gravity of the situation, official arrangements have been made to periodically review the economic conditions of the rural households including their state of indebtedness in the post-independence period. Although a large volume of data relating to rural indebtedness has been generated by the official studies, no academic study with the objective of analyzing the problem in its entirety has so far been attempted, particularly in the North-east India.

There is no denying the fact that even at the national level, studies relating to different dimensions of indebtedness of rural households have received much less importance compared to the huge volume of research work in other areas of rural development.

In Assam/NER, during the pre-independence period, indebtedness scenario was very dismal. The provision of institutional credit was next to negligible. The cooperative movement which was gaining some health in the initial couple of decades after its inception in the very first decade of the last century, had to suffer badly during the great depression in 1930s. Even during the Second World War, when many Indian provinces did register high growth of cooperative societies, the movement failed to recover in Assam. Between 1928—29 and 1945—46, the number of agricultural credit societies decreased noticeably, and the percentage of overdues to outstanding loans rose from 42.7 per cent to 86.6 per cent over the same period.

In a report 'Cooperation in Assam (A New Experiment)' published by RBI, it was noted that 'By the end of the war period, cooperation as a people's movement started and run mostly by themselves was dead in Assam and to the extent that it existed previously, it would appear that more people were ruined than helped by it'. The Rural Credit Survey, 1954 reaffirmed that 'cooperation has failed but cooperation must succeed'.

Nevertheless, today, India's cooperative credit structure (CCS), with over 13 crore members (including six crore borrowers), constitutes one of the largest rural financial systems in the world. The over one lakh primary agriculture credit societies (PACS) can, in many ways, be regarded as the veritable bedrock of India's rural economy. The CCS has 50 per cent more clients than commercial banks and regional rural banks put together. Directly or indirectly, it covers nearly half of India's total population. The CCS services farm input distribution, crop production, processing and marketing as also dairying, weaving and textiles.

Comparative credit scenario (1950-51 – 1970-71)

The Rural Credit Survey Committee (1951) had emphasized in their report the need for a constant review of the main features of the rural credit situation through annual investigations as also more elaborate enquiries from time to time. Accordingly, the RBI conducted four annual follow-up rural credit surveys in selected districts, commencing from 1956 -57 and also, the All-India Rural Debt and Investment survey for the whole of India as also for individual states(RBI, 1969). Since then it has become a decadal exercise (now carried out by the NSSO).

In rural India, both the All India Rural Credit Survey (1951-52) and All-India Rural Debt and Investment Survey (1961-62) reported moneylender as the single most important credit agency. Moneylender was most dominant source of rural credit across the nation in the first two decades after independence, except Assam. In Assam, relatives had constituted the most important agency in 1951-52; but it was taken over by the agriculturist moneylender in 1961-62 (Table 1.1). The institutional sources including cooperatives played an insignificant role during the initial couple of decades after Independence (before the bank nationalization to be precise). In Assam, till 1961-62, a lion's share of the total borrowings came from non-institutional sources, with the cooperatives and government playing an even more insignificant role in the case of non-cultivators than for cultivators.

Table 1.1

Proportion of amounts borrowed from different agencies by rural households as per All-India Rural Credit Survey (1951-52) and All-India Rural Debt and Investment Survey (1961-62)

Attributes	*Assam*				*India*	
	Cultivators		*Non-cultivators*		*All households*	
	A	*B*	*A*	*B*	*A*	*B*
Average debt per household (Rs.)	122.3	35.8	61.4	23.6	160.0	180.0
% share of different agencies to total debt:						
Government	6.2	4.5	9.8	-	3.1	2.3
Cooperatives	0.5	1.7	-	-	2.9	13.8
Relatives	65.7	21.2	62.2	30.6	14.4	8.8
Landlords	-	-	-	-	2.0	0.7
Agricultural moneylenders	17.6	38.1	20.3	26.8	24.8	33.9
Professional moneylenders	7.5	10.8	1.0	4.6	43.8	12.7
Traders and Commission agents	0.9	11.0	6.7	6.0	6.1	10.1
Commercial banks	-	-	-	-	1.1	0.7
Others	1.6	12.7	0.1	31.9	1.8	17.0

A: All-India Rural Credit Survey. B: All-India Rural Debt and Investment Survey.

The relative importance of various credit agencies across the Indian states during 1961-62 can be seen from Table1.2. Almost all the states recorded very high share of agricultural moneylenders in total borrowings, Andhra Pradesh's share was the highest at 59.3. Only in Assam and Gujarat considerable amount of borrowings from the relatives registered by the cultivator households (21 % of the total borrowings each). Most unfortunately, Assam recorded the lowest share of cooperatives (1.7 %) and nil amount of borrowings from commercial banks along with Bihar, Gujarat, Orissa and Punjab. During this period, mortgage of immovable property was very important as security in Assam followed by Bihar and Orissa.

The All-India Rural Debt and Investment Survey reported that, in 1960s, relatively much higher amounts borrowed at higher rates of interest in states like Assam, Orissa, Uttar Pradesh, West Bengal and Bihar – where cooperative credit and extension of branch banking had recorded poor progress. In fact, the amount of borrowings (as percentage of total borrowings) at more than 18 per cent rate of interest constituted 41.1 in Assam, as against the all-India average of 22.9 per cent. The situation was worse earlier particularly in the state of Assam.

The NSS 8th Round observed that in 1953-54, rural people in 'Assam combined with Manipur and Tripura' incurred 64.08 per cent of the total debt at 25 per cent and above rate of interest as against all-India percentage of 17.55. Only a few other states which had recorded sizeable amount of borrowings at 25 per cent and above interest rate were West Bengal (30 %), Uttar Pradesh (28 %), Madhya Pradesh (27 %), Orissa (22 %), Bihar (18 %) and Punjab (19 %).

The Review of Agricultural Development and Cooperative Credit in Assam (1961-1976) highlighted the extremely poor reach of the institutional sources of credit in the Tribal areas of NE-India, where high percentage share of the total credit had to be

Table 1.2

Proportion of cash loans borrowed by cultivator households from different agencies to total amount borrowed during 1961-62 (%)

State	Govt.	Co-operatives	CB	Land-Lord	AML	PML	T & CA	Relatives	Others
Andhra Pradesh	0.5	12.7	1.5	0.4	59.3	9.6	10.2	1.6	4.2
Assam	4.5	1.7	-	-	38.1	10.8	11.0	21.2	12.7
Bihar	1.0	2.6	-	0.1	62.7	14.8	6.3	7.5	4.9
Gujarat	1.1	25.7	-	-	5.8	6.3	11.6	21.2	28.2
J & K	-	11.4	0.2	0.3	7.0	4.6	18.8	15.2	42.6
Kerala	1.1	11.9	4.0	1.2	7.2	3.3	8.3	11.3	51.6
Madhya Pradesh	1.2	17.4	0.3	0.1	34.0	28.1	11.4	3.4	4.2
Madras	2.7	16.5	1.2	0.2	59.8	6.8	2.3	3.6	6.9

(Contd.)

(Contd. Table 1.2)

State	*Govt.*	*Co-operatives*	*CB*	*Land-lord*	*AML*	*PML*	*T & CA*	*Relatives*	*Others*
Maharashtra	8.3	38.3	0.1	0.3	16.2	8.5	3.6	15.5	9.4
Mysore	6.1	20.6	0.6	1.8	43.1	0.9	9.2	6.5	11.2
Orissa	4.2	16.6	-	0.2	15.1	28.8	19.8	3.8	11.5
Punjab	2.1	10.5	-	3.8	30.9	16.5	3.6	13.9	18.7
Rajasthan	0.8	3.8	0.1	-	26.3	23.8	18.3	6.2	20.6
Uttar Pradesh	2.6	16.6	0.4	0.2	35.9	20.0	6.9	9.2	8.2
West Bengal	2.1	5.9	0.1	1.7	28.1	4.0	9.7	16.4	32.1
All-India	2.6	15.5	0.6	0.6	36.0	13.2	8.8	8.8	13.9

* CB : Commercial Bank; AML : Agricultural moneylender

PML : Professional moneylender; T & CA: Traders and commission agents

Source: All-India Rural Debt and Investment Survey.

extended to the cultivator households by the government in the form of Taccavi loans. A Study Team of the cooperation department of the state government which had enquired into the problem of indebtedness in the Goalpara district in 1966 had made a few observations regarding indebtedness of tribal population as follows:

"The private moneylenders are operating in the tribal areas on the basis of the system known as 'Dadan'. Under this system, money is given by the private moneylenders against the advance of the future crops by the tribals. The rate of interest was usually very high and sometimes it was realized in kind viz in terms of paddy. It was found that the rate of interest varied between 1.5 to 2 maunds of paddy for an amount of Rs. 20. The moneylenders charged even higher rates varying from 30 to 40 per cent". Till 1975, there was no special law or machinery in the plains or hill districts to protect the tribal against the exploitation by moneylenders (RBI, 1978).

The 18th Round of the National Sample Survey did record similar frustrating scenario during February 1963 – January 1964. It observed high incidence of indebtedness among the lower income groups both in Tripura and Manipur. Higher income groups (/monthly expenditure groups) recorded nil incidence of indebtedness. During the period, any incidence of loan was often considered as 'sign of poverty'. In the report, 56 per cent of the ST households in Tripura were found indebted, while it was only 11 per cent in Manipur. The above findings substantiated the NSS 8th Round observations.

The NSS 8th Round (July 1954 – April 1955) observed that rural households in Assam during 1954-55, borrowed as high as 72 per cent for domestic consumption, 27 per cent for agriculture and 1 per cent for other purposes. The corresponding all-India percentages were 62, 32 and 6. The report also shows much lower average amount of borrowings in the NE-region, compared to the rest of India. Moneylenders and landlords constituted 60 per cent of the total credit, while the share of institutional sources accounted for merely 7 per cent. The corresponding all-India averages were 62 per cent and 14 per cent.

Rural Indebtedness in NER (1971-1991): Changing Scenario

As reported by the different RBI reports and the All India Debt and Investment Survey (AIDIS – carried out by NSSO) the size of indebtedness (debt per household) had always been low in the NE-states of India. The different Rounds of the All India Debt and Investment Survey (AIDIS – 1971, 1981 and 1991) disclosed some interesting features across the states (Table 1.3). At all India level, the incidence of cash borrowings recorded in 1991 (23%) was found moderately higher than the immediate previous round of 1981 with 20 per cent, but was almost half of the 1971 estimate of 43 per cent. In all the three Rounds of AIDIS, the incidence of cash borrowings in Assam was recorded abnormally low. The incidence of indebtedness in Assam in 1991 (6%) was very close to that of 1981 estimate (5%). However, the 1991 estimate was far lower than the 1971 estimate of 27 per cent. Among the 17 major states, Assam had recorded lowest debt-incidence in all the three estimates, which even did not have a single close follower.

Table 1.4 reveals that all the NE states save Tripura had a very low debt-incidence in 1991. It would be of interest to note that except Assam and Tripura, the sample households of the rest five states were pre-dominantly 'ST'. As many as 7 NE states (including Sikkim) had reported single digit figure. Only Tripura with high share of SC and general population in the sample recorded fractionally higher (23.6) incidence of debt than the national average. However, as mentioned in the different academic studies, the debt scenario in Assam has changed considerably during the last decade or so. In 1989-

Table 1.3
Incidence of indebtedness among the rural households across the states

States	*Incidence of Indebtedness (%)*		
	1971	*1981*	*1991*
Andhra Pradesh	48	26	35
Assam	27	5	6
Bihar	42	13	16
Gujarat	47	19	17
Haryana	35	11	28
Himachal Pradesh	37	12	22
Jammu & Kashmir	48	9	14
Karnataka	50	24	28
Kerala	34	28	31
Madhya Pradesh	42	21	21
Maharashtra	46	22	22
Orissa	37	20	23
Punjab	54	20	25
Rajasthan	57	25	30
Tamil Nadu	49	29	30
Uttar Pradesh	38	18	19
West Bengal	37	18	26
India	43	20	23

Source: 1. NSS 48th Round, Report No. 420.
2. Sarvekshana. 77th Issue, October-December 1998.

Notes: * In 26th and 37th Rounds of AIDIS, 'total household debt' also included 'debt in kind' which formed a very small part (< 3 %) of the total debt. To that extent, any exercise in comparison over different Rounds of AIDIS suffers, since the figures reported on incidence and level of indebtedness in earlier AIDIS Rounds are strictly not comparable with those of 1991 (kind loan excluded). However, the situation of Assam was completely different as seen in Table 1.5.

** Seetha Prabhu et al (1988) and Gothoskar (1988) observed that the estimates derived from 1981-82 survey (as also 1971-72 survey) were underestimated. Gothoskar added that the state sample estimates are generally lower than the central sample estimates for 1981. From the sampling point of view, he suggested that (i) enquiry into financial characteristics of households should not be clubbed with other socio-economic enquiries for the purpose of sample selection; (ii) villages may be grouped into two strata viz, villages having institutional credit facilities and villages not having credit facilities.

90 (NCRL report), Goswami estimated the figure at 91.67 for Assam. In another research study conducted by the author during 1991-92, it was found that as much as 79.33 per cent of the rural labour households were indebted to various sources (here debt-incidence included cash loans, kind loans and other liabilities). Among the landless people of non-labour category, the incidence of indebtedness was relatively low (55.56%), where as it was very high of 89.19 per cent among the rural households with land (Purkayastha, 1997). However, in the year 1999, in yet another study sponsored by the UGC, the incidence of indebtedness among the rural households in Tinsukia district of Assam, was found below 50 per cent. The report recorded much higher size of debt per indebted household (Purkayastha, 2004).

Table 1.4

Incidence of indebtedness and average amount of cash debt per rural household across the North East states in 1991

States	*Incidence of indebtedness (%)*	*Average debt per household (Rs.)*
Assam	6.2	252
Manipur	3.7	98
Meghalaya	0.4	12
Nagaland	3.1	63
Sikkim	4.9	202
Tripura	23.6	1389
Arunachal Pradesh	2.7	135
Mizoram	3.9	351
India	23.4	1906

Source : NSS Report No. 432, Part I, 48th Round.

The average amount of outstanding cash debt per indebted household in 1981 was Rs. 1157 for Assam, the lowest among all the Indian states. It was very high in agriculturally developed states like Haryana (9171), Punjab (7922) and Karnataka (5241), while the national average was being Rs. 3365. Almost all the NE states and eastern states like Bihar (1659), Orissa (1800), and West Bengal (1692) were far less burdened with debt (Government of India, 1987). The situation remains almost unchanged in 1991 as is evident from the Table 5. Punjab continued to top the list of average amount of debt (Rs 5596) in 1991 closely followed by Haryana (5090). The average debt per rural household in Assam experienced sharp fall from Rs. 177 in 1971 to merely Rs. 50 in 1981, only to rise again to Rs. 343 in 1991. In Punjab, Haryana, Assam, Jammu and Kashmir and West Bengal rural households reported high proportion of current liabilities as part of their debt. The recent increase in the average size of indebtedness in Assam, however, partly resulted by steep rise in general price level, and wider coverage of the institutional credit agencies.

Quite surprisingly, Table 1.5 reveals very high incidence of indebtedness in Assam in 1991. It is one of the highest in the country. This is due to the fact that, in the 1991-92 survey, the NSSO presented the analysis on households indebtedness based on cash loans only. However, the RBI had brought out the estimates of total indebtedness of households including current liabilities and made a comparison with similar sets of data (RBI 2000), under the assumption that "current liabilities are of short-term and recurring in nature, which will be outstanding at any point of time during the entire year".

The RBI's fresh treatment of the data (collected by the NSSO) give us some valuable information. As against the significant fall in the incidence of indebtedness during 1971-81,

Table 1.5
Proportion of rural households reporting debt and average amount per household by major states (1971—91)

State	1971*		1981*		1991**	
	P	A	P	A	P	A
Andhra Pradesh	47.4	637	26.3	934	42.1	2731
Assam	25.1	177	4.3	50	37.5	343
Bihar	38.4	288	12.2	202	19.4	645
Gujarat	47.7	930	17.4	848	25.9	1925
Haryana	35.3	921	10.5	962	44.6	5090
Himachal Pradesh	37.5	573	12.3	353	29.0	1435
J & K	47.7	356	8.9	251	37.1	1443
Karnataka	49.2	731	23.8	1249	37.9	2762
Kerala	34.3	366	28.2	951	36.2	3688

(Contd.)

(Contd. Table 1.5)

State	1971*		1981*		1991**	
	P	A	P	A	P	A
Madhya Pradesh	40.3	395	19.7	568	27.2	1860
Maharashtra	45.0	591	22.0	848	34.2	2521
Orissa	29.6	163	19.2	346	28.0	1158
Punjab	54.4	1039	18.9	1499	54.2	5596
Rajasthan	55.9	893	24.2	1157	35.2	3891
Tamil Nadu	49.7	705	28.5	1009	33.2	2580
Uttar Pradesh	37.3	343	17.4	448	24.2	1581
West Bengal	34.5	188	17.5	297	43.5	1589
All India	41.3	487	19.4	653	32.0	2116

P : Percentage of households reporting debt A : Average debt per household

* Relate only to outstanding cash dues payable

** Debt includes cash loans and current liabilities comprising all liabilities arising out of purchase of goods and services for consumption from traders, doctors, lawyers, etc, and other dues payable and trade credit.

Source: RBI Bulletins, May 1999 and February 2000.

there was a steep increase in the proportion of rural households reporting debt between 1981 and 1991 in all the states. Also, there was a multifold increase in the average debt per household in 1991 in all states over those in 1981 (Rao and Tripathi, 2001). In Assam, as many as 31 per cent (37.5 % at the overall level) of the rural households reported current liabilities which, though unfortunately, fails to draw any attention from the analysts. The inclusion of the current liabilities may reduce the overall share of the institutional sources in rural debt in Assam considerably.

According to the NSSO data, at the all India level, the percentage share of the 'nil' and '1-10' interest slabs in the aggregate amount of cash dues outstanding had gone down between 1981 and 1991, while that of highest two interest slabs increased considerably indicating higher burden of debt servicing in recent past. At the national level, two-fifths of the total borrowings were made at the rate of interest between 10 – 15 per cent (this group has gained highest importance as the institutional sources made some inroads into the rural credit market), while in Assam the corresponding share was considerably low i.e., one-quarter of the total cash dues outstanding. In Assam, interest free loans and concessional loans (/below 10 per cent interest category) constituted two-fifths of all loans. Higher interest loans, i.e., above 18 per cent interest category accounted for less than one-fifth of the total debt. The better access of the institutional loans in recent times might have helped in reducing the overall interest burden of loans in Assam.

According to an estimate made by the RBI on the basis of the NSS data on cash and current liabilities, about 4 per cent of rural households and 3 per cent of urban households in India reported loans at the interest rate of '30 per cent or more' in 1991. The corresponding amount outstanding against this high interest range accounted for about 10 per cent and 8 per cent of the total amount outstanding, respectively, for rural and urban households (RBI, 1999).

In order to study the changes in the distribution of loans by purposes during the decades 1971-81, 1981-91, the percentage shares of debt for different purposes at the three points of time in rural India have been presented in Table 1.6. It is clearly evident that the most prominent change in rural areas occurred in the share of debt incurred for productive purposes, which fell drastically to 23 per cent in 1991 after having increased remarkably from 50 per cent in 1971 to 69 per cent in 1981. This could possibly be due to a different procedure being followed in the 48th Round, from that in the earlier Rounds, to record the different purposes for which loans were taken by households*.

Between cultivators and non-cultivators, the fall in the share of productive purpose loan was more pronounced for cultivators – 72 per cent in 1981 to 24 per cent in 1991. The corresponding figures for non-cultivators were 38 per cent and 17 per cent.

Footnotes: * Nearly, half of the debt was shown against 'other purposes' in 1991 as against 8.5 per cent in 1981. However, this category includes debt for purposes of repayment of debt and financial investment besides other purposes. The rise in the expenditure for these two noted purposes, or wrong classification of the purpose could have led to increase in the share of 'other purposes'. Further, one-fifth of the debt was not specified under any purpose in 1991 compared with negligible share in 1981. It is very important that AIDIS, in future, adopt uniform concepts and definitions enabling comparison with the data collected in the earlier surveys (Rao and Tripathi, 2001). The RBI Bulletin, May 1999 clearly mentioned that 'households' expenditure in residential buildings, which is capital in nature, has been included under household expenditure. Thus, the expenditure shown against productive expenditure in the 48th Round of NSS would be an underestimate'.

Table 1.6
Percentage distribution of amount of cash debt by purpose on 30.6.1971, 30.6.1981 and 30.6.91

Purpose	*All Rural Household*			
		India		*Assam*
	1971	*1981*	*1991*	*1991*
In farm business				
Capital expenditure	31.2	42.5	12.0	0.6
Current expenditure	13.5	17.6	2.7	0.5
In non-farm business				
Capital expenditure	3.7	7.3	5.8	4.7
Current expenditure	1.7	1.8	2.0	2.0
Productive purposes	50.1	69.2	22.5	7.8
Household expend.	40.9	22.3	40.1	50.5
Other purposes	8.7	8.3	14.6	21.7
Unspecified	0.3	0.2	22.8	19.9
All purposes	100	100	100	100

Source: 1. NSS Report No. 328 (Sarvekshana, July 1987).
2. NSS Report No. 420.

Table 1.7 presents the inter-state comparison of different purposes of borrowings. It is mentioned earlier that all the NE-states of India experienced extremely low-to-low debt-incidence over the years. The Table shows very low amounts of borrowings for capital expenditure in farm business in all the NE-states save Arunachal Pradesh (32.9%). States like Andhra Pradesh (11), Haryana (11), Orissa (12), Maharashtra (15), Madhya Pradesh (19.2) and Gujarat (10%, not included in the table) recorded higher average shares of borrowings for capital expenditure in farm business than the national average of 9.3

per cent. On the other side, NE-states like Manipur (0.0), Meghalaya (0.0), Tripura (0.1), Sikkim (0.3) and Assam (0.6) incurred debt for the purpose far lower than the national standard. Data on 'current expenditure in farm business' reflect even more disappointing scenario for all the NE-states.

Three NE-states, such as Sikkim (26), Manipur (11) and Nagaland (10) recorded higher percentage share of borrowings for capital expenditure in non-farm business than the all India average of 5.7 per cent. The head 'capital expenditure for residential buildings' constituted a substantial share of 46 and 29 per cent in two NE states of Sikkim and Tripura respectively. It was also found significantly high in two southern states of Kerala (27) and Tamil Nadu (23). The incidence of unproductive loans was found more frequent almost in all states during 1991-92. The debt incurred for meeting household expenditure (other than unspecified category) constituted more than half of all borrowings in states like Assam, Manipur, Tripura, Kerala, Rajasthan, Orissa and Tamil Nadu. Only a few states mostly with high share of 'unspecified loans' did mention relatively low share of the debt contracted for household expenditure. The states were Meghalaya, Nagaland, Arunachal Pradesh, Gujarat, Madhya Pradesh, Bihar, Maharashtra and Punjab—all recorded less than two-fifths of the total cash dues outstanding.

It is worth noting that at the all India level wide extensive gaps and spatial imbalances persist in the availability of institutional credit facilities as is evident from Table 1.8. It is significant to note that since the nationalization of commercial banks the share of the institutional credit agencies in total indebtedness of the rural people with or without land experienced a phenomenal increase across the states. Even in the state of Assam, the rural accessibility of the institutional sources improved significantly during 1980s. However, its overall share (66%) registered in the AIDIS – 1991 was found much less spectacular than many other states including eastern

Table 1.7
Statewise percentage distribution of amounts of cash borrowings by purpose during 1. 7. 91 to 30. 6. 92

	Purpose of Loan									
	In farm business			*In non-farm business*			*In household*			
State	*Capital Exp.*	*Current Exp.*	*others*	*Capital Exp.*	*Current exp*	*others*	*Capital Exp for residential building*	*Current Exp.*	*others*	*Un-Specified*
Assam	0.6	0.8	11.0	2.6	3.0	13.1	5.7	0.3	46.4	16.4
Manipur	-	1.9	0.7	11.4	-	7.3	1.3	0.2	71.8	5.4
Meghalaya	-	-	45.9	-	-	-	-	-	8.1	46.0
Nagaland	4.5	-	3.1	10.1	-	31.9	3.2	0.2	29.3	17.7
Sikkim	0.3	-	7.0	26.4	2.4	7.0	45.7	0.4	0.6	10.2
Tripura	0.1	0.6	-	0.5	-	10.4	29.1	-	48.0	11.3
Arunachal Pradesh	32.9	-	-	4.4	-	28.4	1.3	-	15.7	17.3

(Contd.)

(Contd. Table 1.7)

State	**Purpose of Loan** In farm business: Capital Exp.	In farm business: Current Exp.	In farm business: others	In non-farm business: Capital Exp.	In non-farm business: Current exp	In non-farm business: others	In household: Capital Exp for residential building	In household: Current Exp.	In household: others	Un-Specified
Mizoram	6.8	-	-	6.3	0.7	10.8	5.2	1.1	35.3	33.9
Andhra Pradesh	10.7	3.6	24.6	0.8	0.9	1.7	3.7	4.9	41.4	7.7
Bihar	2.9	0.9	5.3	35.0	0.2	6.2	2.9	0.6	34.1	12.0
Haryana	10.5	0.2	13.3	13.5	2.8	0.9	4.9	-	32.8	21.1
Kerala	6.4	0.3	2.3	14.9	2.2	16.0	26.5	0.5	27.0	3.8
Orissa	11.8	2.4	3.7	1.1	1.3	9.3	0.6	-	57.6	12.3
Punjab	8.3	4.7	31.9	2.1	0.1	3.5	2.0	1.7	31.3	14.6
Tamil Nadu	6.9	3.9	9.6	2.5	2.4	2.3	23.1	1.4	40.1	7.8
U P	6.1	2.9	7.8	4.2	2.6	5.5	8.4	-	36.1	26.5
West Bengal	3.0	4.6	12.7	6.8	8.0	11.9	2.6	1.5	40.5	8.4
India	9.3	3.6	14.5	5.7	1.7	4.1	9.3	1.3	36.1	14.6

Source: NSS 48th Round, Report No. 431 (Part II).

states like West Bengal (82%), Orissa (80%) and Bihar (73%). There is absolutely no doubt that the stranglehold of the usurious money lenders is fast loosening as the different formal sources are making steady inroads into the rural scene.

It is evident from Table 1.8 that the percentage share of institutional sources in outstanding debt of the rural households at the national level jumped up from 29 in 1971 (only 17% in 1961) to 66 in 1991. Interestingly, Assam was the only major

Table 1.8

Percentage share of institutional agencies in outstanding cash debt of rural households in major Indian states in 1971, 1981 and 1991

States	*1971*	*1981*	*1991*
Andhra Pradesh	14	41	34
Assam	35	31	66
Bihar	11	47	73
Gujarat	47	70	75
Haryana	26	76	73
Himachal Pradesh	24	75	62
Jammu & Kashmir	20	44	76
Karnataka	30	78	78
Kerala	44	79	92
Madhya Pradesh	32	66	73
Maharashtra	67	86	82
Orissa	30	81	80
Punjab	36	74	79
Rajasthan	9	41	40
Tamil Nadu	22	44	58
Uttar Pradesh	23	55	69
West Bengal	31	66	82
India	29	61	66

Source: NSS 48th Round, Report No. 420.

state that had observed a significant fall in the share of institutional credit agencies during the 1970s i.e., 31 per cent in 1981 from 35 per cent in 1971, only to rise spectacularly to 66 per cent (shown as 64 % in some reports) in 1991. Nevertheless, the state of Assam's spectacular increase in the share of institutional credit might have looked less spectacular had kind component of loans not been excluded from the consideration.

Table 1.9 presents the percentage distribution of outstanding cash dues of rural households by credit agencies for Assam, other NE-states and all-India. In 1991, the institutional credit covered 64 per cent of total borrowings each in Assam and in India. In order of importance the main sources of loan at the national level were commercial banks (34%), cooperative societies (22%), moneylenders (18%), government (6%) and friends and relatives (6%). For the state of Assam, the important sources were commercial banks (35%), relatives and friends (18%), government (18%) and cooperatives (8%). All other sources such as moneylenders (4%), traders (3%), etc, reported low to nominal shares.

In the NE-states (save Assam and Manipur) different government departments were the major sources of credit. In India, the percentage share of the source 'Government' in outstanding cash debt of the rural households was only 6.1, while it was as high as 97.6 in Mizoram, 67.4 – Meghalaya, 41.6 – Arunachal Pradesh, 26.5 – Tripura, 25.7 – Sikkim (not included in the table), 21.0 – Nagaland, 17.9 – Assam and 9.2 – Manipur. NE-economy is basically a distribution-oriented economy. While the central government is trying to inject resources into the NE-economy by higher budgetary allocation, continuous outflow of resources through the banking system is a major concern. There is no denying the fact that absorption of more institutional credits requires efficiency oriented economic process which is still a far cry in the region. The former Union Minister of State for Finance A. R. V Adsul during his visit to the NER in 2003

Table 1.9

Percentage distribution of amount of outstanding cash dues of rural households by credit agencies (1991)

Credit Agencies	*India*	*Assam*	*Arunachal Pradesh*	*Mizoram*	*Megha-laya*	*Naga-land*	*Manipur*	*Tripura*
Government	6.1	17.9	41.6	97.6	67.4	21.0	9.2	26.5
Cooperative	21.6	8.3	1.5	-	23.2	7.4	31.1	12.8
Banks (+RRBs)	33.7	34.5	4.3	0.6	0.0	27.0	0.4	49.9
Insurance	0.3	0.2	-	-	-	-	3.4	-
PF & OIA*	2.3	3.7	17.6	-	-	-	11.3	0.2
AIA	64.0	64.4	65.0	98.2	90.6	55.4	55.4	89.4
Landlord/ Employer	4.0	0.0	-	-	-	-	-	-
Money Lender	17.6	4.0	8.7	-	-	3.3	2.3	1.9
Traders/shop-keepers	2.5	2.6	-	-	-	-	-	2.4
Friends/Relatives	5.7	17.9	4.4	1.8	9.4	40.3	8.4	6.1
Others	3.0	9.4	13.4	-	-	-	31.4	0.2
All NIA*	32.7	33.9	26.4	1.8	9.4	43.6	42.0	10.6
Unspecified	3.3	1.7	8.6	-	-	1.0	2.6	-
All -Total	100.0	100.0	100.0	100.0	100.0	100.0	100.0	100.0

Source: NSS 48th Round, Report No. 432 (Part-II). AIA : All Institutional Agencies. NIA ; Non-institutional Agencies; OIA : Other International Agencies.

voiced his deep concern at the 'abysmally low' credit-deposit ratio in the region which was only 25 per cent compared to the national average of nearly 60 per cent and directed the top banking officials to expand their activities spatially by forming SHGs.

Indebtedness of cultivator households as per the Reports of AIDIS 2002-03 and SAS 2003

Two important surveys, viz, the Situation Assessment Survey (SAS) and the All-India Debt and Investment Survey (AIDIS) were conducted in the 59th Round of the National Sample Survey Organisation in 2003. The estimates of incidence of debt, extent of indebtedness and also the pattern of debt owed to institutional and non-institutional agencies, showed wide variations among different states and also at the all-India level in the two surveys, mainly because of the adoption of different techniques and definitions. About 49 per cent of the farmer households were reported to be indebted in the SAS, as against 30 per cent in the case of the AIDIS. The incidence of debt was more than 50 per cent in most of the states for SAS, as against less than 25 per cent for the AIDIS.

The share of debt owed to institutional agencies was little higher at 61.1 per cent in the case of AIDIS 2002-03, as against 57.7 per cent in SAS 2003.

Of the total short term and long term direct institutional loans to agriculture and allied activities, the share of cooperatives has steadily declined from 55.8 per cent in 1981-82 to 32.2 per cent in 2001-02. During the same time, the share of commercial banks increased from 41.0 to 57.3 per cent, while the corresponding shares for regional rural banks were 3.2 and 10.5 per cent.

It can be mentioned that the Narasimham Committee viewed an easy and timely access to credit are more important

Table 1.10

Indebtedness of cultivator households (proportions in % and amount in rupees)

State	*Farmer households (SAS 2003)*		*Cultivator households (June 2002)*		*AIDIS 2002-03*	
	PR	*APH*	*APRH*	*PR*	*APH*	*APRH*
Andhra Pradesh	82.0	23965	29226	54.0	16154	29915
Assam	18.1	813	4492	6.7	641	9567
Bihar	33.0	4476	13564	22.5	3336	14827
Gujarat	51.9	15526	29915	33.9	12958	38225
Haryana	53.1	26007	48977	31.7	17340	54700
Himachal Pradesh	33.4	9618	28796	17.9	5843	32643
Jammu & Kashmir	31.8	1903	5984	3.8	1198	31526
Karnataka	61.6	18135	29440	39.1	13422	34327
Kerala	64.4	33907	52651	42.9	27641	64431
Madhya Pradesh	50.8	14218	27988	31.7	12246	38631

(Contd.)

(Contd. Table 1.10)

State	*Farmer households (SAS 2003)*		*Cultivator households (June 2002)*		*AIDIS 2002-03*	
	PR	*APH*	*APRH*	*PR*	*APH*	*APRH*
Maharashtra	54.8	16973	30863	37.8	14268	37746
Orissa	47.8	5871	12282	31.3	3976	12703
Punjab	65.4	41576	63572	28.5	25211	88459
Rajasthan	52.4	18372	35061	36.7	13261	36134
Tamil Nadu	74.5	23963	32165	40.3	14823	36782
Uttar Pradesh	40.3	7425	18424	24.1	5363	22253
West Bengal	50.1	5237	10453	24.7	3820	15466
All India	48.6	12585	25895	29.7	9261	31182

Notes: PR : Proportion of households reporting; APH: Average debt/loan per household; APRH: Average debt per reporting household (APH/PR).

Source: NSSO Reports No 498 and 501 (immediate source: EPW, August 12, 2006)

Table 1.11
Share of different credit agencies in total debt in SAS 2003 and AIDIS 2002-03

Credit agency	*SAS 2003*	*AIDIS (June 2002)*
Government	2.5	1.7
Cooperative banks and societies	19.6	30.2
Commercial banks	35.6	26.3
Other institutional agencies	-	2.9
All institutional agencies	57.7	61.1
Landlord	-	0.9
Agricultural moneylender	25.7**	9.9
Professional moneylender		16.9
Relatives and Friends	8.5	6.2
Others*	8.2	5.0
All non-institutional agencies	42.4	38.9
All agencies	100.0	100.0

Notes: *Others include doctors, traders, etc. **Covers both agricultural and professional moneylenders. Break-up is not available.
Source: NSSO Reports 498 and 501.

than its cost and therefore argued for a phasing out of concessional rate of interest for priority sector loans of small sizes as it would remove the disincentive for banks to expand its clientele in neglected sectors. The Khusro Committee envisaged in developing, in the next 10 to 15 years, an 'autonomous, self-reliant, robust and cost effective system which does not work on crutches and concessions nor on tactics to please the populace temporarily'.

Very recently, the report (June 2004) of the Advisory Committee on the Flow of Credit to Agriculture and Related

Activities from the banking System (Vyas Committee, set up by the RBI) expresses deep concern that 'targets are not being met and that small farmers are being left out, notwithstanding the impressive network of branches that we have'. According to D. N. Ghosh (2005), 'what is proposed in the report is the same old remedy: comprehensive credit planning and monitoring, stricter guidelines, refinement of targets with higher sub targets for the disadvantaged sections, etc'.

References

1. Ghosh, D N (2005), 'A Policy Approach for Agricultural Lending', EPW, January 8.
2. Government of India, July 1987 'Sarvekshana' Vol. XI, No 1, NSSO.
3. Government of India, 'Sarvekshana' Vol.XXII, No. 2, 77th Issue.
4. Government of India (1998) 'Debt and Investment Survey', NSSO 48th Round (5 Vols.).
5. Government of India (1969) 'Tables with Notes on Indebtedness of Scheduled Tribe Households' National Sample Survey, 18th Round.
6. Government of India (1962) 'Tables with Notes on Rural Indebtedness' National Sample Survey, 8th Round. No. 68.
7. NEDFi Databank Quarterly – Various issues, 2003 .
8. Purkayastha, G. (1997) "Rural Labour Indebtedness in Assam", Mohit Publications, New Delhi.
9. Purkayastha, G (2004) 'Human Development and Rural Indebtedness in North East India', Anmol Publications Pvt. Ltd. New Delhi.
10. RBI's Banking Statistics: Basic Statistical Returns. Various Issues, 2000 – 2003.
11. Rao, K S R and Tripathi, A K(2001), 'Indebtedness of Households:Changing characteristics' EPW, May, 12 - 18.
12. Rao, K G K Subba (2006) 'Indebtedness of Cultivator Households Some Puzzling Results' EPW, August 12.

13. RBI Bulletin' May 1999, Vol. LIII. No. 5.
14. Reserve Bank of India (undated) 'Cooperation in Assam (A New Experiment)' Agricultural Credit Department, Bombay, p. 20.
15. Reserve Bank of India (undated) 'Cooperation in Assam (A New Experiment)' Agricultural Credit Department, Bombay, p. 20.
16. RBI (1969) 'Report of the All India Rural Credit Review Committee 1969', Agricultural Credit department, Bombay).
17. RBI (1978) 'The Review of Agricultural development and Cooperative Credit in Assam (1961-1976)' Bombay.
18. Shah, Mihir et al (2007) 'Rural Credit in 20th Century India Overview of History and Perspectives', EPW, April 14.
19. The Assam Tribune, December 1, 2004
20. The Assam Tribune, June 25, 2003.

2

A Brief Description of Sample State, Districts, Villages and Households

Assam is a landlocked state which is connected to the rest of India by a narrow Siliguri Corridor popularly known as 'chicken neck'. For all the North East states (save Sikkim), Assam is the gateway to India. In 1945, Jawaharlal Nehru said, 'I have no doubt great highways by road, air and rail will go across Assam connecting China with India, and ultimately connecting East Asia with Europe'. Undoubtedly, the landlocked Assam/NER with only 2 per cent of its border connected with the main land of India can become a major trade corridor for India to the world's fastest growing economic zones. This will also act as an adequate corrective to regional imbalances.

Assam falls in the world map of 25 bio-diversity hotspots. Essentially it is agricultural. Though the seeds of industrialization were sown in later part of 19th century by establishing Tea industry, and the Asia's first oil refinery in 1901, industrially the region is less developed. Service sector contributes highest share to the state domestic product. According to Jayanta Madhab (2004), Assam/NER has the potential advantages on the following areas:

- Surplus energy resources, mainly hydro resources, estimated at 40000 MW at 60 per cent plant load factor, untapped gas resources and limited oil.
- Water for irrigation, water supply, navigation, fisheries and horticulture.
- Forest resources, Wild Life alongside an ancient civilization.
- Tourism prospects, and
- Surplus tea.

To live up to the potentials, the region need better and adequate infrastructure, investment and market oriented government economic policies and friendly environment to grow. Most unfortunately, all these critical infrastructural inputs for development are missing in the state.

In comparison with the rest of India, NER had acute deficiency in areas like roads, railways, power, ports and funding sources. In the report "Level and Structure of Development in North-East India – 1997-98" sponsored by the NEC, S.C. Srivastava stressed the fact that 'transport and communication should be given top priority in the NE-states especially in view of the liberalization and globalisation of the Indian economy which has a significant bearing on NE-economy due to the sheer fact that 98 per cent of the Region's territories are international'.

Some reports mentioned that the rural poverty ratio has increased considerably in the region during the post-liberalisation period. The Assam government's BPL Survey shows that rural poverty in Assam has increased from around 40 per cent in 1993-94 to nearly 60 per cent in 1999. However, according to the 55th Round of NSSO , 36 per cent people were lying below poverty line in 1999-2000. In this flood prone state, the ratio of poverty-ridden population widely fluctuated from time to time.

It is a matter of concern that local entrepreneurs are not getting adequate amount of assistance (loan) from commercial banks. In the post-liberalisation period, the NE-region's credit-deposit ratio has steadily slipped to lower level (from about 40% in early 1990s to 26% in 2003). Between March 1994 and March 2001, the credit-deposit ratio in rural areas of Assam has declined from 56 per cent to 34 per cent. In rural area of the Southern India, the credit-deposit ratio was above 67 per cent in March 2001, though it was lower compared to 1994. The rural credit-deposit ratio in Southern India was highest in the country mainly because of the presence of a large number of NGOs, women organizations, formation of a number of successful SHGs in the recent past which led to high recovery ratio and to some extent better local administration. On the other hand, the lukewarm presence of NGOs (consequently, SHGs) in larger part of the NER, limited role of the women bodies, demoralized (superficial) local self governments, banker's indifferent attitude and poor recovery ratio (around 20%), etc., were the main hurdles in getting credit from the banks. It is a matter of great concern that frequent shifting of the rural bank branches to semi-urban/ urban areas on the ground of insecurity to bank deposits posed by the ultras has been responsible for creating even more distance between the bank staff and the rural beneficiary households (potential borrowers) – affecting the frequency, size, timings and recovery of loans. This has slowed down the participation of potential local entrepreneurs in those activities which came up because of the government's liberal and renewed economic policies.

On the one hand, private investment in Assam/NER has not increased in the post-reform period. On the other, Government has adopted a policy of phasewise withdrawal of its direct investment in certain fields. Between August 1991 to September 2001, while only 5 states viz. Maharashtra (20.7%), Gujarat (17.0%), Andhra Pradesh (11.0%), Tamil Nadu (6.4%)

and Karnataka (5.0%) accounted for as high as 60.1 per cent of the proposed investment of Rs.10,41,962 crores at the national level, the state of Assam received around 0.7 per cent of such proposals. The concentration of private investment proposals in the aforesaid five high profile states has increased by 2 percentage points during 1998-2001. In the background of Government's overall shrinking role in developmental activities, its (government) role as a facilitator has become ever important in recent times particularly in states like that of NE-region. It is sad to note that the cumulative share of financial assistance disbursed by all-India financial institution up to March end 1997 again was found extremely low for infrastructurally backward states like Assam (0.5), Bihar (1.4), Orissa (1.8) as compared to Maharashtra (21.0), Gujarat (13.5) or Tamil Nadu (9.0). Globalization has so far created more investment opportunities in metropolitan/big cities at the cost of rural/semi-urban/small towns. During the post-liberalisation period (financial sector reforms) the credit-deposit ratio in metropolitan/urban areas has increased significantly, at the cost of the countryside. In 1994, national credit-deposit ratio in urban areas was below 60 per cent which increased to 70 per cent in 2001. The major beneficiary was the western region where credit-deposit ratio jumped from 55.9 per cent in 1994 to 83.2 per cent in 2001. A considerable gain was also recorded by the Northern and Southern region. On the other hand, NER along with Eastern and Central regions all having low level of infrastructures are on the losing side. The overall credit-deposit ratio in the predominantly rural Assam dropped almost 9 percentage points in just 7 years, i.e., from 41 per cent in 1994 to 32 per cent in 2001. This abnormally low credit-deposit ratio has resulted in a continuous liquid drainage amounting several thousand crores of rupees. If the above trend continues unchecked the regional disparities may increase further thereby causing more damages to the credibility of institutional arrangements for better distribution of resources in the region.

The recent political developments in South Asia, South-East Asia and between India and China (ushering regional cooperation within the regions over a wide range of subjects) may prove extremely beneficial for the landlocked North East India, Assam in particular. The NER is projected as the high potential trade corridor between the world's fastest growing economies such as China, North Asia and ASEAN (labeled as the engine economy of the world for the next 25 – 50 years) and the rest of India. Opening up of the border trade through the ancient Stilwell road (apart from the already agreed Silk route which is the best route for tourists wanting to visit Lhasa, mount Kailash and the holy Mansarovar lake) would generate huge employment opportunities in trade, transport, tourism, and related services for the youths which may subdue the tendencies of militancy and other anti-social activities in the region. The UNCTAD study reported that NE-states had a potential of generating exports up to 1 billion $ in non-wood trade to China. However, the pre-requisite to get maximum benefit from the world's fastest growing trade hub at its doorsteps is an all out effort from all the 8 North East units to form economic union for closer coordination on check on insurgency, tourism, export promotion, an integrated transport system, among other matters of common interest (for faster regional development).

As reported in the NEDFi Databank Quarterly (October 2002), Assam is relatively most developed amongst the north eastern states but, the most underdeveloped among the major Indian states. During the period 1993-94 to 2000-01, the NSDP at constant prices grew at a compound annual growth rate of 2.70 per cent as compared to the NNP growth of 6.21 per cent. The per capita income of Assam at constant 1970-71 prices was Rs. 50.40 higher in 1950-51 than the average per capita income of India. However, in 2000-01, the state's per capita income at constant prices was only Rs. 6157 as compared to the All India average of Rs. 10254.

Agriculture forms the backbone of Assam's economy, although only two-fifths of the total geographical area is available for cultivation on the state. The food grain yield was 1406 kg per ha in 1999-00 compared to the national average of 1700 kg per ha.

Although an increasing trend is observed as regards consumption of fertilizers in absolute terms in Assam, its consumption in terms of NPK is far below the level achieved by other Indian states/national average.

As reported in the Economic Survey, Assam 2002-03, the flow of bank credit to the farmers of the state is insignificant. The position of flow of credit for last three years through Assam Cooperative Apex Bank Ltd. were as below.

Table 2.1

Year	*Short Term (Rs. in lakh)*	*Medium term (Rs. in Lakh)*
1998-1999	95.48	153.25
1999-2000	22.87	114.23
2000-2001	13.41	18.67

In respect of the programme for issue of KCC, only 7388 cards were issued in Assam as on December 2001 as against 45,28,261 in Andhra Pradesh.

It is important to note that in the southern states of Andhra Pradesh (1222%), Kerala (1596%) and Tamil Nadu (974%), as against the national increase of 667%, the amount of rural borrowings per head rose significantly between 1971-72 & 1991-92. The percentage increase of the average amount of cash borrowings in 1991-92 over 1971-72 for eastern states (with low base year average debt) like Assam (761%), Bihar (492%), Orissa (508%) and West Bengal (615%) was not very significant. There is no gainsaying that the bank or other formal sources of credit play twin roles in the world of indebtedness of the rural households. The increase in the share of institutional credit simultaneously leads to a fall in the household's burden of high interest borrowings besides boosting (productive) economic activities for the needy households. However, the most worrying feature is that almost all the survey conducted by the government institutions or individual researchers on indebtedness revealed least access to these sources by those who need their service most. Of the cumulative number of 2.64 lakh SHGs provided with bank loan as at the end of March 2001, as high as 47.9 per cent were in Andhra Pradesh alone, distantly followed by Tamil Nadu (12.4%), Uttar Pradesh and Uttaranchal (8.8%—combined share) and Karnataka (7.1%). Assam's share was nominal. By August 2003, there were nearly 66000 registered SHGs in Assam of which more than two-thirds were women groups. However, till recently, merely 5000 SHGs have accessed institutional credit.

The state of Assam registered relatively low debt-incidence over the years mainly because of the low level of commercialization of the agricultural sector and the shortages of indigenous entrepreneurship.

In terms of the different socio-economic developmental parameters, the state is placed at the bottom of the list, among the 17 major Indian states.

In recent years, the Assam's finances have been under severe pressure as reflected in various fiscal indicators, such as fiscal deficit, revenue deficit, primary deficit, the level of debt and rise in debt service obligations. The increase in revenue deficit has resulted from inadequate buoyancy in revenue receipts and rising level of revenue expenditure.

Table 2.2

State wise and population group wise statement of credit-deposit ratio of banks in India: all scheduled commercial banks. (Credit-deposit ratio in percentages)

Region / State	*March 2001*			*March 1994*		
	Rural	*Urban / Metropolitan*	*Total*	*Rural*	*Urban / Metropolitan*	*Total*
Northern Region	39.1	74.3	63.1	39.4	67.6	57.7
Haryana	41.9	43.8	41.7	51.0	51.3	47.9
Punjab	50.9	44.9	41.4	44.6	43.9	39.6
Rajasthan	47.6	56.7	48.2	54.0	52.4	49.2
Delhi	23.3	83.9	82.9	11.2	76.4	75.1
NE- Region	33.4	31.0	28.1	50.6	35.3	38.8
Arunachal Pradesh	18.8	-	17.3	14.1	-	14.1
Assam	34.4	39.3	32.4	56.4	39.8	41.2
Manipur	79.4	27.1	38.9	126.6	45.5	65.2
Meghalaya	22.9	15.7	16.8	33.0	13.8	17.3
Mizoram	61.1	16.1	25.5	39.2	-	24.5
Nagaland	33.1	-	13.9	52.7	-	42.0
Tripura	37.2	14.5	23.0	86.3	41.4	58.6

(Contd.)

(Contd. Table 2.2)

Region / State	March 2001			March 1994		
	Rural	Urban / Metropolitan	Total	Rural	Urban / Metropolitan	Total
Eastern Region	25.9	47.1	36.9	48.5	47.3	44.0
Bihar	22.5	21.6	21.3	45.9	30.7	35.2
Orissa	42.6	45.0	41.5	71.9	56.8	60.0
West Bengal	23.4	52.7	44.1	43.1	50.4	45.9
Central Region	29.3	36.8	33.4	41.6	43.3	42.0
Madhya Pradesh	43.8	56.4	48.3	56.2	60.0	54.9
Uttar Pradesh	27.2	30.0	28.8	37.5	36.7	37.2
Western Region	48.4	83.2	75.0	46.9	55.9	53.2
Goa	12.6	-	22.8	11.2	-	18.1
Gujarat	38.0	58.5	49.4	45.5	48.9	46.0
Maharashtra	73.1	88.6	85.4	59.3	57.1	56.3
Southern Region	67.1	76.5	65.8	75.8	69.0	67.3
Andhra Pradesh	77.4	64.4	63.3	82.6	73.9	70.7
Karnatake	68.5	58.9	59.3	72.9	68.0	65.6
Kerala	55.0	59.4	43.1	54.2	64.6	43.9
Tamil Nadu	59.6	109.0	90.6	82.7	89.1	82.4
All India	40.2	69.9	58.5	50.0	59.8	54.2

Table 2.3

Select socio-economic features of the sample state/districts

Attributes	*Tinsukia*	*Nagaon*	*Kamrup*	*Karimganj*	*Assam*
Area (Sq. km)	3790	3831	4345	1809	78438
Population (million)	1.15	2.31	2.51	1.0	26.6
% of rural population	80.51	88.0	64.19	92.67	87.28
Population Growth rate (1991-2001) %	19.52	22.30	25.75	21.35	18.85
Sex ratio	909	939	894	944	932
Density	303	604	579	555	340
Literacy (%): All	63.28	62.28	74.69	67.21	64.28
Male	72.16	68.52	81.24	73.87	71.93
Female	53.40	55.57	67.31	60.09	56.03
No. of habitations	905	3777	5148	2147	70669
With drinking water facilities(2001)	821	2470	3115	1395	47580
Per capita GDDP*	7244	6982	16577	8105	8989

(Contd.)

(Contd. Table 2.3)

Attributes	*Tinsukia*	*Nagaon*	*Kamrup*	*Karimganj*	*Assam*
Primary sector (%)	30.72	49.04	14.25	48.10	45.50
Secondary sector	24.06	18.88	19.04	17.81	16.59
Tertiary sector	45.22	32.08	66.71	34.09	37.90
Total Main workers as % of total population	36.50	29.26	28.71	26.92	31.19
Main (male) workers as % of male population	48.56	49.78	48.30	47.45	48.38
Main female workers as % of female population	22.96	7.18	6.40	5.21	12.57
Total marginal workers as % of total population	4.18	6.20	3.88	1.98	4.89
Male marginal workers as % of male population	1.75	0.90	0.67	0.65	1.07

(Contd.)

(Contd. Table 2.3)

Attributes	*Tinsukia*	*Nagaon*	*Kamrup*	*Karimganj*	*Assam*
Female marginal workers as % of female population	6.91	11.90	7.54	3.39	9.04
Cultivators as % of total main workers	35.41	54.80	35.05	43.14	50.9
Agricultural Labourers as % of main workers	5.82	14.77	8.22	16.64	12.08
Other workers as % of main workers	58.77	30.43	56.74	40.22	37.01

*Per capita Gross District Domestic Product. Tinsukia's per capita GDDP seems to be underestimated.

Source: Statistical Hand Book, Assam, 2002 (Compiled data).

Table 2.4

Other socio-economic parameters (miscellaneous) of the sample districts/Assam.

Attributes	*Tinsukia*	*Nagaon*	*Kamrup*	*Karimganj*	*Assam*
Rainfall in MM (normal)	1772	2626	2127	3312	2584
Sub-division (31-5-02)	3	3	3	1	49
SC as % of total population (1991)	2.61	10.02	7.54	14.58	7.40
ST as % of total population (1991)	5.35	3.69	10.72	0.17	12.82
Forest (%)	34.94	21.98	26.14	30.13	24.59
Land not available for cultivation (%)	30.0	13.14	20.06	21.05	31.98
Fertiliser (NPK) consumption (in tonnes-2001-02)	6464	20256	11139	2785	152946

(Contd.)

(Contd. Table 2.4)

Attributes	*Tinsukia*	*Nagaon*	*Kamrup*	*Karimganj*	*Assam*
Crop intensity -- 1998-99 (%)	139.94	156.56	138.92	151.65	145.89
Irrigation potential utilized in 1999 -- 2000 (%)	6.98	99.16	44.33	7.31	23.66
No. of registered factories (2001)	350	115	521	63	2512
Installation of STW (1997-98 to July 2002) under ARIASP and SKY*	2230	16996	16265	-	146292
No. of scheduled commercial banks (2002)	69	87	171	45	1232
C-D ratio (March 2002)	0.25	0.22	0.38	0.16	0.31
Linked by	Rail, Road & waterways	Rail, Road & waterways	Rail, Road, air & waterways	Roadways & railways	Siliguri corridor & airways

*Assam Rural Infrastructure and Agriculture Services Project (ARIASP) and Samriddha Krishak Yojana (SKY).

Composition of the Sample Households

Occupation wise distribution of sample households:

* Agriculture	260
Industry	25
Tertiary	215

Caste wise distribution:

ST	104
SC	62
OBC	157
General	177

Land status wise distribution:

Landless hh. (< 1 bigha)	115
Marginal Farmer (< 8 bigha)	190
Small Farmer (8 – 16)	115
Semi-medium Farmer (16+)	80

Village location-wise distribution:

Remote Village	250
Village nearby towns	250

* Further break-up of agricultural households:

Landless households	26
Marginal Farmer	80
Small Farmer	90
Semi-medium farmer	64

* Break-up of tertiary households (including 67 government employees):

Landless households	84
Landed households	131

* Break up of industrial households:

Landless households	5
Landed households	20

District wise distribution:

1. Kamrup (lower Assam) : 140 households.
   Remote Villages: Malukhatal(ST) and Pub-Borichuka (61).
   Villages Nearby Towns: Dwigunpar(OBC) and Rangmohal (79).
   Sub-divisions: Rangia and Guwahati.

2. Nagaon (Central Assam) : 120 households.
   Remote Villages : Heragaon(SC) and Panjabari/Mosoka, (47).
   Villages Nearby Towns: Bamungaon and Begenati (73).
   Sub-divisions: Nagaon and Hojai.

3. Tinsukia (Upper Assam) : 120
   Remote Villages: Powaimukh(ST), Manmou Ulup/ Barmura (IV – 78).

Villages Nearby Towns: Balijan and Bozaltoli (42).
Sub-divisions: Margherita and Tinsukia.

4. Karimganj (Barak Valley) : 120
RemoteVillages: Eraligul and Nayabari (64).
Villages Nearby Towns: Sridurgapur (/Das gram -SC) and Batarashi (56).
Sub-division: Karimganj (North and South Karimganj blocks).

Positive sides of the sample

1. A detail questionnaire was prepared, tested and then canvassed among the sample households directly and personally.
2. The author spent considerable time with the sample households, for which he had to stay in the villages sometimes for weeks together. (On few occasions, lack of motorable road compelled the author to do so).
3. The author took the help from local youth clubs/ social workers/local NGOs at the time of survey — for introduction, getting an easy access to the village - which, at the same time, allowed the author with an extra advantage of cross verification of the facts collected from the interviewee.
4. Sample districts and villages were selected purposively with the objective of making the sample truly representative of the state population. Each sample village was then stratified on the basis of the broad socio-economic characteristics of its residents. The sample households were drawn on the basis of stratified random sampling method.

Limitations of the sample

1. Hill districts are not covered in the sample.
2. Proportionate representation of the different social groups (in relation to each district's population composition) has

not been made in the sample. Scheduled Caste population constitutes a low percentage share in the state population. However, since SC population receive special significance in the government developmental schemes and as their presence in certain economic activities can be felt in all the sample districts, this group of population has been given a fair representation in the sample. In other words, (fair) representation of the different social groups in the sample is to be seen only in terms of the size of the sample.

3. Only 20 per cent to 25 per cent (depending on the size of the village) of the total households in each sample village were included in the present study. However, care was taken to include fair number of households belonging to the different social and economic groups.

A brief description of the sample villages (district wise)

Kamrup district — hub of commercial activities and also, moderately developed in agricultural sector – is taken from the lower Assam. The district has the highest number of financial institutions in the state. The sample villages from the district were taken from the north bank of the Brahmaputra which is relatively less developed and more agrarian.

Major minerals found in the district : Granite, quartz and feldspar.

Major plantation in the district is tea.

Dwigunpar

The village Dwigunpar is located 3 km away from Kamalpur under the jurisdiction of Rangia sub-division in Kamrup district. It was under Bordek par GP. The geographical area of the village was over 2000 bigha, of which nearly 1500 bighas were cultivable. Around 300 households inhabit the village. The village is linked to Kamalpur town by a kutcha road. The condition of road was not found good because of floods during the last two consecutive years. In fact, high floods in recent times, had snapped its road connectivity with Borka. Regular markets, commercial banks/RRBs, one private bank, educational institutions, etc. were located within 4 km radius.

The village was largely inhabited by backward caste people. The primary occupation of the villagers was agriculture. However, non-agricultural occupation has been on the rise as it was located just 3 km away from Kamalpur/National Highway leading to Guwahati (30 km).

Due to the breach of embankment over the Puthimari river, the villagers were exposed to severe floods and loss of standing crops has become a regular feature. Early cropping was not possible due to uncertainity of floods (late Sali was in practice), while rabi crops was not possible due to water shortages. Government minor canal irrigation scheme from Puthimari river was lying abandoned since 1989. However, the office still exists, but employees were not getting salaries for past many months. Subsidised STW scheme has not been offered to this village till the date of survey. Only one sample household had STW, 3 households owned pumpsets and a tractor. Most surprisingly, KCC holders were not reported at all. Only 2 women-SHGs were formed just before the survey. Wrong conception about the rules of formation of SHGs and indifferent role of the PRIs/blocks, etc. were responsible for much late entry of the SHGs in this village. One block official had visited the village in mid-September 2002 to encourage villagers to form SHGs. He explained the village women that only BPL women can form SHGs and get the benefits of the government schemes including revolving fund.

Very interestingly, almost all the women members (also, a large majority of the males) were members of thrift and credit groups. The basic difference between these groups with the

SHGs was that the credit and thrift groups were formed for a fixed period of 1 – 3 years, at the end of which the accumulated group funds are distributed among the members according to their respective contributions. Old groups break down at regular intervals, while new groups are formed. Some members join 2 – 4 groups at a time for 2 – 3 years. The credit and thrift groups used to give loan at 3 – 5 per cent monthly rate of interest to the group members, but only at higher rate of interest (5 – 7 %) to non-members. According to the individual members' strength, the monthly contribution varied from Rs. 5 per weak to Rs. 200 per month.

Electricity was there, although it was concentrated only in the central part. It is very sad to note that to start a rice mill, one household was compelled to pay Rs. 10000 to ASEB for extension of the high voltage line to the factory site. Also he had to pay Rs 15000 as speed money to the officials of the Assam Financial Corporation to get two loans with high subsidy provision. There is no denying the fact that the extra costs in terms of 'lost time, energy, money, and faith in the bureaucratic system' is quite high in Assam which often discourages entrepreneurial activities among the potential local entrepreneurs. The prevailing unethical practice has also negatively contributed to the region's poor repayment ratio.

Pub-borichuka

This village was located 7 km away from Kamalpur. The approach road to the village was kutcha which turns unmotorable during rainy season. The village was located 4 km from kamalpur-Borka road which was in bad shape due to flood devastation and subsequent inaction by the PWD department. Since 1989 (when a few culverts were badly damaged by floods), Guwahati-Rangia passenger buses had stopped plying on this road. Apart from National Highway 31, this was the only road which links Guwahati with Rangia, Mangoldoi, Goreswar, etc. This was also the shortest route, but presently in dilapidated condition.

This is pre-dominantly a tribal village. The main occupation of the villagers was agriculture. Absence of irrigation facilities was responsible for sustaining the practice of mono-cropping.

The village was covered under anti-poverty loan scheme. However, like most of the villages in Assam, misuse of loans, poor motivation for repayment and lack of follow up services from bank / NGOs were responsible for almost no impact of the anit-poverty schemes on their economy. Consequently, the repayment ratio was extremely poor.

The village was partially covered by electricity supply. For past few months there was no electricity, due to out-of-shape transformer. As many as 50 households had not paid electricity bill due quite some time, ranging from Rs. 500 to Rs. 7000. Now the ASEB want at least 50 per cent of the arrears to be cleared first for replacement of the transformer.

Poor infrastructure was responsible for isolation of the village from the main stream. In fact, non-availability of all-weather road connectivity and irritating distance from regular organized market (which can provide remunerative price and motivation for commercial cultivation) were responsible for subsistence nature of the economy.

Nature product (fish catch from wetland) constitute a significant portion of the villagers' income (+ nutrition). However, population explosion led over-exploitation of these vital but ill-managed resources was responsible for falling income from common property resources in recent times.

The village was affected by floods for last few years. Although, in this village as well as in Dwigunpar, silt deposition has not assumed a problem, uncontrolled flood has caused huge erosion of the other village assets including vital infrastructure.

Rangmohal

Rangmohal was a village of mixed population. It falls under the Rudreshaw Gaon Panchayat in Bezera Block. Rangmohal has around 1600 population. Since it was located very close to north bank of the Brahmaputra, near ferry services which leads to Guwahati, a large number of households in non-agricultural profession were reported even among the ST households.

The village has electricity connection and an all weather motorable road. A number of shops – grocery stores, electrical appliances, panshops, cosmetic items, PCO, etc. – were seen in the outskirt of the village, on the road side. The village has the added advantage of bi-weekly market on Sunday and Wednesday in the locality. Two nationalized banks (apart from a private bank) were located within 4 km radius. One degree college was also there within walking distance from the village.

Most unfortunately, almost all the cooperative societies were found in dying condition, as was the case in all other districts of Assam. 'Fulung Rangmohal Bhaiyam Janajati Samabay Samiti' (Farmers Cooperative Society) worked for 7 years effectively. The society got a tractor from the government and 150 bighas of government land on lease. However, after giving service for 7 years, when the tractor developed some technical problems, the society failed to motivate a mechanic to visit their remote field where tractor was lying abandoned.

Lack of cooperation, integration and faith among the members led to its failure. The 16 powerful members divided the 150 bighas of land equally between them, which led to the complete break down of the cooperative inside 10 years of its birth.

Quite a few educated women (simple graduate/HSSLC) in the village, were working as Sahara/Peerless/LIC agents. Non-agricultural activities were on the rise.

Malukhatal

It was a remote village largely inhibited by ST community. The main occupation of the villagers was agriculture. The total number of households in the village was around 100. It was located 12 km away from Guwahati. The village falls in Bezera block under Guwahati sub-division. The approach road was pucca in most of the part and motorable in all seasons. The village has electricity supply. Tapping underground water by pumpset (individual effort) was the only source of irrigation. The village was covered by government's anti-poverty scheme.

Just one km from the village, on the road side, there was a regular market. It is observed that many tribal educated youths were very keen to leave agricultural activities (mostly given to the tenants on lease) and engaged themselves in non-agricultural activities.

The villagers have a unique tradition of group savings (thrift and credit groups) for past 3 decades or so. Few such groups have recently transformed their thrift and credit groups (which were temporary in nature) into SHGs (supposed to be more permanent in nature) with uniform contribution. In thrift and credit groups, any member can save any amount. The interested members have the provision to save in the name of their children as well. These groups were formed for a fixed period of 2 to 3 years. Sometimes, savings were kept in post offices in which case members misses the loan facilities from group funds. However, most of the groups used to keep a certain portion of their savings in fixed deposit and the rest amount was made available for lending in small amounts to the members. Very interestingly, the interest rate varied between groups (and also between members and non-members), from 2 per cent to 5 per cent per month (Occasionally, interest rate even went up to 10 % per month, but only from the non-member borrowers). Almost all the adult (male and female) were the members of credit and thrift groups. Few people were members of 2 – 3 groups simultaneously.

Nagaon: Nagaon district is centrally located and agriculturally developed (but industrially backward) district of Assam located in the south bank of the Brahmaputra. Cropping intensity, irrigation facilities (STW and canal irrigation), use of fertilizers, intensity of crop diversification etc. are much higher in this district. However, other infrastructural facilities are not satisfactory in the district. The district is considered as the vegetable belt of Assam.

The distribution of a large number of shallow tube wells (STWs) to the farmers at a highly subsidized price during 1990s under the World Bank scheme adequately supported by the government/NABARD was instrumental in ushering green revolution in certain districts of central and lower Assam. Nagaon district is one of the few districts in Assam which has witnessed green revolution along with the rest of India. The district produces surplus rice, fish and plenty of seasonal vegetables (including 'early and late seasons' vegetables and off season vegetables) and exports it across the state, sometimes to the neighbouring states. These progressive farmers mostly belonging to the immigrant population (some times termed as '*na-asomia*') are by nature very hard working and have the capacity to learn quickly. Largely settled in geographically disadvantageous areas (char areas) the minority people are trying hard to cope with the recurring devastating floods in the state and experiment with different crop combinations, often successfully in low lying fields or heavily silted land.

Particularly in Nagaon district, few big farmers reported about employing (*halua*/ploughmen) tied labourers. The halua (cannot be termed as bonded labour) was engaged either on monthly or yearly contract basis. The *halua* works for more than 10 – 12 hours a day in the field. Also, they have to look after the comforts of domestic animals. These tied landless agricultural labourers (aged between 13 – 50 years), hardly get Rs. 10000 to Rs. 13000 per year.

There was another group of *halua* who works on monthly basis. They generally get Rs. 1200 per month. However, these workers can be discontinued at any point of time.

Major minerals found in the district: Granite and Quartz.

Major plantation crops in the district: tea, rubber and coffee.

Begenati

The village is located four km away from Nagaon town, a district headquarter in central Assam. The village has 300 families with a population of little less than 1800. The village is linked to the Nagaon market by a graveled motorable road. It is a very developed and agriculturally surplus village. The successful implementation of the STW scheme in the village has brought about 80 per cent of the village cropped land under irrigation facilities.

In Begenati village, the incidence of institutional loans to the farmers irrespective of land status was found higher also because the village FMCs and one NGO were reported to have been pressurizing the lending agencies to provide loans, KCCs in particular.

At the time of investigation, the local NGO of Begenati got 4 projects from DRDA. The sanctioned amount was Rs. 22.50 lakh per project. The Project Director's (who was also the FMC Secretary) main function was to encourage the formation of SHGs among women, awareness campaign, supporting seed capital/working capital for dairy, poultry, tailoring, weaving, mushroom cultivation, etc. The maximum limit of fund support per group was fixed at Rs. 25000. The system followed was that two-thirds of the project cost will be funded by the NGO, while the rest one-third of the cost to be contributed by the SHGs from their accumulated funds.

Promoting 'user group' (members having land above 7 bigha) and development of pond, land, crop demonstration, community hall, construction of approach road to fields, small irrigation, culvert and embankment, etc were incorporated in water shed development schemes. Ironically, all the projects were taken up far outside the Begenati village.

The village was well covered by one SBI branch, Lakshimi Gaonlia Bank and Assam Cooperative Apex Bank. Besides, private credit agencies were also accessible to the villagers. Being adjacent to Nagaon town, it has good access to educational institutions, agricultural extension services, health care, etc. The village has two Field Management Committees: Agragami FMC (120 members) and Pub-Begenati FMC (105 members).

About 30 Agragami FMC members owned individual pumpsets for irrigation. An equal number, i.e. 30 Pub-Begenati FMC members had also owned pumpset (STW) for irrigation. The village was covered under government irrigation scheme. However, the Government minor canal irrigation facilities was found unsatisfactory for water was never distributed in time and in adequate amount. This was the main reason for which a large number of farmers have managed their individual pumpsets. Many small farmers reported that they have used hired pumpset, tractor/power tiller from the neighbours as and when required. The FMCs also collect tractor from block office (currently, captured by a powerful rich farmer) during agricultural season to be used by the members only.

The villagers have a cooperative society viz. Pathori Samabay Samiti. Its main function was limited to drawing ration for the members and providing small loans to the members at moderate to high rate of interest.

As many as 52 households received Kisan Credit Card (KCC) of which 8 numbers were distributed during 2002.

Another 10-12 households were in the process of getting KCC. This is quite high in comparison to other villages in Assam. The level of implementation of KCC scheme in Assam was extremely poor in comparison to other states of the country. Lack of up-to-date land documents and the cumbrous procedure of transfer of land rights, etc was acting as stumbling block for the farmers who have not yet got the KCCs in the village.

In 2002, SBI Khutikutia branch distributed crop loans worth Rs. 5 lakh to its 37 KCC holders, while the Assam Cooperative Apex Bank (11 KCCs) and Lakshimi Gaonlia Bank (4 KCCs) together advanced Rs. 1.5 lakh to the farmers of Begenati. Only 3 years back this village was in the bank's defaulter list. In recent times, quite a few KCC holders were approached by the bank officials to take much higher amount of loans (for power tillers, tractors, etc.). The credibility of the KCC holders has increased considerably because of the bumper production which was made possible by increasing mechanization, crop diversification and more use of manures, HYV seeds, etc. through credit. The initiative taken by a bank manager to recover the IRDP loan overdues from a couple of farmers after distributing KCCs (to them) had also positively contributed to the overall recovery and repayment culture in the village. Another encouraging feature was that, of late, quite a few self help groups (including women SHGs) have been formed in the village, under the influence of village FMC.

The western part of the village was often affected by floods where rice, mustard seeds and jute were grown. The per bigha productivity of rice was found 5.2 quintals in the case of *sali* rice (kharif season) and 9.4 quintals in the case of *boro* rice (*rabi* season). During *rabi* crops relatively high dose of organic and chemical fertilizers were used, apart from pesticides.

In the East Begenati, the farmers grow vegetables all the year round on the 84 hectares of land which were not flood affected. The crop intensity was found above 330 per cent in this flood-free arable zone. There was no seasonal unemployment problem in the village. Not a single family was short of two square meals a day. The unique farm practice adopted by the villagers yielded net income of Rs 18000 to 22000 per bigha per year (Farm income is equal to the value of gross output minus all costs excluding imputed value of human labour charge provided by the farms family and interest on fixed capital). The land use pattern of Begenati village is ideal for thousands of marginal and small farmers living below the poverty line particularly in upper Assam region where the normal practice is mono cropping (rain fed sali crops). During 2001, a large number of villagers grew potato, brinjal, ridge-gourd and one or two leafy vegetables on the 84 hectares of land which was entirely covered under the STW scheme.

The farmers of the village raise one or two leafy vegetables for a short period of 30 – 45 days on a small plot of land and get Rs. 1500 – Rs. 1600 per bigha. In the case of potato cultivation (October – December), roughly one month after sowing potato seeds they sow one row of brinjal seedlings on 2 : 1 basis i.e, after every two rows of potatoes, one row of brinjal seedlings is sown. It is done in such a unique fashion that when the potatoes are ready for harvesting, the brinjal plants start flowering. Then the farmers put ridge-gourd seedlings (when potato harvesting is over) besides the flowering brinjal plants. The creepers (*jhinga*) will thus have a free growth on the old brinjal plants at the point when it (brinjal) no longer bears fruit. This system reduces the costs of bamboo support to the climbing plant to the minimum for the farmers, apart from increasing the intensity of land use.

The successful crop-combination adopted by the villagers were as follows:

* Potato + brinjal + ridge-gourd + 1 or 2 leafy vegetables.
* early season cabbage + seasonal cabbage + late season cabbage.
* 10 – 12 varieties of seasonal leafy vegetables (spinach) ideal for tiny farmers owning 1 to 3 bigha land.
* Mustard seeds + paddy/ jute + paddy – weather permitting in the case of flood affected land.
* Mustard seeds + jute + leafy vegetables.

As already mentioned these hardworking farmers grow vegetables round the year with application of power tillers, irrigated water, chemical fertilizers, pesticides and plenty of cow dung. They have already developed a good 'experimenting temper' and plant as many seedlings as possible so that not an inch of land remains unexploited.

It is a matter of concern that because of the excessive use of pesticides and chemical fertilizers by many farmers, a few respondents reported about the frequent problems of stomach disorder and poor eye-sight. Sometimes vegetables (/slightly rotten vegetables) taste so much bitter that even livestock refuses to eat. Nevertheless only recently, two one-day awareness campaigns about the judicious application of chemical fertilizers and pesticides were organized by the FMC of the village.

It is because of the lack of cold storage facilities, absence of cooperative marketing network and government collection centres (the presence of a large number of commission agents and illegal check gates between the farm house and the wholesale market also adds to their woes), the farmers of Assam have to sell their crops at throw-away prices particularly during the peak seasons when markets are flooded with vegetables (paddy

Table 2.5

The average yield of different crops in Begenati village during 2001-2002.

Crops	*Average yield per bigha (in quintal)*	*Average price (in Rs.)*	*Value of the product*	*Cost of production per bigha per year (all crops)*	
Potato	30	4.00	12000	Cow dung (one truck)	1200
Brinjal	40	2.50	10000	Chemical fertilizers	2000
Ridge Gourd	20	3.00	6000	Pesticides	500
Leafy vegetables	*		1500	Irrigation	600
				Seeds	600
				Power tiller(hired)	400
				Wages paid	2300
				Transportation, others	1600
			29500		9200

* Normally raised in 1- 1 ½ bigha land & sold in a lot. ** 1 bigha = 0.13 hectare.

* Farm income is equal to the value of gross output minus all costs excluding imputed value of human labour charge provided by the farms family and interest on fixed capital.

in some pockets). The farmers hardly get 15-20 per cent of the actual price paid by the consumer. The sample village is getting much better price (remunerative price) because it is located near Nagaon wholesale market. Moreover, these farmers give stress on producing early and late season crops so as to get higher prices of the product.

Subsidising access to public infrastructure services is often more useful for the poor than price subsidies. (World Bank, 1994). There is no gain saying that by establishing all weather road connectivity to the villages with surplus production, the income of the farmers can easily be raised up to 20-40 per cent which is more important than any other infrastructure including credit support to the poor. All weather road connectivity quickens the transportation of perishable commodities, reduce transport cost which sometimes constitutes above 50 per cent of the farm price, facilitate access of the farmers to nearest organized markets thereby free them from the clutches of the unscrupulous commission agents and above all, it gives big incentive (by allowing them remunerative price) to produce more thereby directly contributing to the state GDP. It is the need of the hour that stress is given on creating cold storage facilities in some of the developed rabi crops belt by the FMCs with adequate support from the NABARD, NEDFi, district administration and NGOs. This will definitely add to the income of the progressive farmers by allowing them a much better price and reducing the volume of discarded rotten vegetables.

Heeragaon

Heeragaon was a SC village located 6 km away from Nagaon town. It was mainly an agricultural village, although quite a few households reported to have been working in informal sector in Nagaon town. There were 25 SC households in the village. An equal number of non-SC households were also living in the village, mostly farmers.

The approach road of the village was kutcha, although motorable in all seasons. The village was fully electrified. The source of drinking water was tubewell and well.

The village was moderately covered by the government's anti-poverty loan schemes.

A couple of decades back, the villagers used to grow sugar cane. However, all the farmers, in recent times, switch over to vegetables/multiple cropping. According to them, in case of sugar cane production, the gestation period was high, i.e., one full year. Moreover, the second year income from sugar cane was also less. But in the case of vegetables, gestation period is hardly 3 months. It is also more remunerative and the chances of 'flood loss' as often experienced in the case of *Sali* paddy is much less.

The cropping intensity in this village was above 200 per cent. Like Begenati village, the farmers of this village also reported that lack of smooth up-dating of land record (quick transfer of ownership rights of land as and when such a situation arises) was the crucial obstacle in the way of their access to KCCs.

Bamungaon

This village falls in Udali Block under the jurisdiction of Hojai sub-division in Nagaon district. It is a road side village, 5 km away from Lanka town. In spite of the location of the block development office at a stone's throw distance from the village, the villagers failed so far to take the advantage of government schemes.

The village falls in the rain shadow area. For a brief period only, land can be irrigated from ponds, without which cultivation is very unsafe in this belt. No government irrigation schemes exist in this village. Only a couple of deep tubewell were provided by the government for meeting the drinking water needs of the village.

No organized watershed development schemes could be observed in this critically placed sample village or in its surroundings except a small number ponds at the individual level which can supply small amount of water to the vegetable fields till the end of December. From January to May, the area becomes very dry.

Due to harsh weather and absence of peoples' organized action (also, may be because of the unwise selection of crop variety which requires more water), the villagers were compelled to lead a subsistence living. Regular threats of drought and crop failures restricted financial institutions to extend KCCs or any other agricultural loans. Even the IRDP/ SGSY scheme (which emphasized on livestock/ milking cow, poultry and weaving) was found less familiar and ineffective in the region because of the shortages of fodder/grass land particularly in the case of dairy farming.

Nevertheless, the scope of watershed development was there, if and when adequate amount of funds are made available to appropriate professional organizations which would also help in the development of fisheries.

Only one women SHG was formed in the village by the 'deprived' Muslim women till the date of investigation.

Punjabari (Mosoka)

The village falls in the Dhalpukhuri Block under the Hojai sub-division. It is located 6 km away from Lanka town. The kutcha approach road was in dilapidated condition. It is a village of mixed population. The village economy was affected by shortages of water, as it was also located in rain shadow area.

However, the region has good scope of storing monsoonal run off which mainly comes from the nearby hills, presently untapped.

The primary occupation of the villagers was agriculture, dairy farming and commercial activities in Lanka town. Only a few households have pumpsets for irrigation from ponds.

The village was spread over 1500 bigha of agricultural land with population of around 1200. Wage earners (agricultural and non-agricultural) constituted about 20 per cent of the total population. Cultivators, mainly marginal farmers, accounted for majority of the village population. The village was sparsely covered by electricity supply. Like Bamungaon, government development schemes have largely by passed this remote village.

Although the villagers formed FMC few years back, at the time of investigation, it was almost non-functioning. Lack of coordination between FMC, block office, PRIs and financial institutions was vividly realized which had also restricted the spread of SHGs or KCC movement in this region.

It was very discouraging to note that a few women respondents belonging to the religious minority expressed that male members of the family dislike to admit their wives to the hospital at the time of delivery, which also reduces the incidence of immunization rate. Relatively low socio-economic condition might be responsible for it.

As in Bamungaon, the villagers were largely unaware of the SHGs formed in large numbers in other blocks of the district. Only one SHG was formed by the ST women.

Tubewell was the main source of water.

Lawlessness was its another problem. In this region, the high incidence of dacoity, theft, etc. was reported.

Tinsukia

Tinsukia district is relatively developed in industrial sector (and plantation sector) but less developed in terms of the different agricultural parameters. The district has experienced considerable fall in income/ certain economic activities (cottage and small scale industries) in recent times mainly because of the Supreme Court's ban on tree felling since 1996.

Major minerals found in the district: Crude oil and coal.

Major plantation crops in the district: Tea and rubber.

Powaimukh

This was a tribal village, although non-tribal population has outnumbered them in recent past. It is located 14 km away from Margherita town under the jurisdiction of Margherita sub-division in Tinsukia district. The connective road is kutcha which becomes unmotorable during the rainy season.

The number of ST families in the village was 42, while the non-tribal constituted another 50 households. The village was spread over 1600 bigha of agricultural and high land. Not a single labour household was recorded among the tribal households. However, among the non-tribal communities, nearly 15 agricultural labour households with or without small amount of agricultural land were reported.

Quite a few big farmers were reported among these people. The primary occupation of the villagers was agriculture (mono-cropped). Sali rice was the main crop in the village. Orange and tea were the main cash crops of the village. The villagers reported sizeable amount of income from bamboo, tokou palm leaves, arecanut, oranges and very recently, from the sale of 'green tea leaf'. Of late, tea plantation in very small scale has received importance amongst the villagers thereby creating considerable amount of pressure on the community land, which may badly affect the interests of the poorer households in near future.

It is because of the out of shaped transformer, there was no electricity for the past 3 years. Government's canal irrigation system was also non-functioning (rather washed away by devastating floods in 1995). A few households got pumpsets for irrigation purposes at a subsidized price. These pumpsets were used for irrigation in the tea gardens and/or, for running the rice mills. The area under irrigation was nominal and the cropping intensity quite low. The per bigha productivity of Sali rice was around 8 maunds.

The Powaimukh FMC has got one power tiller from the government. It also collects seeds, etc from the block office as and when made available by the government. However, neither the government nor the bank has so far tried to use the FMC platform to improve the recovery ratio.

Banks and regular markets were located 14 kms away i.e., in Margherita. Nabard/World Bank's STW scheme was availed by a couple of households only. Few small tea growers took loans from the purchaser of 'green tea leaf' for cutting, toning, purchasing fertilizers or pesticides on condition that they will sell their green leaves only to them (i.e., repayment in kind / fixed business relation).

Only one grocery shop and a pan shop were there in the village. Two LP schools and one ME school (within 1 km) and one high school were located within 4 km from the village.

The village was covered by the government's anti-poverty schemes. However, its impact was nominal as most of the households who received government assistance (/bank loan) diverted to non-productive use. The repayment culture was missing in the village, as was the case in most of the other villages except Begenati. It was observed that quite a few youth expecting bigger amount of loans (PMRY, etc.) with high amount of subsidy from the government. They have shown much less interest in KCCs and SHGs. Very recently, two SHGs were constituted – one by the male members and the other, by females.

One cooperative society was functioning in the area with 51 members. Members were mostly from non-tribal communities of the adjacent villages. The society got two permanent sheds from the government – one for poultry and the other, for piggery. However, in early 1995, in one night, all the pigs were killed by unidentified person by poisoning, while the devastating floods in the mid-1995 which last for quite some times completely destroyed the poultry farm. The second tragic incident had also sealed the fate of the cooperative society. Both the poultry and piggery sheds, which may require minimum to considerable amounts for repairing, currently lying abandoned.

There were few rich households in the village who were both lenders as well as borrowers at the same point of time.

During the cultivation season, even the rich farmers were seen taken loans from the shop-keepers, and repaid the same in kind immediately after the harvesting.

As already said, the village was affected by occasional floods. It was losing large size of arable land due to massive soil erosion/river bank erosion. It was also occasionally affected by storms.

It was either because of floods or storms, a few households had to mortgaged some amount of land for repair or reconstruction of badly damaged house (chang ghar) and also, for food consumption.

In this village, quite a few households reported loan against mortgage of land. In normal situation, maximum of Rs. 5000 could be borrowed against mortgage of one bigha land, although the market value of land may be higher by 6 to 7 times. When the productivity of land was low and the mortgaged land was only suitable for rice cultivation (low lying, flood affected or drought prone land), the amount of loan made available was even less. In Powaimukh, Bamungaon or in Dwigunpar, where the usual practice was mono-cropping (Sali crops), one bigha land yields crop value of around Rs. 2200. The cost of production was at least, one-third of the total production. If the moneylender than leased out the piece of which was mortgaged-in (often to the borrower himself), he gets one-third of the crop value of Rs. 2200. In other words, he will go on receiving Rs. 733 as interest in all the normal years till the borrowers fully repay the loan amount. Loan repayment in parts is always discouraged by such moneylenders.

However, in Begenati (also, in Heeragaon), the terms and conditions of such loans differed widely. In the vegetable belt, one bigha land can produce crop value worth Rs. 10000 (flood affected land where jute and boro paddy is grown) to as high as Rs. 28000 (3 – 5 cash crops are grown on the same plot of land).

In the vegetable belt, Rs. 20000 was also borrowed against mortgaged of one bigha land. Generally, the lender force the borrower to make an informal agreement so that land can be released only after 5 years. The borrowers can release their land at any time only after the completion of 5 years term, by paying the full amount of loan of Rs. 20000.

If the borrower borrows in the range of Rs. 5000 – Rs. 10000, or even less, in such cases mortgaged land can be released at any point of time by repaying the principal amount.

Only two households, out of the 45 cases of borrowings against mortgage of land, had also required to pay 10 per cent additional rate of interest on the borrowed amount. In both these cases, quality of mortgaged land was poor and regularly affected by natural calamities.

In the flood free vegetable belt, if a borrower borrows in the range of Rs. 5000 – Rs. 10000, he will get back his land automatically after 5 years. In this case he need not repay the principal amount borrowed. However, the mortgaged land can be released even before 5 years. But in that case, the borrower will have to pay back the entire loan amount.

The author has also interviewed some households from Manmau Ulup, a remote village occupied mainly by ex-tea communities. The socio-economic condition of these people was very low in the state of Assam. The sample village was also completely by passed by the different government's developmental schemes. This was done to make the sample truly representative of the state population.

The villagers were mostly farmers. Of late, orange and tea cultivation has received some importance among the few better off households.

The village was located 18 km away from Margherita town. The approach road was mostly kutcha and was very difficult to ride on during rainy days.

Sali crops was pre-dominant (10 maunds per bigha), although a few households also practiced Ahu (7 maunds per bigha). The cropping intensity was found around 130 per cent.

Interestingly, in this village, the incidence of borrowings against land mortgaged has gone down significantly since the SHG movement had started in this region. However, loans which were taken against mortgage of land 5 – 10 years back remains yet active.

In this village, by taking the advantage of ignorance and simplicity, even government officials/*gram sevaks* brutally cheated few farmers. For instance, in 1998, two farmers deposited with the gram *sevak* Rs. 9500 each for STW. But till the date of survey (mid 2003), STW was not delivered to the concerned farmers. The gram sevak, as reported by the respondents, blamed the already transferred Block Development Officer for the unusual delay in releasing the STW.

The village has recorded quite a few school-drop outs and never attended children. Government's universal literacy campaign had no impact (in fact, till mid-2003 no officials related to literacy campaign visited this village).

The incidence of women employment in temporary jobs/ seasonal jobs was very high in the sample villages in Tinsukia district. It was mainly because of two factors: (i) women from ex-tea communities often takes part in plucking tea leafs, due to poor socio-economic condition (also, because it has almost become a culture) and (ii) mushrooming growth of tiny tea gardens where mostly family labour is used.

Of late, quite a few SHGs were formed in the village mainly under the influence of one father who had visited the local missionary school from outside Assam. Also, one NGO member was working in this area for last one year to promote SHGs and user groups. Zila Pather Parichalana Samity (District FMC) Tinsukia has appointed a community Organiser – Monmaujan NWDPRA w.e.f September 1, 2002. The NGO worker strongly expressed his dissatisfaction that in neighbouring villages, DRDA deposited sum of Rs. 10000 each with a couple of SHG accounts as revolving fund, when the actual number of SHG members were not more than 5 – 6 and that all of them were not genuine.

The Government's old age pension scheme for the BPL families was found of limited use, so was the case with IAY. Only a few households reported to have got pension for some months, maximum for two years. Much lower aged women/

relatively better off widowed and even , one wife of a retired government employee got pension, in spite of highly competitive market.

Balijan

This village was located 3 km away from Digboi town. It was under Margherita sub-division in Tinsukia district.

It was a village of mixed population. A considerable number of tribal and SC population are also living in this areas. This falls in the flood free zone.

The village was spread over 1700 bigha of arable land. Quite a few nationalized banks and one each RRB and Cooperative bank (almost inactive) have been functioning in this region. In terms of educational and medical facilities, markets and transportation, the village was advantageously placed.

It was a surplus village in terms of rice and vegetable production. Of late, considerable amount of investment was made on tea cultivation extending into homestead land, vegetable garden, horticultural land, paddy field and also forest land. Nearly half of the households were dependant on non-agricultural activities including petty trade, contractors, salaried jobs, mechanics, transport workers, etc.

The village was covered by different anti-poverty schemes. However, repayment ratio was extremely poor. Of late, the villagers were taking some interest in forming SHGs particularly by the women.

Most unfortunately, irrespective of 'male and female SHGs', at least half of the SHGs were formed in the sample villages with the primary objective of getting 'high subsidy based loan scheme'/revolving fund. This general tendency of the SHG members may not help in improving the repayment ratio in the state from 20 – 30 per cent to at least 90 per cent in near future.

Few households reported of having savings accounts in bank. Most unfortunately, in most of the cases no transaction was made during the last year or two. This was the general trend in the sample villages. However, all the bank account holders were reported in the table irrespective of the fact that most of these accounts were inactive.

Bozaltoti

This was located 3 km away from Tinsukia town. The approach road was mostly pucca and motorable throughout the year.

The majority of the households in the village were engaged in non-agricultural activities. The households were largely from OBC communities. The cropping intensity was below 130 per cent. Pumpset irrigation was the main source of agriculture during rabi season.

In terms of financial institutions, regular markets, remunerative price of the produces, and scope for non-agricultural activities, this village was advantageously located. A couple of group loans were taken by few households. However, the loan-assets was mainly utilized by the richest member of the group. This was tactfully done by a couple of rich farmers to take the advantage of hefty government subsidy allowed on power tiller when purchased by a group of farmers.

The incidence of leased in land was high among the land poor. Many rich farmers who have recently shifted to or expanded their non-agricultural activities leased out their agricultural land. The amount of rent varied from one-third to one-half of the production. If the owners of land provide all inputs (plough, seeds, etc), other than labour, then their share rises up to 50 per cent of the total production. In other cases, where the tillers use his own bullock but borrowed seeds from the owners, rent varies between 33 per cent to 40 per cent.

It was observed that when the rent was fixed at one-third of the total production (the normal charge prevailing in the state) and if the tenant households who undertakes leased in land also required to borrow all other agricultural inputs except labour, the cost of production comes to around (sometimes even more than one-third of the total production) 33 per cent of total yield. It means that the tenant households would get one-third of the total production which was just sufficient to maintain a subsistence living (except vegetable belt of Nagaon). Moreover, they had to take full risk of natural calamities which is a recurrent problem in Assam. In the case of monsoon failures, the tenant households become indebted to the input suppliers (although they need not pay any amount as rent to the land owner) and at the time when he looses his own share of production/scope for casual work.

Barmura

It was a flood affected remote village. It was located 6 km away from Dholla, a semi-urban area. The approach road to village was kutcha.

The village was spread over 1000 bighas of agricultural land. Agriculture was largely mono-cropped. The villagers were mostly small farmers. Agricultural labourers constituted 10 per cent of the total population. Some amount of arable land was under irrigation facilities. Few households were exploiting under ground water for irrigation through diesel operated pumpsets. The cropping intensity was less than 130 per cent.

The village was thinly covered by different anti-poverty schemes. Continuous threats from Dholla river has been responsible for limited economic activities in the village. The bank shows indifferent attitude to individual proposals like fishing or poultry schemes, since there was high risk of floods which may in all probability washed away the loan assets. While a few households expressed that they were also not interested to invest in fishery, etc, till flood problem was solved permanently.

In fact, devastating flood has been responsible for slowing down of the economic activities in a large number of villages in Assam, as most of the villages lack sufficient knowledge about how to live with flood. It was also responsible for increasing burden of unproductive loans in the countryside, in the severely affected villages.

Table 2.6a

Socio-economic characteristics of the sample households (district wise and village location wise distribution).

Attributes	*All households*			*Kamrup*	
	VNT	*IV*	*All*	*VNT*	*IV*
No. of households	250	250	500	79	61
Total Population	1443	1577	3020	416	347
Male (all age group)	741	839	1580	202	166
Female (all age group)	702	738	1440	214	181
Male (0 – 6 age group)	70	90	160	12	11
Female (0 – 6 age group)	71	78	149	18	21
Literates (6+) : Male	613	663	1276	171	138
Female (ever enrolment basis)	509	502	1011	155	133
Illiterates (6+): Male	58	86	144	19	17

(Contd.)

(Contd. Table 2.6 a)

Attributes	*All households*			*Kamrup*	
	VNT	*IV*	*All*	*VNT*	*IV*
Female	122	158	280	41	27
Never attended school : (6 – 15 age group) male	1	4	5	-	-
Female	2	9	11	1	1
(16 – 25 age group) Male	9	5	14	1	1
Female	5	6	11	-	-
Graduate and Technical degree holder: Male	48	29	77	12	10
Female	36	9	45	12	6
Drop outs (PE): < 15 age group: Male	6	11	17	-	-
Female	3	6	9	-	1
(16 – 25 age group): Male	16	21	37	3	1
Female	17	20	37	5	1
Above 25 age group: Male	66	62	128	13	6
Female	82	74	156	19	11
Drop outs (ME): < 25 age group: Male	31	56	87	8	9
Female	33	27	60	5	4
Above 25 age group: Male	33	37	70	7	4
Female	27	41	68	5	12
Employment Status: Employed (< 15 years age): Male	9	11	20	-	2
Female	2	5	7	-	-
15+ age group (> 180 days) : Male	310	340	650	78	74
Female	13	19	32	6	12
Temporary (30 – 180 days) : Male	55	73	128	18	9
Female	96	112	208	41	11
Unemployed (16 – 40 years) : Male	47	39	86	19	21
Female	27	22	49	6	18

Table 2.6 b

Socio-economic characteristics of the sample households (district wise and village location wise distribution).

Attributes	*Nagaon*		*Tinsukia*		*Karimganj*	
	VNT	*IV*	*VNT*	*IV*	*VNT*	*IV*
No. of households	73	47	42	78	56	64
Total Population	482	315	228	434	317	481
Male (all age group)	264	170	117	237	158	266
Female (all age group)	218	145	111	197	159	215
Male (0 – 6 age group)	24	14	11	27	23	38
Female (0 – 6 age group)	21	13	11	18	21	26
Literates (6+) : Male	213	138	99	179	130	208
Female (ever enrolment basis)	163	104	82	128	109	137
Illiterates (6+): Male	27	18	7	31	5	20
Female	34	28	18	51	29	52
Never attended school : (6 -- 15 age group) male	1	2	-	1	-	1

(Contd.)

(Contd. Table 2.6b)

Attributes	*Nagaon*		*Tinsukia*		*Karimganj*	
	VNT	*IV*	*VNT*	*IV*	*VNT*	*IV*
Female	-	1	-	7	1	-
(16 – 25 age group) Male	5	1	2	2	1	1
Female	4	4	1	2	-	-
Graduate and Technical degree holder:	16	5	13	3	7	11
Male						
Female	3	2	17	-	4	1
Drop outs (PE): < 15 age group:	2	-	-	7	4	4
Male						
Female	2	-	-	2	1	3
(16 – 25 age group): Male	7	4	-	3	6	13
Female	11	4	-	10	1	5
Above 25 age group: Male	21	15	8	18	24	23
Female	40	16	8	22	15	25

(Contd.)

(Contd. Table 2.6b)

Attributes	*Nagaon*		*Tinsukia*		*Karimganj*	
	VNT	*IV*	*VNT*	*IV*	*VNT*	*IV*
Drop outs (ME): < 25 age group: Male	13	8	1	22	9	17
Female	7	7	2	11	19	5
Above 25 age group: Male	10	12	6	9	10	12
Female	8	10	5	6	9	13
Employment Status: Employed (< 15 years age): Male	6	-	-	4	3	5
Female	2	-	-	4	-	1
15+ age group (> 180 days) : Male	107	61	52	97	73	108
Female	2	4	3	2	2	1
Temporary (30 – 180 days) :Male	20	15	10	36	7	13
Female	29	17	13	74	13	10
Unemployed (16 – 40 years) :Male	18	8	6	3	4	7
Female	7	1	9	1	5	2

(Contd.)

Table 2.7a

Other socio-economic information about the sample households (district and village location wise distribution)

Attributes	*All households*			*Kamrup*	
	VNT	*IV*	*All*	*VNT*	*IV*
No. of households	250	250	500	79	61
Leased in land (No. of households reported the incidence)	45	70	115	14	10
Leased out	27	36	63	11	12
Mortgage in	7	34	41	3	1
Mortgage out	14	31	45	7	1
Average productivity of rice*( ) kg per hectare / maunds per bigha)	2038	1460	1865 kg	7-13 mns	6—10 mns
Cropping intensity	-*	-	150 %	135 %	130 %
No. of househlds used/owned: Power tiller/tractor	49	11	60	27	8
Pumpsets/STW for irrigation	47	24	71	4	4
Fertilisers	46	41	87	17	2

(Contd.)

(Contd. Table 2.7a)

Attributes	*All households*			*Kamrup*	
	VNT	*IV*	*All*	*VNT*	*IV*
Pesticides	31	39	70	8	-
No. of hhs owned cattle/bird population: Cow	75	66	141	44	15
Bull	84	127	211	25	15
Goat / Pig	55	34	89	36	10
Duck / hen	78	88	166	43	18
Housing structure : Kutcha	182	202	384	60	47
Pucca	51	25	76	14	13
Mixed	17	23	40	5	1
No. of hhs having sanitary latrine	20	14	34	8	7
Source of water: Tap/Tubewell	204	189	393	79	61
Well/pond/river	46	61	107	-	-

(Contd.)

(Contd. Table 2.7a)

Attributes	*All households*			*Kamrup*	
	VNT	*IV*	*All*	*VNT*	*IV*
Energy: Fuelwood	181	202	383	54	27
Gas	70	33	103	29	27
Owned following facilities: Electricity	131	86	217	39	32
Phone	16	10	26	4	3
Scooter/car	21	15	36	9	3
Television	79	56	135	26	18
Bank/post office account	72	42	114	20	13
Agricultural Wage rate (Rs.) Male	50 – 60	50	55 (+ 1 meal)	50-60	50-60
Female	40 – 45	40	40 *	40	
Rent charges for leased in land	33%	33%	33 %	50 % *	33 %

Notes: *Rent charges goes up to 50 %, when most of the inputs except labour are supplied by the owners.
* During off season no meal and tea is provided to the agricultural labourers.
* Cropping intensity data for all-IV and all-VNT groups not shown separately.

Table 2.7 b

Other socio-economic information about the sample households (district and village location wise distribution).

Attributes	*Nagaon*		*Tinsukia*		*Karimganj*	
	VNT	*IV*	*VNT*	*IV*	*VNT*	*IV*
No. of households	73	47	42	78	56	64
Leased in land (No. of households reported the incidence)	17	15	9	27	5	18
Leased out	8	7	3	5	5	12
Mortgage in	4	9	-	24	-	-
Mortgage out	4	14	2	16	1	-
Average productivity of rice* (kg per hectare / maunds per bigha)	10-24 mns	6—12 mns	8 – 12 mns	7-11 mns	8-12 mns	9-13 mns
Cropping intensity	<300%	> 150 %	130 %	125 %	160 %	150 %
No. of households used/owned power tiller/tractor	18	-	2	1	2	2
Pumpsets/STW for irrigation	38	8	3	9	2	3
Fertilisers	22	13	4	-	3	26

(Contd.)

(Contd. Table 2.7b)

Attributes	Nagaon		Tinsukia		Karimganj	
	VNT	IV	VNT	IV	VNT	IV
Pesticides	18	15	4	10	1	14
No. of hhs owned cattle/bird population: Cow	12	11	16	21	3	19
Bull	34	27	15	50	10	35
Goat / Pig	4	3	14	18	1	3
Duck / hen	12	9	13	56	10	5
Housing structure : Kutcha	48	36	30	71	44	48
Pucca	22	2	9	1	6	9
Mixed	3	9	3	6	6	7
No. of hhs having sanitary latrine	4	2	4	1	4	4
Source of water: Tap/Tubewell	63	42	42	78	20	8
Well/pond/river	10	5	-	-	36	56

(Contd.)

(Contd. Table 2.7b)

Attributes	Nagaon		Tinsukia		Karimganj	
	VNT	IV	VNT	IV	VNT	IV
Energy: Fuelwood	60	47	25	78	42	50
Gas	12	-	21	-	8	6
Owned following facilities:						
Electricity	48	19	24	17	20	18
Phone	7	-	3	-	2	7
Scooter/car	6	6	2	3	4	3
Television	26	12	18	9	9	17
Bank/post office account	25	8	15	13	12	8
Agricultural Wage rate (Rs.)						
Male	50	50	50 – 60	35 -50	60-70	50-60
Female	40	40	40	30 -40	60-65	40-50
Rent charges for leased in land	33%	33% -- 50%	40 %	50 %	50 %	50 %

Karimganj

Karimganj district is very backward in terms of different industrial as well as agricultural parameters. Infrastructural facilities are abysmally low. Provision of irrigation is extremely low; soil condition is unsuitable for installation of STW.

Major plantation crops of the district: tea and rubber.

Sri Durgapur

It is located 6 kms away from Nilam Bazar under the jurisdiction of South Karimganj development block. It is linked with Nilam Bazar by a kutcha road (Nilambazar is famous for fingerling trade). However, the most important highway which connects Nilambazar with Karimganj on one end and Agartala on the other was in dilapidated condition.

The number of households in the village was 229 with 1504 population. The shares of male and female population were 788 and 716 respectively. Two-thirds of the village population were living below the poverty line.

It is a general caste dominated village (182), although quite a few SC artisans households (22) were also found in the village. The main occupation was agriculture. However, a considerable number of wage earners, sales worker and petty businessmen and (government) salaried people were also reported. Cachar Grameen Bank, commercial bank, Sr. secondary schools, one venture college, regular markets were located within 6-7 kms radius. The village has also electricity supply. SHG or KCC schemes are yet to make any dent in these areas. The source of water was ring well, pond and hand pump.

The provision of irrigation was very little in the village, purely on individual basis. The average productivity of rice was found to be 1700 kg per hectare. High population pressure and consequently, low per capita land and relatively slightly better scope of non-agricultural activities were responsible for intensification of land use pattern in the village in recent times.

Nearly, 20 per cent households were landless, most of whom walks up to Nilambazar for casual works during the lean season. Marginal farmers constitute the single largest majority in the village. Petty business, lowly paid salaried jobs in Nilambazar commercial centres, government jobs etc. constituted one-fourth of the total employment.

About 70 per cent of the village population were literate. During 2001, the incidence of births among the 185 village couples (13 – 45 years) was 33. The number of deaths recorded during 2001 calendar year was 11. Of the 11 deaths, 6 were infant. The IMR was very high in this region. This was also supported by the fact that 52 per cent of the 143 under five children of the village were partially immunized (including only a few fully immunized children), while the rest 48 per cent were not at all immunized.

Of the 185 couples in the 13 to 45 age groups, only 24 couples had accepted family planning methods till 2000. During 2001 and 2002, 26 more couples were motivated by a local club turned NGO, constituted by the educated youths of the area. All these newly motivated couples were in the 18 to 30 age groups and most of them had more than 2 children. It is important to note that of the 50 protected families as many as 30 women have accepted pills, while laparoscopy (19) and others (1) were found less familiar.

It can be noted that Rainbow Sporting Club cum Community Centre is a voluntary, non-government organization, which has been working for socio-cultural uplift of the rural people in the survey village and in its neighbourhood for last 3 – 4 years. It is considerably because of the this club constituted by the local youths that more and more pregnant and nursing mothers had, of late, showed interest to visit the health camps organized by the club occasionally. Child immunization rate as well as couple protection rate has also improved a bit, otherwise in a very conservative male-dominated society. The author was informed by social activists that few households of a particular community/religion, under the influence of a few influential religious persons, refused to give polio drops to their kids, lest it may reduce fertility of their children. In such families, pregnant women were not allowed to consult a doctor. These critical free health services were propagated as the government's policy only to reduce fertility of the present and future generations.

Eraligul

It was a remote village under the Bandarkuna GP in the jurisdiction of South Karimganj Development Block. The only means of transportation for the villager was one morning train which connects the village with Nilambazar and Karimganj. The closer of the Putni Tea Estate was responsible for much higher incidence of joblessness among the tea pluckers. Quite a few people gained marginally in terms of extension of agricultural land on the abandoned tea land.

The village was pre-dominantly agricultural. Marginal farmers were predominant among the farming community. The extremely poor infrastructure has been responsible for the continuity of the subsistence village economy. The village lacks irrigation facilities. Quite interestingly, Navarun, a local NGO was found working in the region for last 3 years to enthuse poor people to work on cooperative basis for their socio-economic uplift. Within a very short span of three years, nearly 160 SHGs have been promoted by Navarun – all under the Bandarkuna GP. Out of these, 30 SHGs got revolving fund and also loan under the SGSY schemes. Three SHGs (including one owned by the President of Navarun) have also been selected for DRDA's Golden Cow scheme sponsored by the World Bank. Navarun's initial stress was on quick yielding projects, viz. dairy schemes, goat tending, poultry, banana and ginger farming, and fishery. As many as 35 SHG members got KCCs at the time of survey. Quite a few SHGs (18) were reported from the sample village as well.

The village was located very close to Bangladesh border. In terms of all critical infrastructure, the village was found lagging. The village has no road connectivity. In the areas of education, finance, health care, etc. it has gross deficiencies. The sources of water were pond and tubewell.

It can be mentioned that in the sample villages under Karimganj district, incidence of widowed and deserted women were found much higher than the average village of Assam. Men often get remarried quickly after the failure of their first marriage (due to divorce, separation or death of their first wives). But this was rarely true in the case of women.

The divorcee/deserted women often try to return to their parents' home. In a poverty ridden society, these deserted women with 2 – 3 children put heavy burden on their parents. On many occasions, their position was found less than a maid servant. Very surprisingly, these women were found completely by passed by the SHG movement. It is also important to note that from the sample villages in Karimganj and Nagaon districts as many as 35 women headed households reported their main earning members not living with them. All these 35 households had 1 to 3 male members working in the neighbouring states viz. Nagaland, Meghalaya, Mizoram and sometimes, in foreign countries like Saudi Arab and UAE. Quite a few such households constituted mainly by senior women, grown up girls and children who had to suffer from irregular remittances more often than not.

Although, Karimganj district was a border district, the Grameen Bank concept has not yet well received by the people.

In fact, only a few people have heard (except Eraligul/ Bandarkuna GP) about the group movement and its advantages. Consequently, not a single woman SHG member from the religious minority group was found in the sample villages in Karimganj district. Quite surprisingly, under Navarun, not a single women- SHG was formed till the date of survey. This speaks volume about the plight of the women in the sample villages.

Batarashi and Nayabari

These two villages were taken from the North Karimganj Development Block. Batarashi was primarily a non-agricultural village located just 2 km away from Karimganj town. It is a very big village with thick population. The agricultural land of the village was limited. However, quite a few households reported agricultural land 3 – 5 km away from the village. Quite a few SC households were also reported from the village. Most of them were engaged in non-agricultural activities. A large number of households were seen engaged in self employment activities in non-agricultural sector (petty traders, mechanics, tailors, hawkers, etc). Quite a few households reported salaried jobs both in government offices and commercial centres in Karimganj town. Although the village was located close to Karimganj town, so far, it has failed to take the advantage of better infrastructures and government facilities.

Incidence of dairy or poultry farming was found extremely limited in the village. Although the village did record highest wage rates both for the male (Rs. 60 – Rs. 70) and female (Rs. 60 – Rs. 65) wage earners, the incidence of women wage earners (contractual maid servants were considered as permanent workers) were very few. It is a matter of concern that in all the sample villages, women wage earners were treated inferior to men for which they received 10 rupees less than their male counterparts. Loss of 10 rupees accounted for 20 – 25 per cent of their daily income, which they had to forgo simply because it has become customary to pay less to women workers than their male counterparts.

The village was fully electrified. There were provision of tap water in some areas, while some people were using tubewell or pond water.

Nayabari was primarily an agricultural village. Farm size was found very small. Landless households constituted nearly one-fourth of the total village population. During agricultural season, they work in the village field, while during the off seasons, most of them move to the nearest town Karimganj for casual/contractual work. Few households have their own irrigation facilities, using pumpset to tap tank/pond water. No household has STW, since the irrigation department found it unsuitable for irrigation purposes in the region. The yield of paddy per bigha was reported at 10 maunds. Sali was the main crop. Due to the shortages of irrigation facilities, the village remains largely mono cropped, particularly when compared with the Nagaon district.

Almost in all villages, the cost of raising paddy or vegetables was reported at around one-third of the total yield. Quite a few farmers in Nayabari had reported about the regular use of chemical fertilizers and pesticides, apart from cowdung. In the vegetables field, the application of urea per bigha was around 30 kg; super – 10 kg, potash – 8 kg while for paddy , the application of DIP was 20 kg and potash – 20 kg. The hiring cost of pumpset per hour was reported at Rs. 90. During off season, the motor meant for irrigation was used in rice mills.

Quite a few petty traders, salesworker, mechanic, etc. were also reported from the village. Most of them were employed in Karimganj town which was located about 6 km away from the village. The link road between Nayabari and Karimganj town was kutcha, difficult but motorable.

The main sources of water were well and tubewell.

Changing occupational pattern in rural Assam

In the sample, non-farm workers constituted more than 44 per cent (461) of the total workers (1045). A large number of educated unemployeds (undergraduate to graduate level) were reported in the 20 – 40 age group. Only a few of them were taking interests in small tea gardens, while few others were simply waiting for the PMRY loans to start their own enterprises.

Among the non-farm workers, only government (/ corporate sector) services accounted for 22 per cent. Teachers constituted above two-fifths of all government employees. Quite a few workers were working on temporary basis for last 5 – 10 years and drawing a monthly salary of Rs. 300 to Rs. 1000 only. Some people aged 50 – 55 years accepted VRS. None of them have pursued any economic activities (other than agriculture) since then. Many youths aged 20 – 35 years migrated to the neighbouring states (Mizoram, Nagaland, Arunachal Pradesh and N. C. Hills in Assam) and got themselves self employed in trade and services.

Only 3 per cent non-farm workers were engaged in household enterprises (bakery, toy/doll making, bamboo, cane and wooden furniture, etc.). Household and cottage industries were in decaying condition due to shortages of raw materials, lower government support and sometimes, freer market competition. Ban on tree felling has affected all wood based village industries in Assam thereby by further straining the supply of raw materials for these industries.

Quite a few educated youth were found involved in medicine business (pharmacy, medicine distributorships to village/semi-urban markets). Soft drink distributor, electricity bill distributor, gas cylinder arranger, service under private security agencies, etc were also recorded among the respondents. Small savings collectors – Sahara agent and insurance agent – constituted 3 per cent of all non-farm workers. Auto, truck and bus driving (/handimen) created employment opportunities for another 5 per cent workers. Small traders (grocery, vegetables vendor, pan shop, stationery, PCO, etc.) accounted for 28 per cent of all non-farm workers.

A large number of women thrift and credit groups were formed in some villages. They used to extend small loans to the members at 2 – 5 per cent monthly rate of interest for contingency needs and also to assist household industries (weaving, handicrafts, knitting, agro-service centres, poultry, etc) among the group members. Sometimes, many groups together make arrangements for display of their products at nearby /important public gatherings, festivals, exhibitions, fairs, etc. Many of these groups used to provide loans to outsiders but only at higher rate of interest, 5 – 10 per cent monthly rate of interest. At the end of the year, quite a few group members were able to earn Rs. 500 to 1000 (plus around Rs. 1000 from household industries) in the form of interest income on their own savings as well as income from the micro lending. Facilitating the involvement of NGOs having linkages to the SIRD and NABARD's 'research, training and promotional programmes (related to SHGs) can help these women groups to expand their activities and give their present part time occupation a permanent shape. Already, quite a few 'SHG Marketing Complex' were established in important places across the states with the active participation from NGOs, SHG-members and government, etc. Of late, SIRD, NEDFi, etc. were seen making special efforts to display the different products of SHGs by organizing trade fairs, etc. However, all these efforts are still very much concentrated in some pockets in the surroundings of the capital city Guwahati.

Particularly in Nagaon district, the increasing mechanization of the agricultural sector is associated with crop diversification and much improved intensity of cropping. In fact, increasing mechanization of agriculture has not affected the growth of employment in the farm sector. It has facilitated surplus production of paddy, vegetables, fruits, etc. thereby created self employment opportunities in transportation and trading of surplus production in village markets, wholesale markets and retailing in nearby towns. Few agro-based industries, such as rice mills and agro-service centres have also facilitated some employment.

References

1. EPW Research Foundation, (2002), 'Special Statistics-31' EPW, Feb. 2.
2. Karmakar, K.G, (2001), "Rural Credit and Self-Help Groups" Sage Publications, New Delhi.
3. Kurian, N.J, (2000), 'Widening Regional Disparities in India – Some Indicators' EPW, Feb.12.
4. NEDFi, (2002), NEDFi databank Quarterly, Vol. I, Issue II, October.
5. Srivastava, S. C, (1998), 'Level and Structure of Development in North East India' in NIRD's 'Research Highlights 1997-98' Hyderabad.
6. Vyas, V. S, (2002), 'Globalisation: Hopes, Realities and Coping Strategy' EPW, March 23.
7. Wadhwa S.C, (2002), 'Bank-NGOs Collaboration for Better Rural Lending to the Poor', Financing Agriculture, AFCL, April-June.

3

Incidence, Extent and Nature of Indebtedness

In the present study, all households who had taken loans either from informal or formal sources during the current year and / or, past years and the full amount of loans or a part thereof remained unpaid at the time of investigation, were treated as indebted households.

A loan borrowed for a shorter period may remain outstanding for a long period of time owing to the inability or unwillingness of the households to repay the amount within the stipulated period (This is a familiar situation in the case of institutional loans particularly in the eastern and north eastern region). A loan may also be taken on a long term basis to be repaid over a number of years. This is more common in the case of loans drawn against mortgage of properties and sometimes, when it was raised from friends and relatives, etc.

It is also important to mention that loans were classified on the basis of the original purpose of borrowings, even when the entire amount or a part thereof was diverted to other purposes after the release of loans. There were quite a few households who were found taken loans from more than one sources and for multiple purposes. For better estimation and analysis, two types of tables were constituted. In some tables, the purpose for which the maximum amount of loan was originally intended to was considered, i.e., smaller loans were merged with the bigger ones (one household one loan). In some other tables, all loans were estimated separately so that relative position of all purposes/sources could be estimated more accurately.

* Kind loans constituted a small fraction of the total loans. Only a few kind loans were recorded against shopkeepers (grocery items) and traders as trade credit (/current liabilities). These loans were treated as cash loans.

* Contracting loans at compound rate of interest constituted a nominal amount for which it was not shown in a separate column.

* SHG-bank linkages indicate the bank loans extended to the groups either directly or under the SGSY schemes. Only the respondents' individual share in group loan was considered and shown against the source 'bank'.

In the present study, 215 households constituting 43 per cent of the total 500 households, were reported indebted at the time of survey. In the remote villages (IV), 35.2 per cent of the total 250 households were indebted, while 50.8 per cent of the another 250 sample households drawn from the villages nearby urban centres (VNT) had borrowed from the different credit agencies at the time of interview.

It is very clear from Table 3.1 that the incidence of indebtedness widely differed across the state. In Kamrup and Nagaon districts, incidence of indebtedness was found quite high at 53.6 per cent and 53.3 per cent respectively. In Tinsukia

Table 3.1

District and village status wise distribution of number of indebted households, population, principal amount of loan, repayment, outstanding debt and overdues.

District/ Village (VNT & IV)	*No. of households/ Indebted hhs (%)*	*Total population (indebted Population)*	*Principal amount of loan (Rs.)*	*Repay-ment (Rs.)*	*Outstandin g debt (Rs.)*	*Overdues (Rs.)*
Kamrup:						
VNT	79 (73.4)	416 (308)	821600	263340	817200	196800
IV	61 (27.9)	347 (90)	192800	66900	212300	198000
ALL	140 (53.6)	763 (398)	1014400	330240	1029500	394800
Nagaon:						
VNT	73 (49.3)	482 (260)	590200	158600	661800	226600
IV	47 (59.6)	315 (200)	310800	12800	315300	19000
ALL	120 (53.3)	797 (460)	901000	171400	977100	245600

(Contd.)

(Contd. Table 3.1)

District / Village (VNT & IV)	*No. of households / Indebted hhs (%)*	*Total population (indebted Population)*	*Principal amount of loan (Rs.)*	*Repay-ment (Rs.)*	*Outstanding debt (Rs.)*	*Overdues (Rs.)*
Tinsukia:						
VNT	42 (47.6)	228 (108)	318200	108500	264700	75000
IV	78 (38.5)	434 (180)	183550	41100	191950	38000
ALL	120 (41.7)	662 (288)	501750	149600	456650	113000
Karimganj						
VNT	56 (23.2)	317 (74)	137700	13000	141800	27000
IV	64 (20.3)	481 (116)	105500	38800	103100	6300
ALL	120 (21.7)	798 (190)	243200	51800	244900	33300
All-VNT	250 (50.8)	1443 (750)	1867700	543440	1885500	525400
All-IV	250 (35.2)	1577 (586)	792650	159600	822650	261300
All-Total	500 (43.0)	3020 (1336)	2660350	703040	2708150	786700

VNT: Village Nearby Town; IV : Interior Villages.

district, two-fifths of the total sample households were indebted, while the Karimganj district reported lowest debt-incidence at 21.7 per cent.

In all the districts save Nagaon, remote villages recorded lower debt incidence than that of the villages located near urban centres. In Nagaon district, VNT group included a village which falls in the rain shadow area where economic activities were limited and the scope of raising loans was low. While in the other village (Begenati), higher incidence of KCC loans of much larger amount has reduced the number of households who had borrowed smaller loans earlier from informal sectors. Few KCC holders' savings has also improved. They take loans only in time of need, i.e., during the major cultivation season and repay the amount immediately after the harvesting season was over. In contrast, IV group included one SC village which was covered fairly by the different government's anti-poverty schemes. Although this group also incorporated one village from the rain shadow area, its overall economic condition and water position was a bit better. All these factors together contributed to much higher incidence of loans in remote villages under Nagaon district.

Among the four sample districts, it was only in Kamrup where incidence of indebtedness (73.4 %) in VNT group was found substantially higher than the IV group (27.9 %). In the former group of villages, apart from higher incidence of institutional loans, a large number of households reported small loans from savings and credit groups. Although, in the IV group, a sizeable number of savings and credit groups were reported among the sample households, the incidence of loans from group funds was far less (These two villages were surveyed just after the harvesting season was over).

The incidence of indebtedness among the different groups of people on the basis of their religious belief also depicts almost the same picture. It was highest among the Buddhists (total households – 46) with 45.7 per cent indebted households, closely followed by Hindus (Total households – 281) with 44.1 per cent and Muslims (Total households – 141) with 43.3 per cent. The Christian households (Tea Tribes – 32 households) registered the lowest debt-incidence of 28.1 per cent.

It can be noted that a few Muslim households from Karimganj district reported that borrowing money or making profit by lending money is not permitted in their religion. However, this has almost no impact on the overall incidence of debt among the Muslims population.

The Christian households were drawn from the ex-tea communities. The incidence and intensity of poverty, illiteracy and landlessness was very high among these people. The access of these people to different institutional credit agencies was also very low over the years.

Table 3.2 reveals the social group wise distribution of incidence of indebtedness. It is interesting to note that just above one-third of the SC households recorded incidence of borrowings, which was lowest among all the social groups. The corresponding shares for ST and general households were 43.3 and 44.6 per cent. In the author's two earlier studies (survey periods: 1991-92 and 1999 calendar year) also, incidence of indebtedness among the SC and ST households were found high, but not higher as compared to the general households. It seems that in the Brahmaputra and Barak valleys, unlike the national trend, SC and ST households were not heavily burdened with debt as compared to the general households. Very interestingly, the incidence of poverty was highest (56.45 %) among the SC households (the incidence of poverty over the different social groups has not been shown separately in a tabular form), while their debt-incidence was the lowest (33.9 %). The incidence of poverty was less pronounced among the ST (37.50 %) and general households (41.0 %). However, relatively much higher incidence of indebtedness was recorded among these people.

Table 3.2
Social group wise distribution of incidence of indebtedness.

social group	*No. of household*	*Incidence of indebtedness (%)*	*Debt per household*	*Debt per indebted household*
SC	62	33.9	2844	8395
ST	104	43.3	3907	9030
Others	334	44.6	6364	14265

The incidence of indebtedness was found highest in the highest income bracket/asset value group (Table 3.3 and Table 3.4) and lowest among the people in the lowest income/ asset group. In the middle groups, however, no clear trend could be observed. The reasons might be as follows:

Institutional loans have made visible inroads into the rural credit market, although in selective pockets.

Table 3.3
Distribution of incidence of indebtedness by Asset value groups.

Asset group (Rs.)	*Incidence of indebtedness (%)*	*Debt per indebted household*	*Debt-asset ratio*
Up to 50000	38.5	2955	0.10
50001 – 1 lakh	41.2	5500	0.08
> 1 lakh – 2 lakh	39.5	13408	0.08
> 2 lakh – 3 lakh	39.7	8714	0.04
> 3 lakh – 4 lakh	45.3	14300	0.04
> 4 lakh – 7 lakh	51.3	14646	0.03
> 7 lakh – 11 lakh	38.9	17381	0.02
Above 11 lakh	55.6	32860	0.02

- Bad institutional advances (directed micro loans) against which no repayment was recorded during the past 10 years or so, and which had not been written off, were also included in the table.

- All liabilities including very small loans of above Rs. 100 were estimated.

Table 3.4

Distribution of incidence of indebtedness by income groups.

Income group (Rs.)	*Incidence of indebtedness (%)*	*Debt per indebted household*	*Debt-income ratio*
Up to 11000	34.6	4850	0.54
11001 – 22000	47.6	5682	0.32
22001 – 26000	36.1	5385	0.23
26001 – 30000	44.2	7491	0.27
30001 – 36000	39.5	8127	0.24
36001 – 75000	41.5	8398	0.14
75001 – 2 lakh	42.9	22086	0.13
Above 2 lakh	56.3	41783	0.12

It is evident from Table 3.5 that except Dwigunpar and to some extent Begenati village (both located near urban centres and where a large number of landless households were engaged in non-agricultural sector such as, salaried jobs in private and government offices, self employment in trade and business) landless households recorded very low debt incidence. In remote villages, where reach of the institutional agencies was very limited and land acted as good security (in the informal loan market, in particular), landless households were in absolute disadvantage even in the beginning of the 21st century. It can be mentioned that of the total 115 landless households, only 26 households were engaged in the agricultural sector, primarily as agricultural labourers. There were quite a few households

Table 3.5

Land status wise and village group wise distribution of number of households, indebted households, principal amount of loan, repayment, outstanding debt and overdues (part I).

Land status	*Village groups*	*No of hhs.. / indebted hhs.*	*Amount of loan taken*	*Amount of Repayment*	*Amount outstanding*	*Overdues (Rs.)*
Land less	Dwigunpar	15 (20)	25650	1000	26750	3500
	Malukhatal	5 (17)	44300	22000	29800	27000
	Begenati	10 (18)	83200	10900	123700	69500
	Punjabari	- (4)	-	-	-	-
	Balijan	5 (12)	19000	6500	15000	2000
	Powaimukh	- (2)	-	-	-	-
	Sridurgapur	7 (33)	84200	7000	88700	14500
	Eraligul	- (9)	-	-	-	-
	Sub-total:	42 (115) **(36.51 %)**	256350 **(6104)***	47400	283950 **(6761)**	116500 **(41.03)***

(*Contd.*)

(Contd. Table 3.5)

Land status	*Village groups*	*No of hhs.. /indebted hhs.*	*Amount of loan taken*	*Amount of Repayment*	*Amount outstanding*	*Overdues (Rs.)*
1- 4 B	Dwigunpar	14 (21)	217600	88700	203700	64100
	Malukhatal	7 (21)	28500	6000	38000	32500
	Begenati	2 (10)	28000	-	36000	16000
	Punjabari	5 (5)	17300	-	17400	-
	Balijan	7 (10)	79200	30000	58700	31000
	Powaimukh	1 (5)	21000	10000	19000	-
	Sridurgapur	2 (8)	28000	-	28600	-
	Eraligul	3 (19)	16300	2000	15600	300
	Sub-total:	41 (99) (41.41)	435900 (10632)	136700	417000 (10171)	143900 (34.51)

(Contd.)

(Contd. Table 3.5)

Land status	*Village groups*	*No of hhs.. /indebted hhs.*	*Amount of loan taken*	*Amount of Repayment*	*Amount outstanding*	*Overdues (Rs.)*
4–8 B	Dwigunpar	10 (16)	150100	25840	179900	11500
	Malukhatal	2 (9)	94500	35200	122000	120000
	Begenati	13 (22)	149500	17200	178500	81000
	Punjabari	2 (8)	7000	-	7000	-
	Balijan	3 (7)	91000	62000	52000	19000
	Powaimukh	3 (13)	5300	-	6800	1500
	Sridurgapur	2 (6)	12500	1000	15000	6500
	Eraligul	3 (11)	25700	16500	19400	-
	Sub-total:	38 (92) **(41.30)**	535600 **(14095)**	157740	580600 **(15279)**	239500 **(41.25)**

*Figures in brackets show average debt per indebted household.

** Overdues as percentage of the outstanding debt.

* Total households shown in brackets, while indebted households are shown outside the brackets.

Table 3.5 (Part II.)

Land status	*Village groups*	*No of hhs../indebted hhs.*	*Amount of loan taken*	*Amount of Repayment*	*Amount outstanding*	*Overdues (Rs.)*
8–12 B	Dwigunpar	11 (12)	202300	104100	171700	96700
	Malukhatal	1 (5)	5000	1000	8500	8500
	Begenati	4 (11)	51500	12500	63100	25100
	Punjabari	8 (9)	44500	5000	46700	5000
	Balijan	3 (7)	118000	8000	128000	12000
	Powaimukh	8 (16)	34000	6500	31500	-
	Sridurgapur	1 (2)	8000	3000	6000	6000
	Eraligul	1 (8)	5000	-	5500	-
	Sub-total:	37 (70) **(52.86)**	468300 **(12657)**	140100	461000 **(12459)**	153300 **(33.25)**

(Contd.)

(Contd. Table 3.5 part II)

Land status	Village groups	No of hhs.. / indebted hhs.	Amount of loan taken	Amount of Repayment	Amount outstanding	Overdues (Rs.)
12–16B	Dwigunpar	4 (4)	91150	18800	83850	6000
	Malukhatal	- (1)	-	-	-	-
	Begenati	1 (4)	10000	-	12000	-
	Punjabari	5 (9)	29000	4800	27200	-
	Balijan	1 (3)	2000	-	2000	2000
	Powaimukh	9 (13)	59750	600	64050	15400
	Sridurgapur	- (1)	-	-	-	-
	Eraligul	4 (9)	54000	19800	55100	-
	Sub-total:	24 (44) **(54.55)**	245900 **(10246)**	44000	244200 **(10175)**	23400 **(9.58)**

(Contd.)

(Contd. Table 3.5 part II)

Land status	*Village groups*	*No of hhs.. / indebted hhs.*	*Amount of loan taken*	*Amount of Repayment*	*Amount outstanding*	*Overdues (Rs.)*
16–32B	Dwigunpar	3 (5)	51300	24900	31300	15000
	Malukhatal	2 (8)	20500	2700	14000	10000
	Begenati	5 (7)	225000	88000	228500	35000
	Punjabari	5 (8)	105000	-	105000	-
	Balijan	1 (2)	9000	2000	9000	9000
	Powaimukh	8 (24)	48500	24000	55000	20500
	Sridurgapur	1 (6)	5000	2000	3500	-
	Eraligul	2 (8)	4500	500	7500	6000
	Sub-total:	27 (68) **(39.71)**	468800 **(17363)**	144100	453800 **(16807)**	95500 **(21.04)**

(Contd.)

(Contd. Table 3.5 part II)

Land status	*Village groups*	*No of hhs.. / indebted hhs.*	*Amount of loan taken*	*Amount of Repayment*	*Amount outstanding*	*Overdues (Rs.)*
32B +	Dwigunpar	1 (1)	83500	-	120000	-
	Malukhatal	- (-)	-	-	-	-
	Begenati	1 (1)	43000	30000	20000	-
	Punjabari	3 (4)	108000	3000	112000	14000
	Balijan	- (1)	-	-	-	-
	Powaimukh	1 (5)	15000	-	15600	600
	Sridurgapur	- (-)	-	-	-	-
	Eraligul	- (-)	-	-	-	-
	Sub-total:	6 (12) **(50.00)**	249500 **(41583)**	33000	267600 **(44600)**	14600 **(5.46)**

who worked 4 – 6 months in the agricultural sector and rest of the year in non-agricultural sector.

It is estimated from Table 3.5 that incidence of indebtedness among the landless households (agricultural plus non-agricultural) stood at 36.5 per cent. Above 41 per cent of the marginal farmers (defined in terms of land holding of less than 8 bigha, irrespective of their primary occupation) were indebted as against 53.51 per cent and 41.25 per cent reported among the small farmers and semi-medium (/large) farmers.

Important observations:

- Incidence of indebtedness widely differed between villages.
- Incidence of indebtedness among the villages located near urban centres was found substantially higher than that of the remote villages. Nagaon district was the only exception.
- In Tinsukia district, households from remote villages had a larger representation, while in Nagaon district, households from nearby villages had a much larger share in the sample. The above feature might have contributed at least to some extent in showing lower incidence of debt in the former district, although in Nagaon district, one SC village in remote areas recorded much higher debt-incidence.
- Incidence of debt was much higher among the landed households, compared to their landless counterparts.
- Incidence of indebtedness was higher among the higher income brackets and asset value groups. Thus, incidence of indebtedness can not be taken as a sign of poverty. It can not be, at the same time, accepted as a sign of prosperity (productive economic activities) as long as its

composition, end use, purpose, source and terms and conditions of loans are explored in a systematic manner.

- To some extent, the incidence of indebtedness in a village was influenced by time of data collection – agricultural season or lean season, festive season, etc. The better access to KCCs, SHGs, etc. have also influenced the debt-incidence in some pockets.

- Incidence of indebtedness was found higher in the agriculturally advanced village.

- Higher or lower incidence of indebtedness can not be established on caste basis. Caste has nothing to do with incidence of indebtedness. However, certain government sponsored loan schemes have a slight caste bias. Two villages – one ST village in Karmrup district and the other, SC village in Nagaon district – were fairly covered by the IRDP/SGSY schemes.

- The incidence of debt was found considerably low among the SC households, although the poverty ratio was much higher. The incidence of poverty was lower and indebtedness relatively higher among the ST households and the 'non-ST non- SC' other households. This was also found true in the author's one earlier study (Purkayastha, 1997). This may dispel wrong notions about the caste-class/ caste-debt linkages in our society (if indebtedness is taken as a sign of poverty/ prosperity).

- It is also observed that the extent of debt burden of the SC and ST households was less than the other households. The national level observations that STs and SCs were in debt-trap (in most of the states) because of their high amount of debt to exploitative moneylenders, was not true in this region.

Extent of Debt

As already noted in the introduction chapter, a rise or fall in the level of indebtedness can not be taken as a sign of health or absence of it unless and until the composition of loans being explored. The relative importance of productive and unproductive components of loan, rate of interest and other explicit as well as implicit terms and conditions that may be associated with loans, particularly when drawn from the informal market are the important aspects of indebtedness which needs to be explored exhaustively. Extent of indebtedness is an important aspect of the study of indebtedness which has direct impact on the socio-economic condition of the borrowers.

The size of debt per household was found to be Rs. 5416, while the debt per indebted household was substantially higher at Rs. 12596. It seems that compared to the 1980s or 1990s, the volume of debt per household/indebted household has increased significantly in recent times, even if we take into consideration the inflationary rise in the price level and much higher incidence of borrowings in recent times.

It is evident from Table 3.6, which is derived from Table 3.1, that the rural people of Assam was indebted to the tune of just less than Rs. 900 per head at the beginning of the 21st century. In the remote villages, — where the incidence and intensity of poverty was of more serious nature, access of institutional credits were infrequent, DRDA/Block officials were conspicuously missing, PRIs members were almost inactive and uninformed about the government schemes, etc. – the burden of indebtedness per head was much less at Rs. 522, than their VNT counterparts (Rs. 1307).

The Table clearly shows that in Karimganj district, rural people were much less indebted than other districts. The per head average size of debt in Karimganj district was Rs. 307 as against Kamrup district's average of Rs. 1349, Nagaon – 1226 and Tinsukia – 690. Karimganj district was backward in terms of agricultural diversification and institutional arrangements for boosting rural activities through credit.

Tinsukia district, which is yet to cope with the ban on tree felling resulting in closer of many small and bigger sized forest based industries which has significantly reduced the flow of income to the village economy both directly and indirectly, also reported relatively lower amount of debt. The practice of mono-cropping and the conspicuous absence of bank loans to small tea growers, etc were also responsible for lower incidence of debt in the district.

Nagaon, a poor district in terms of per capita income, made visible strides in the agricultural sector during the past decade or so. It has achieved significant milestones in the sphere of agricultural productivity, cropping intensity, etc. It has been transformed into a surplus rice producing district, the vegetable belt of Assam/ NER. In this district, the per capita debt was recorded at 1226. It is because of the much diversified and high input based agricultural and related activities, the district has recorded per head debt of above Rs. 1000 both in the IV and VNT groups.

In Kamrup district, — blessed with all major commercial activities in the capital Guwahati and all major head / zonal offices of institutional credit agencies (and better focused by media, critics, politicians, etc.), VNT group recorded highest per head debt of Rs. 1964. However, IV group recorded far lower amount of debt per head at Rs. 612, which compares poorly even with Nagaon district.

Debt per indebted household column shows considerably higher average amount of debt per loanee household (15267) in Nagaon district, particularly in VNT group. Among these households, quite a few KCC loans of much higher amount were reported. It was observed that in Begenati village, in the initial stage, FMCs and a local NGO had to put some pressure on banks/block officials to issue KCCs to the villagers. In no other villages, in spite of huge unmet needs for seed capital/ working capital, individual people/FMCs/SHGs/PRIs, etc. were seen to be demanding as it was the case in Nagaon. One good thing was that, in Nagaon, FMCs (Begenati village) were also taking at least some interest in timely repayment of loans by the KCC holders.

Kamrup district has also recorded considerable amount of debt per indebted household both in VNT (14090) and IV (12488) groups mainly because of relatively high incidence of housing loans and PMRY loans. It is very interesting to note that the spread of institutional loans across the state was not similar, neither evenly distributed between villages, income groups, occupational groups within the district. Politically active members could manage PMRY and power tiller loans at ease.

In Kamrup district, a large share of institutional loans went to the house building purposes, while a lesser amount was taken under the government sponsored schemes viz. IRDP/ SGSY and PMRY.

In Nagaon district, institutional advances were made mostly against KCCs (Begenati), while loans under anti-poverty schemes were mostly concentrated in Heeragaon SC village.

In Tinsukia district, institutional loans had limited access. Only a few ST households had access to the government directed loan schemes comprising IRDP/SGSY, etc. A couple of consumer loans were also recorded.

In Karimganj district, a few SHG-bank linkages and KCC loans were recorded – mostly in the remote villages. This was the reason for which debt per indebted household was found to be Rs. 7931 in remote village group, although overall debt incidence /debt per household was found quite low in the district.

It is also evident from Table 3.3 that average debt per indebted household had increased continuously through the higher asset value groups. It was only Rs. 2955 in the lowest asset group to as high as Rs. 32860 in the highest asset group, with the only exception of the 2 — 3 lakh asset value group, where magnitude of debt was found to be Rs. 8714, which was much lower than the immediate previous group (13408).

A similar trend was found true across the different income groups. The extremely poor income group shown relatively low level of debt per indebted household of Rs. 4850, whereas the very rich group registered the amount at Rs. 41783. The higher income groups represented much higher size of debt per indebted household, while the lower income groups accounted for much lower debt burden. Only 22001 – 26000 income group shown debt burden slightly lower (5385) than their immediate previous group (5682).

It can be mentioned here that the higher 4 asset groups constituted 42.8 per cent of the total sample households, while its share in total loan accounted for 66.53 per cent. Similarly, the income wise distribution shows that households in the 4 higher income brackets although constituted less than 58 per cent, raised 79 per cent of the total debt outstanding. In other words, the poorer households in the 4 lower income brackets constituted 42 per cent of the total sample population, but they could only accessed 21 per cent of the total borrowings.

Table 3.4 also shows the debt-income ratio for the lowest income group at 0.54 which continuously declined (with a minor exception in the middle) with the higher income groups to 0.12 in the topmost income bracket. In other words, among the extremely poor households, their debt constituted 54 per cent of their annual income. This is in spite of the fact that these households were not mostly allowed access to both informal and formal sources of credit because of their perceived poor credibility. The successive three lower income groups also recorded high percentage share of debt, as it constituted one-third to one-fourth of their annual income. However, the above poverty line income brackets (highest three income brackets) registered considerably lower debt-income ratio of 0.14, 0.13 and 0.12 respectively. A similar trend followed in the case of debt-asset ratio. In this case, the lowest asset-holding group registered debt-asset ratio at 0.10, which sharply falls as one moves higher asset brackets to as low as 0.02 at the highest asset group.

Table 3.6

District and village status wise distribution of per capita and per household outstanding debt

District / Village (VNT & IV)	*Debt per household*	*Debt per indebted household*	*Debt per head*	*Debt per indebted person*
Kamrup:				
VNT	10344	14090	1964	2653
IV	3480	12488	612	2359
ALL	7354	13727	1349	2587
Nagaon:				
VNT	9066	18383	1373	2545
IV	6709	11261	1001	1577
ALL	8143	15267	1226	2124
Tinsukia:				
VNT	6302	13235	1161	2451
IV	2461	6398	442	1066
ALL	3805	9133	690	1586
Karimganj				
VNT	2532	10908	447	1916
IV	1611	7931	214	889
ALL	2041	9419	307	1289
All-VNT	7542	14846	1307	2514
All-IV	3291	9348	522	1404
All-Total	5416	12596	897	2027

From the above observations, it can be said that in terms of debt-income ratio as well as debt-asset ratio, income poor and asset poor people were heavily burdened with debt repayment obligation, compared to their more affluent counterparts.

The major occupation wise distribution of the extent of debt also shows some interesting features. The average debt per agricultural household was estimated at Rs. 4902 as against Rs. 5974 recorded by the non-agricultural households.

It is seen from Table 3.7 that the average outstanding debt per landless agricultural households was Rs. 1465, as against the corresponding figures for marginal farmers of Rs. 4441, small farmers – 4428 and bigger farmers – 7541.

Among the non-agricultural households engaged in services sector, the landless households' average size of debt-outstanding was Rs. 2925, while the landed households registered the above average at Rs. 8698 (the highest among all the groups classified on the basis of occupation and broad land status). At the overall level, the households in services sector registered outstanding debt per household at Rs. 6442. This group of people recorded quite a few government employees and sound businessmen where the incidence of bigger institutional loans (particularly housing loans) was much higher.

The households engaged in industrial sector constituted a very small section of the sample (25 households). Cottage and small scale industries were in decaying condition in the sample villages. Doll/toy making, wooden furniture, bamboo and cane products, mosquito net making, etc were all in bad shape either due to lack of fund or shortages of raw materials, or because of the unremunerative prices in the absence of easy access to the organized market. The landless households engaged in industrial sector registered outstanding debt at Rs. 40, while the landed household's average was Rs. 2420. The overall debt-outstanding for the households engaged in industrial sector was estimated at Rs. 1944.

At the overall level, the size of outstanding debt was higher than the principal amount of borrowings (Table 3.1). This was found true in the case of Kamrup, Nagaon and Karimganj districts. The only exception was Tinsukia district where outstanding debt was found lower than the principal amount of borrowings. Village group wise analysis shows that in VNT group in Kamrup district, VNT group in Tinsukia district and IV group in Karimganj district, total outstanding debt was lower than the principal amount of borrowings. All IV group average and all VNT group average, however, shown higher burden of outstanding debt as compared to the initial amount of borrowings, in spite of recording some amount of repayment on both heads.

Table 3.5 shows that landless household group recorded much higher amount of outstanding debt, in spite of recording some amount of repayment (Rs. 1192 per indebted household). The landed households, such as, 4 – 8 bigha and '16 +' groups also recorded higher outstanding debt over principal amount of borrowings, although these households recorded Rs. 4151 and Rs. 5500 respectively as repayment per indebted household.

It is important to note that repayment here means all part or full payment made against current or previous loans in the current year and/or, all part repayments made before the current year against the old loans which are yet to be repaid in full. The outstanding loan was higher than the principal amount of borrowings mainly for two reasons: (i) accumulation of the institutional loans due to non payment of interests regularly and also, the principal amount of loan, and (ii) the much higher frequencies of current year institutional loans (KCCs, direct loans, SHG loans, etc).

It would be relevant to note that landless household group recorded 41 per cent of their outstanding debt as overdues. The overdue position was little better in the case of marginal farmer (less than 4 bigha group – 35 % and 4 – 8 bigha group – 41 %). The small farmer recorded much lower level of overdues (8 – 12 bigha group – 33 % and 12 – 16 bigha group – 9.58 %). Although the bigger farmer i.e., '32 bigha +' (5.46 %) registered very low level of overdues, the 16 – 32 group recorded 21 per cent of their outstanding debt as overdues. Needless to mention that frequencies of fresh loans and accumulation of old loans were the two main factors which have significantly influenced the overdue position of each groups. Other factors which have directly or indirectly influenced the overdue position across the different sources/ income groups/purposes, etc were explained in the later part of this chapter and the following chapter.

Important observations:

- The volume of indebtedness has increased manifold in recent times. Only a portion of the rise in the size of debt can be attributed to the rise in price level and increase in the incidence of indebtedness.

- Lower the level of income/asset- value, lower the access to the loan market. Consequently, debt-asset ratio (/debt-income ratio) was found much higher in the lower asset/ income brackets compared to the higher asset/income brackets.

- In spite of apparently better coverage of the villages by the government schemes, SC and ST households registered substantially lower debt burden. Very interestingly, SC households registered high incidence of poverty and much lower level of debt incidence. Among the ST households, incidence of poverty was lower, but their debt burden was relatively higher. Thus, the caste-class linkage or caste-debt linkage can not be established in the state of Assam, as it was the case at the all-India level.

- Extent of debt was found higher among the non-agricultural households than that of the agricultural households. This new trend might be because of the increasing incidence of housing loans among the non-agricultural households, particularly incurred by the salaried people.

- Volume of debt was found much higher in the much diversified agricultural belt of Nagaon. It was also higher in the villages with expanding non-agricultural sector in the Kamrup district. Slow growth districts like Karimganj and Tinsukia (in recent times), where agriculture was more or less mono-cropped and irrigation facilities were also limited, recorded lower volume of indebtedness.

- Land was still the most important factor in rural areas to have the access to both the formal and informal credit market. With the faster growth of the non-agricultural sector (and also, much wider reach of consumerism), 'other than land' factors have gained some mileage in the sphere of securing access to the loan market. This is also supported by the fact that non-agricultural households recorded higher amount of debt than the agricultural households.

- On the one hand, credit-deposit ratio in the state has gone down in the recent past. On the other hand, high incidence and size of debt per household had been registered among the sample households. The reasons might be : (a) accumulation of old institutional debt; (b) high incidence of personal loans in recent times, and (c) resurgence of moneylenders.

Table 3.7

Distribution of the amount of debt per household by occupational groups and broad land status

Agricultural households		*Tertiary households*		*Industrial households*	
Land status	*Size of debt per household*	*Land status*	*Size of debt per household*	*Land status*	*Size of debt per household*
Landless	1465	Landless	2925	Landless	40
Marginal farmer	4441	Landed households	8698	Landed households	2420
Small farmer	4428				
Semi-medium farmer	7541				
All	4902		6442		1944

There were significant differences between the sample districts in the sphere of loan incidence and size of loans incurred from the different credit agencies as may be seen from Table 3.8 and Table 3.9. In the former table, all institutional loans and non-institutional loans according to the size of loans were presented in different columns. It is important to note that if a household was found taken two loans – one from institutional source and the other from non-institutional source – both were shown in their respective columns according to their sizes. However, if a household had incurred a loan from a particular source for two or more purposes, it was considered as single loan in this table.

Of the 250 incidence of borrowings (total incidence of borrowings may go up further by purpose wise distribution), 23 households borrowed in the range of Rs. 100 – Rs. 500. More than 50 per cent of these loans were taken from shop-keepers (credit purchase), quite a few loans were taken from friends and relatives, while savings and credit groups and moneylenders had also recorded a couple of very small lending.

In the range of Rs. 501 to Rs. 1000, 16 loans were incurred mostly from the SHGs and 'other' sources. Apparently, these 39 incidence of loans of Rs. 1000 or less seem insignificant. However, quite a few (at least 10 households) reported their inability to repay even such a small amount of loans for quite sometime.

In the next range of borrowings (Rs. 1001 – Rs. 2000), nearly 32 households were reported. Once again, SHGs and friends were found providing the highest number of loans in this category. It can be mentioned that SHGs, friends and relatives and shop-keepers (2 shopkeepers extended loans against mortgage of land were shown in 'mortgage of land' column) did extend only small loans mostly for household expenditure. In

Table 3.8

Distribution of the incidence of loans according to their sizes and sources

Range of borrowings (Rs.)	*Bank +*	*SHGs +*	*Moneylenders*		*Friend & Relatives*	*Shop keeper*	*Others*	*All*
			With interest	*Against land mortgaged*				
100 – 500	-	2	3	-	5	12	1	23
501 – 1000	-	5	2	-	2	2	5	16
1001 – 2000	2	14	3	3	4	2	4	32
2001 – 5000	25	8	8	10	5	-	3	59
5001 – 10000	39	2	3	18	-	-	-	62
10001 – 25000	18	1	5	12	1	-	1	38
25001 – 50000	8	1	-	2	-	-	-	11
50001 – 75000	3	-	-	-	-	-	1	4
Above 75000	5	-	-	-	-	-	-	5
All-Total	100	33	24	45	17	16	15	250

* All institutional loans were shown against 'bank+'. If a household borrowed both from formal and informal sources, entry was given in both heads, according to their individual size of loan.

* A couple of shopkeepers provided loans against mortgage of land shown in the moneylenders column.

* SHGs also included other savings backed sources like school welfare fund and village societies.

* 'Bank+' also included (institutional) current liabilities, 9 cases of electricity bill dues. In the following section, these liabilities were shown in 'other' heads, unless otherwise specified.

the table, only a couple of medium size loans can be seen against SHGs /welfare societies (both were actually taken from school welfare societies).

In 2001 – 5000 group, 59 incidence of loans were recorded. As many as 23 loans from banks were recorded in this group, followed by moneylenders ('loan against mortgage of land' – 10, others – 8), SHGs (8) and friends (5). Contribution of all other sources stood at 5. The highest number of borrowings (62) was recorded in the range of Rs. 5001 to Rs. 10000. Banks constituted about 63 per cent of all loans in this category, followed by moneylenders who had made advances 18 times against mortgage of land (and 3 additional loans on simple rate of interest). No loan was registered in this category against friends, government, shop-keepers and others. In the 10001 – 25000 category, once again banks top the list with 18 numbers of loans, followed by moneylenders (against mortgage of land – 12 , and others – 5). Other sources showed nominal or blank account. The last three groups of borrowings together recorded only 20 incidence of loan. As many as 16 numbers were recorded against bank. All other credit agencies were found non-existent or at best, insignificant in the spheres of lending higher amount of loan of above Rs. 25000.

It appears that most of the demand for credit in the rural areas was micro in nature. One earlier study in Assam carried out by NEIMB (IIBM) in 1997 also found that about 72 per cent of the rural loans were below Rs. 10000 and another 22 per cent loans were in the range of Rs. 10000 – Rs. 25000. In other words, 94 per cent of the rural borrowings were below Rs. 25000 (Gogoi, 2004).

At the aggregate level, the contribution of different credit agencies in the borrowings of the sample households were as follows: Bank and other institutional agencies — 100, moneylenders (against mortgage of land – 45 plus 'with interest'

– 24) – 69, SHGs/ welfare societies – 33, friends and relatives – 17, shop-keepers – 16 and others – 15. The break-up of the institutional loans were as follows: bank : 87; PF/cooperative/ tribal development board: 4 and electricity bill dues/current liabilities: 9.

Table 3.9

District wise distribution of the incidence of loans according to their size groups

Range of borrowings (Rs.)	*Kamrup*	*Nagaon*	*Tinsukia*	*Karimganj*
100 – 500	12	3	4	4
501 – 1000	9	3	4	-
1001 – 2000	21	3	6	2
2001 – 5000	19	14	16	10
5001 – 10000	14	28	14	6
10001 – 25000	9	16	7	6
25001 – 50000	3	5	3	-
50001 - 75000	2	1	-	1
Above 75000	4	-	1	-
All	93	73	55	29

The highest incidence of borrowings (93) was recorded in Kamrup district (even if we take into consideration the fact that larger number of sample households were drawn from the district), followed by Nagaon district with 73 cases, Tinsukia district with 55 cases, while it was lowest in Karimganj district with only 29 cases of borrowings. It was observed that SHGs (on a couple of occasions, school welfare fund) extended 29 loans in Kamrup district, as against nominal 4 in all other districts (SHG-bank linkages were shown against bank). Almost all these were of small loans.

Shop-keeper, as a source of credit, was found active only in Kamrup district. Very interestingly, friends as a source of credit was found very weak in Kamrup and Karimganj districts where a large number of SHGs were formed. In Kamrup, where the culture of group savings was at least 20 – 30 years old, quite a few loans were recorded from SHGs, while in Karimganj district, a large number of people were seen forming SHGs only very recently and in some selective remote pockets. Incidence of loans from traders, employers, etc were found less frequent and mainly of smaller value.

Important Observations:

- Banks constituted above one-third of all borrowings in terms of incidence.
- Institutional sources, other than banks, were seen disappearing from the rural credit scenario.
- Institutional agencies constituted nearly three-fifths of all incidence of loans of above Rs. 10000, while moneylenders' corresponding share was around one-third of the total.
- Apparently, institutional agencies (banks) looked very active in the region, among the sample households. However, the reality is not so impressive. A large number of borrowings from institutional agencies were made long back where no repayment was recorded since its release. To some extent, the accumulation of the institutional loans – old and new ones alike – was responsible for apparently much higher incidence of institutional loans.
- Poor repayment of loan taken against mortgage of land was also responsible for swelling size of this category of loans.

- The credit agencies viz SHGs, friends, shopkeepers and 'others' extended either no loans or one or two loans of higher amount of above Rs. 5000.

Current Year Borrowings and Repayment

Information on current year borrowings and repayments may give us some important insights into the changing scenario of rural indebtedness. It is an important part of any study on indebtedness since it gives valuable information on the latest repayment position, nature of demand for loans, relative position of the different credit agencies, etc.

Table 3.10 and Table 3.11 show the amount borrowed and repayments made in the current year by the village groups and source of loans. Altogether 81 loans were taken by the sample households during the current year. The incidence of loans (24) during the current year was found highest in the VNT group in Kamrup district. Ironically, the lowest incidence of loan was also recorded by the Kamrup district in the IV group. Among the four districts, Tinsukia recorded very low incidence of loan (VNT – 3 and IV – 7), followed by Karimganj district (VNT – 5 and IV – 11). Only Nagaon district recorded higher incidence of current year loans both in the VNT (16) and IV (11) groups.

The total amount of current year borrowings stood at Rs. 931050. Very interestingly, institutional loans constituted as high as 73.7 per cent in the total borrowings. In other words, informal sources (including savings and credit groups, village welfare societies) constituted slightly higher than one-quarter of the total loans.

It is a matter of concern that the distribution of institutional loans was found extremely uneven across the villages, and also, among the different socio-economic classes (not shown separately in the table). Direct loans from banks constituted as high as 60 per cent of the total institutional loans.

Merely, one-fifth of these loans constituted by one tractor loan and one small trade loan. The rest four-fifths of the total direct loan from banks were taken by the well-to-do families for house building. This clearly shows that bank advances are, of late, directed more towards meeting the demand for personal loans often stems from consumerism.

Table 3.10
Distribution of the incidence of current year borrowings, size of debt and repayment by village groups

Village groups	*Incidence of borrowings*	*Total amount of borrowings*	*Average size of loans*	*Amount repaid (Rs.)*
Kamrup:				
Dwigunpar+(VNT)	24	298000 (32.01)	12417	91650 (38.94)
Malukhatal+ (IV)	4	800 (0.09)	200	1200 (0.51)
Nagaon:				
Begenati+(VNT)	16	312500 (33.56)	19531	62500 (26.56)
Punjabari+(IV)	11	39800 (4.27)	3618	12400 (5.27)
Tinsukia:				
Balijan+(VNT)	3	108000 (11.60)	36000	33500 (14.23)
Powaimukh+(IV)	7	16750 (1.80)	2393	16100 (6.84)
Karimganj:				
Sridurgapur+(VNT)	5	87700 (9.42)	17540	4000 (1.70)
Eraligul+(IV)	11	67500 (7.25)	6136	14000 (5.95)
All-Total:	**81**	**931050 (100.0)**	11494	235350 (100.0)

It is encouraging to note that KCCs constituted more than one-third of all institutional loans incurred in the current year. The problem here was that as much as 83.16 per cent of the borrowings made against KCCs were concentrated in one village in Nagaon district. The rest amount i.e., less than 17 per cent of all KCC loans were taken by the households in Karimganj district. Not a single household from Tinsukia and Kamrup districts reported KCC loans. Some other areas of concern were as follows:

- Not a single PMRY loan was reported during the current year.
- Not a single loan was reported from Cooperative banks.
- The most disappointing feature was that SGSY and SHG–bank linkages constituted merely 6.30 per cent of the total institutional loan.
- A lion's share of the institutional loans went to the better off section.

Nevertheless, loans from savings and credit groups/SHGs (which had not yet received revolving fund or loans from banks) constituted above 19 per cent of the total informal loan. The percentage of loan incurred against mortgage of land constituted less than 13 per cent of the total informal loan.

Both 'interest free' and 'with interest' loans (other than SHG loans) constituted more than one-third each in the total informal loan. Interest free loans also included one relatively big trade loan of Rs. 55000. Incurring trade loans and subsequently, its repayment becomes recurring in nature. Apparently, these loans look interest-free. But in true sense, these were not. Normally, the retail traders looses certain concessions on wholesale price when they maintain a part of their stock through trade credit.

Table 3.11
Distribution of Current Year Borrowings (CYB), Repayments against CYB and Repayments against old loans (RAOL) during the current year by sources over the village groups/ districts. (Rs. in '000)

Attributes	*Kamrup*		*Nagaon*		*Tinsukia*		*Karimganj*		*Total*
	VNT	*IV*	*VNT*	*IV*	*VNT*	*IV*	*VNT*	*IV*	
CYB From:									
KCCs	-	-	195	-	-	-	16.5	23	234.5
SHG/ SGSY/ PMRY	-	-	-	-	-	-	-	43.2	43.2
Banks (Direct loans)	208.5	-	100	-	100	-	-	-	408.5
From informal sources:									
With interest	30	-	17	11.3	5	3	16	1	83.3
Interest free	1.8	0.8	-	18.5	-	6.7	55.2	0.3	83.3
Mortgage of land	14	-	-	10	-	7	-	-	31
Savings & Credit group +	43.7	-	0.5	-	3	-	-	-	47.2
RA- CYB: (all)	21	-	8.5	4.4	0.5	2.1	2	14	52.5
RAOL:	57	1	54	-	25	9	-	-	146
Banks +									
Savings & Credit groups +	8.1	0.2	-	-	8	-	1	-	17.3
Other informal agencies	5.5	-	-	8	-	5	1	-	19.5

It seems that interest free loans, which did constitute a very high percentage share of loans in Assam in the past, is drying up in recent times (as it constituted a meager 3 % of the total borrowings, if trade loan is not considered as interest free). The reasons for such a drastic fall are many: (i) The formation of SHGs/savings and credit groups by a large number of people in some pockets of Assam, which has a provision of micro lending to the members at moderate to high interest rates. (ii) A few SHGs were also seen lending to the non-members at high rate of interest (In the sample, only a few high interest borrowings from the SHGs were included). (iii) Friends and relatives, who used to provide loans at nil rate of interest, have become (on many occasions) members of the different savings and credit groups . (iv) A few MFIs have come up in some pockets of the state (Begenati and Mulakhatal in sample villages). (v) In a couple of villages, banks have made significant inroads into the agricultural loans through KCCs, which has definitely helped in reducing the incidence of crop loans from the big farmers and friends, particularly, raised by the marginal farmers/tenant households during cultivation seasons.

It is also seen that across the village groups, distribution of loan was extremely unequal. Level of economic activities (diversification of agricultural and non-agricultural activities), access to SHGs, KCCs and other institutional loans, time of investigation (generally during the lean season, incidence of consumption loan was found higher, while during the cultivation season, few households took loans for purchasing agricultural inputs), pre or post flood situation, etc had influenced the incidence of loan.

Only two village groups – VNT in Kamrup and Nagaon districts – constituted two-thirds of the total current year loans. Similarly, these two groups also recorded almost two-thirds of the current year repayments.

Current year borrowings in remote villages of Kamrup and Tinsukia districts were negligible. It is significant to note that both remote villages (7.25 % of the total current year borrowings) as well as villages close by towns (9.42) in Karimganj district registered considerable amount of loans in the current year, as compared to the past few years' borrowing record. This is largely because of the distribution of KCCs among the farmers in a couple of villages, and the formation of a large number of SHGs in a remote village.

The repayment column shows current year repayment at Rs. 235350, constituting 25.28 per cent of the current year borrowings. Out of these, only Rs. 52500 i.e., 22.31 per cent of the total was meant for repayment of the current year loans.

A lion's share of the repayment made in the current year was meant for the loan taken in the previous year or even before that. In fact, the repayment made in the current year against old loans constituted nearly 78 per cent of the total repayment. One interesting fact was that repayment against old institutional loans constituted 62 per cent. However, a large part of which went to the KCCs account (30.14 %) and personal loan/ direct bank loan account. Societies/ SHGs constituted above 7 per cent, while other non-institutional sources registered repayment of 8.29 per cent.

Non-institutional sources (moneylenders and interest-free sources) registered low repayment rates. The reasons behind such a low repayment ratio were explained in the next chapter.

It is very clear from the tables (3.10 and 3.11) that the frequency and size of borrowings have increased considerably in recent times. Savings backed borrowings has increased considerably in some pockets, as also loans against KCCs (apart from personal loans from banks). All these loans recorded satisfactory repayment ratio which was in sharp contrast to the state's long established poor record of repayment. There is no gainsaying that repayment culture is slowly picking up because of the change in the nature of loan distribution.

It is significant to note that no fresh loans at concessional interest or below 10 per cent interest rate was reported. The rate of interest charged on KCC loans was 11 per cent or more. The SGSY/bank loans to SHGs carried interest rate of 12.5 per cent plus 2 per cent charged by the groups/NGOs for loan administration. However, even above 14 per cent rate of interest looked very low compared to the rate of interest charged by the savings and credit groups (varied from 2 per cent per month to as high as 10 per cent per month). In fact, the interest rates charged by the informal credit agencies are usually much higher than those charged by institutional agencies, showing that the rural poor are willing and often able to pay higher interest rates. What they need most is improved access to funds, not subsidized loans that hardly reach them (Muhammad Yunus, 1997 and Jacob Yaron, 1997).

A much larger amount of rural credit is, in recent times, seen going to big farmers/salaried persons. Narasimham Committees's influence can be seen in lending practices adopted by the banks where banks were seen trying to achieve lending targets by issuing much bigger amount of loans to a few better off rural households.

In spite of the appointment of Gupta and Kapoor Committees in December 1997 for speeding up credit delivery in agriculture and small scale industries respectively, the share of agriculture in total credit has steadily declined from about 15 per cent in the early 1990s to less than 10 per cent as of March 2002 (in Assam, agricultural credit came down to 9 per cent). The SSI units recorded even bigger fall (EPW Research Foundation, 2003). The present study also confirms that banks have moved away from the productive sectors in their lending programme, which may act as a major stumbling block in the healthy capital formation in rural areas in the near future.

The findings of the present study had also substantiated by another study at the national level. The relatively high rate of interest was charged by the banks both from the poor and rich (in case of term loans) when the depositors were allowed less than 6 per cent interest rate on term deposits for over three years and PLRs have been declared in the range of 9 to 12.25 per cent. But in March 2002, nearly 50 per cent of commercial bank advances were at 14 per cent and above. A number of public sector banks have 60 per cent of business at rates of interest of 10 to 14.50 per cent, with higher rates charged for term loans (EPW Research Foundation, 2003).

Nature of Borrowings

The study of indebtedness by type of security which controls the supply of credit in rural areas is another important aspect. The availability of good security (sign of prosperity) increases credit flow both from the formal as well as informal sources of credit, which increases over all economic activities. However, absence of good security often distorts the composition of the rural credit business, where both the borrowers and lenders (institutional agencies in particular) fail to make use of credit as an important instrument for bringing about socio-economic changes in rural areas. The type of security against which loans are advanced often act as an important constraint that sometimes forced the loanees to raise unfavourable loans carrying high interest rates.

Table 3.12 shows the village wise and social group wise outstanding debt by type of security. At the aggregate level, the largest proportion of the total debt, i.e., 52.17 per cent was based on primary security (PMRY loans and KCCs also included in this category where no security as such is provided). The actual share of loans drawn on the basis of personal security (primary security) will be much higher as it was also the main indicator in the subsequent three columns. Only a small proportion of loans (less than 5 %) was taken on the basis of third party

Table 3.12

The village group wise and social group wise percentage distribution of outstanding debt by type of security.

Village groups & Total Debt	*Mort-gage of land*	*Primary / Personal security*	*Salary cut (Bank, pvt. Bank +)*	*SHGs, societies(savings backed*	*High interest (37 % and above)*	*Others (+ current liabilities)*
Kamrup:						
VNT: 817200 (100.0)	7.28	40.14	34.51	12.08	3.67	2.33
IV : 212300 (100.0)	-	97.88	-	2.12	-	-
Nagaon:						
VNT: 661800 (100.0)	7.25	76.49	15.11	0.09	1.06	-
IV: 315300 (100.0)	78.97	20.52	-	-	0.51	-
Tinsukia:						
VNT: 264700 (100.0)	2.15	34.38	43.45	17.76	-	2.27
IV: 191950 (100.0)	51.05	35.35	9.90	-	3.70	-

(Contd.)

(Contd. Table 3.12)

Village groups & Total Debt	*Mort-gage of land*	*Primary/ Personal security*	*Salary cut (Bank, pvt. Bank +)*	*SHGs, societies(savings backed*	*High interest (37 % and above)*	*Others (+ current liabilities)*
Karimganj:						
VNT: 141800 (100.0)	14.10	70.03	-	2.47	13.40	-
IV: 103100 (100.0)	-	46.56	-	27.93	25.51	-
All total:						
2708150 (100.0)	17.73	52.17	19.05	6.76	3.36	0.92
Social group wise break ups:						
SC: 176300 (100.0)	21.55	53.37	19.85	-	5.22	-
ST: 406350 (100.0)	26.95	34.49	21.90	11.47	2.98	2.21
G : 2125500 (100.0)	15.65	55.45	18.44	6.42	3.28	0.75

VNT : Village Nearby Town; IV: Interior Village.

guarantee or surety security. However, this segment of loan was incorporated in the 'salary cut' and 'savings backed' columns.

In the Table, the heads 'salary cut' and 'savings backed' were included with the objective of highlighting certain important changes that are, of late, taking place in the rural credit scenario. As RRBs and commercial banks have shown increasing interest in extending consumer loans (housing loans, scooter/car loans) to the fixed income earners, i.e., salaried people (and /or, against savings certificates, insurance policies), this category of loans may increase further in near future. Among the sample households, the proportion of loans taken against salary security (with/without savings certificates, insurance policies, etc.) constituted above 18 per cent of the total.

SHGs (savings and credit groups) and village societies (also, banks-SHG linkages) give emphasis on the amount of savings of the potential borrowers at the time of lending. SHGs were seen extending small loans to the members quite frequently, although the rate of interest charged on these loans may be quite high. The amount of loan depends on the individual borrowers' savings with the SHG funds. Non-members can also borrow from SHGs, but only when any SHG member gives surety security of loan recovery. Although, these loans were also raised on personal security, these were distinct from the other categories of security. Regular savings with the group account (/group pressure) as security constituted 6.76 per cent of the total outstanding debt. Loans provided against high interest (37 per cent above) constituted just above 3 per cent. Largely, moneylenders and a few SHGs had extended these loans. Often these loans were not backed by surety security, mortgage of properties, or government securities/ savings certificates. A sizeable amount of these high risk loans were provided for household consumption, during natural calamities. More often than not, where the relationship between lenders and borrowers were found weak, moneylenders charged higher interest rate so as to ensure healthy returns even if some borrowers fail to make repayment in full or a part thereof.

It is important to note that nearly no loan was registered against mortgage of immovable property other than land. Standing crops or agricultural commodities as security for borrowings were found almost absent. A couple of tiny loans taken from the traders of green tea leaves were of personal nature, although taken for cultivation. The head 'others' accounted for current liabilities and one old cooperative loan of Rs. 10000.

'Mortgage of land' was found very important as security in Assam. Nearly 18 per cent of all borrowings were made under this category of loans. Among the social groups, incidence of borrowings against mortgage of land was found highest among the ST households, followed by SCs, while the 'non-SC and non-ST' other households recorded lowest incidence.

After the personal security, mortgage of land was found very important as security among the three major social groups. The predominant position of loans on personal security was found almost common across the villages. The proportion of such borrowings ranges from 97.88 per cent of the total debt in Malukhatal to 20.52 per cent in Punjabari. It can be noted that in remote villages in Nagaon district and also, in remote villages in Tinsukia district, loans against mortgage of land respectively constituted 78.97 per cent and 51.05 per cent. In both these village groups, loans against personal securities constituted much lower share of 20.52 per cent and 35.35 per cent. It is very interesting to note that Punjabari village falls in the rain shadow area, while Powaimukh was badly affected by storms in recent times.

Another very interesting feature was that in Malukhatal and Eraligul, a large number of SHGs /savings and credit groups have come up in recent times. Both these village groups recorded no loan against mortgage of land. In contrast, Dwigunpar did record 7.28 per cent of its total debt under the category 'loans against land mortgaged'. This group of villages had also managed 12 per cent of the total debt against borrowers' own savings (SHGs/welfare societies).

Personal security was pre-dominant in the rural credit scenario. Collateral security was found less frequent even among the institutional loans. There was a good beginning of the savings backed credit business, which seems to be the best type of security from both ends. However, this category of loan has not yet constituted a substantial amount. In fact, this culture has not developed in many villages yet. Thus, too much emphasis in this respect may also cause more unequal distribution of loans across the different economic classes, at least in the initial years. In some areas, 'mortgage of land' was found the only security against which moneylenders extended loans which raises questions about the effectiveness of the government developmental schemes in removing this social menace.

Duration of Loan

The break-up of loans into short term (up to one year), medium term (1 – 3 years) and long term (more than 3 years) is very important in the sense that this will give us the idea about the nature of credit needs of the rural households. In fact, to facilitate adequate flow of credit in time and extensive institutional arrangements to meet the demand for different types of loans of varying durations, etc. regular information (i.e., time series data) on the above aspect of indebtedness is a must.

Table 3.13 shows the village wise percentage distribution of outstanding debt by duration of debt. Contrary to the general belief, only 13.36 per cent of all debt were contracted for duration of one year or less. Out of this, the shares of institutional loans and non-institutional loans were 9.69 per cent and 3.68 per cent respectively. The entire amount of institutional loans in this category was drawn against KCCs, for cultivation purposes. The KCC loans, were concentrated in Nagaon and Karimganj districts. Sample villages in the other two districts had not yet open their KCC account. Very short duration loans taken from informal sources mainly comprises of consumption loans and trade loans.

Loans taken for medium term constituted 14.12 per cent of the total borrowings. In this category, the shares of institutional and non-institutional sources were 6.90 and 7.22 respectively. The institutional loans were mostly of productive in nature. Apart from a few small SGSY loans (individual *swarojgaries*), loans to SHGs by banks were also registered in this category.

Quite a few loans were drawn from SHG funds for household consumption. A couple of housing loans (/repairing) from school welfare fund were also registered by the salaried people. Small loans for education (for instance, to pay examination fees), health care, etc were also recorded in the informal loan category.

As high as 69.92 per cent of all borrowings were made for long term purposes (including the unspecified loans), while 'others' constituted 2.60 per cent. Long term loans constituted abnormally high proportion in the total borrowings because of the following reasons:

- All loans – institutional and non-institutional – which were taken for unspecified period were shown as long term loans.

- All loans against mortgage of immovable property was incorporated in this category. These loans were mostly taken for long term/unspecified period.

Table 3.13

Percentage distribution of outstanding debt by duration – village group wise.

Attributes	*Up to 1 year*		*1 – 3 years*		*Above 3 years & mortgaged loan*			*Others*
	IA	*NIA*	*IA*	*NIA*	*IA (Fresh loan)*	*IA (NPA)*	*NIA*	
Kamrup								
VNT (100)	-	0.43	5.51	14.00	44.30	21.30	13.36	1.10
IV (100)	-	0.38	-	0.94	-	88.08	-	10.60
Nagaon								
VNT (100)	34.38	1.84	7.71	1.15	12.84	34.83	7.25	-
IV (100)	-	7.26	-	3.30	-	6.66	82.78	-
Tinsukia								
VNT (100)	-	-	7.18	9.44	43.45	24.93	2.15	12.84
IV (100)	-	2.42	9.90	7.97	-	15.11	62.0	2.60
Karimganj								
VNT (100)	12.06	38.93	-	13.75	-	19.04	16.22	-
IV (100)	17.17	0.29	51.21	1.26	-	5.82	24.25	-
Total (100)	9.69	3.68	6.90	7.22	20.75	27.35	21.82	2.60

IA : Institutional Agencies. NIA : Non-institutional Agencies.

- Few loans (carrying interest rate) from moneylenders and even SHGs were also included. That portion of the loans where borrowers were required to pay the annual interest accrued regularly till the principal amount was paid back in full is considered in this category.

- All the big institutional loans (housing loans in particular) taken from banks during the recent times were of long term in nature.

- All institutional medium term loans which were in default were included in this category under the sub-head 'NPA'. Even the overdues against KCCs (short term loans) were also included in this category. These two together constituted over 27.35 per cent of the total debt. This explains why the share of short term and medium term categories recorded substantially lower percentage shares in the sample.

The distribution of outstanding debt by duration of loans across the sample villages reveals certain important features. Both in Kamrup and Tinsukia districts, where KCC scheme has not yet created any impact, short term loans constituted merely 1 to 2 per cent of the total borrowings. In contrast, Nagaon and Karimganj districts recorded considerable amount of short duration loans mainly because of the agricultural loans against KCCs and trade loans (trade loan was found in VNT group in Karimganj district). Medium term loan was found very important only in Karimganj district, particularly in remote villages, where a few SHGs reported loans from banks. In all the backward villages (8), not a single loan was recorded from the institutional sources for long term duration. This speaks volumes about the inaccessibility of these households to long term institutional loans. However, 3 VNT groups save Karimganj did record moderate to substantial amount of long term loans in recent times. In a sense, the NPA column also establishes the fact that remote villages were deprived of institutional loans in the past, as NPA loans (except Karimganj district) were also found substantially lower in the remote villages than their VNT counterparts.

In most of the districts (other than Karimganj), a sizeable amount of the long term debt was incurred from the informal sources, particularly against mortgage of immovable property. The reasons for such borrowings were health care, marriage and on a few occasions, to expand productive operations.

Interest Rate

The study of interest rates at which borrowings are made is extremely important as it gives information about the money costs (explicit costs) to be borne by the indebted households. Needless to mention that usury loan retards development and accentuates the problems of borrowers even when such borrowings were made for productive purposes. The high interest burden may push the weaker sections into debt-trap, if incremental income from loan assets fall short of the interest burden of debt and also, when such loans are raised for health care, marriages, etc.

Table 3.14 presents interest slab wise distribution of outstanding debt over the sample villages. It is observed from the table that merely 5.48 per cent of the total debt was interest free, although this group constituted 19 per cent of all debt-incidence. The borrowings made against mortgage of land constituted above 17 per cent of the total. As many as 17.77 per cent of the indebted households (loan incidence) reported borrowings against mortgage of land. The outstanding debt in the 1 – 10 per cent interest group accounted for 2.91 per cent and was reported by 3.72 per cent of the total indebted households.

About three-fifths (59.75 %) of the total outstanding debt was contracted at 11 – 15 per cent interest rate. Less than 37

Table 3.14

Village wise percentage distribution of outstanding debt by interest groups.

Attributes	*Rate of Interest (%)*							
	Nil	*1 - 10*	*11-15*	*16-20*	*21-36*	*37-50*	*51 & Above*	*Mortgage of land*
Kamrup								
VNT	3.05	3.16	56.11	20.68	6.33	0.40	4.47	5.81
IV	0.38	9.42	89.26	-	0.94	-	-	-
Nagaon								
VNT	0.03	-	89.76	1.81	-	-	1.15	7.25
IV	6.82	-	6.66	7.04	-	-	0.51	78.97
Tinsukia								
VNT	12.84	6.04	75.56	-	3.40	-	-	2.15
IV	5.97	-	25.01	12.40	1.88	-	3.70	51.05
Karimganj								
VNT	38.93	7.76	25.81	-	-	-	13.40	14.10
IV	0.29	5.82	68.38	-	-	24.25	1.26	-
Total	5.48	2.91	59.75	8.38	2.45	1.04	2.70	17.29

* Percentages were shown against the respective totals of each village group.

per cent of the total loan-incidence occurred in this group. This group covered a lion's share of the institutional loans viz SGSY, KCCs, PMRY loans, where interest rates varied mostly between 11 – 14 per cent. The next higher group of interest, 16 – 20 per cent, constituted 8.38 per cent of the total debt and below 5 per cent of the total loan incidence. This group included one large institutional loan, one loan from private bank for consumer goods, and the rest from the moneylenders. A considerable number of small loans raised by the SHG members (from group funds) were recorded in the 21 – 36 per cent interest slab. This group, although constituted nearly 11 per cent of the total indebted households (loan incidence), had registered merely 2.45 per cent of the total debt. The highest two interest slabs together constituted less than 4 per cent of all debt. However, the loan incidence was much higher at 7.44 per cent.

Areas of concern:

- It is observed that '21 per cent and above' interest slabs constituted more than 6 per cent of the total outstanding debt. However, the highest 3 interest slabs accounted for above 18 per cent of all loan-incidence.

- At least one-third of the apparently interest free loans were borrowed from traders which carried hidden interests in the form of lower concessions allowed on the wholesale price to the loanee retail traders.

- More than 17 per cent of the total debt were contracted against mortgage of land indicating thereby erosion of opportunities to grow paddy on the mortgaged out land till full repayment is made by the borrowers. The moneylenders enjoy interest in kind in terms of annual crop yields from the land taken in mortgaged.

- At least one-third of all the indebted households were found shouldering either high interest burden or had to mortgage out a piece of arable land.

- Interest free sources of loan were found much thinner in recent times. To some extent, this might be due to the formation of SHGs in certain pockets where 'friends and relatives' participated in large numbers. A few SHGs were found acting as MFIs which was responsible for high percentage share of 'with interest' loans and drying up of the interest free sources.

- There is no immediate sign of falling interest burden in the sample villages. In spite of government's initiative to lower the rate of interest, the effective rate of interest for KCCs (11 – 12 %), and SHGs (12.5 – 14.5 %, including 1 % each charged by NGOs and SHGs for loan management and supervision) was still high in comparison to the rest of India (or, housing loans in particular).

It seems that the interest burden of both institutional and non-institutional loans has increased in the state in recent times.

The debt incurred in the range of 11 – 15 per cent – which accounted for 59.75 per cent in total debt at the aggregate level – were found very high in nearby villages under Nagaon district (89.76 %); remote villages in Kamrup district (89.26 %); VNT group in Tinsukia district (75.56 %) and IV group in Karimganj district (68.38 %). The nearby villages under Kamrup district also reported fairly significant amount (56.11 %) in the above category of loan. The IV group in Tinsukia (25.01 %) and VNT group in Karimganj (25.81 %) also recorded moderate proportion of debt in the above category. The remote villages of Nagaon (6.66 %) was the only exception.

It is observed that only in two remote village groups, the proportion of debt against mortgage of land was very high. These village groups were respectively in Nagaon (78.97 %) and Tinsukia (51.05 %) districts. In sharp contrast, the other two

Table 3.15

Percentage distribution of outstanding debt by interest groups over the land status and occupational groups.

Interest Groups (%)	*Non-agricultural households*		*Agricultural households*				*All Total*
	Landless	*Landed*	*Landless*	*MF*	*SF*	*Bigger farmer*	
Nil	24.43	3.36	18.64	2.25	7.85	0.41	5.48
Mortgaged	1.63	10.33	3.94	19.42	23.71	36.57	17.29
1 – 10	9.97	2.40	-	7.26	-	-	2.91
11 – 15	48.40	69.46	47.24	51.51	46.05	59.99	59.75
16 – 20	-	11.38	-	11.26	10.24	2.28	8.38
21 – 36	2.97	0.77	30.18	4.93	4.32	0.75	2.45
37 – 50	-	0.11	-	-	6.78	-	1.04
51 – 99	8.54	1.99	-	3.38	1.05	-	2.25
100 +	4.07	0.19	-	-	-	-	0.45
All-Total	100.0	100.0	100.0	100.0	100.0	100.0	100.0

remote village groups in Kamrup and Karimganj districts registered 'zero' loan in this category. All the VNT groups recorded some amount of debt against mortgage of land which varied from 14.10 per cent in Karimganj district to very low 2.15 per cent in Tinsukia.

Another important range of interest was that of 16 – 20 per cent, accounting for more than 8 per cent of total debt. In this group, highest amount of debt was recorded by VNT group in Kamrup (20.68 %), IV group in Tinsukia (12.40 %) and IV group in Nagaon (7.04 %). Others registered either nil or negligible amount of debt. Debt incurred at the higher rates of interest though constituted around 6 per cent at the aggregate level, were found having a sizeable share in VNT group in Kamrup where 29 loans were recorded in the highest 3 interest slabs. In all other village groups, loan-incidence was much less frequent viz VNT group in Karimganj – 3, IV (Tinsukia) – 3, IV (Karimganj) – 2, VNT (Tinsukia) – 2, IV (Nagaon) – 2 and IV (Kamrup) – 1.

Table 3.15 presents the distribution of debt by interest groups over the land status and occupation of the sample households. It is evident from the table that landless households (agricultural wage earners — 26 households and non-agricultural landless households – 89, where quite a few petty businessmen and salaried people were recorded) registered fairly significant amount of interest-free debt, while the proportion of debt incurred against mortgage of property constituted negligible amount. Landless households borrowed prominent amount at 11 – 15 per cent rate of interest which mostly incorporated institutional loans. Few small loans from SHGs were also recorded at 21 – 36 per cent interest rate. No loan was recorded at 37 per cent and above rate of interest by the agricultural labour households, while non-agricultural landless households incurred nearly 13 per cent of their debt at 37 per cent and above interest rates.

Non-agricultural landed households (including 20 households engaged in the industrial sector) incurred much fewer numbers of loans at 37 per cent and above interest slabs. Merely 2 per cent of the total debt were incurred against the highest 3 interest groups. Landed non-agricultural households borrowed as much as 69.46 per cent at 11 – 15 per cent interest rate, which also contains high proportion of institutional loans. Interest free loans and 1 – 10 per cent interest categories constituted very low percentage share in total debt, although loan-incidence was found not negligible at 13 per cent. As many as 10 cases of loans against mortgage of land was reported which constituted 10.33 per cent of total debt.

The presence of interest free sources of credit among the farmers was seen drying up. It constituted merely 0.41 per cent among the large farmers, 2.25 per cent among the marginal farmers and a moderate amount of 7.85 per cent among the small farmers. Farmer households, as expected, reported high percentage share of debt against mortgage of land. Quite surprisingly, larger farmers reported above one-third of the total debt in this category, followed by small farmers (23.71 %) and marginal farmers (19.42). The major asset viz land was found the most sought after security in the informal credit market for raising big loans.

Marginal farmers borrowed 7.26 per cent of the total debt at 1 – 10 per cent interest rate. This group constituted a couple of institutional loans, although nearly 50 per cent of such borrowings was made from moneylenders who charged simple annual rate of interest of 10 per cent on the principal amount which was in addition to the land security provided by the loanees. No such loans were registered by the small farmers and bigger farmers. In the 11 – 15 per cent interest slab, bigger farmers reported two-thirds of their total debt; slightly lower at 51.51 per cent was reported by marginal farmers; while small farmers reported the lowest percentage share of 46.05.

One interesting feature was that no farmer did report (neither agricultural landless households) any debt at 100 per cent and above rate of interest. It was reported only by the non-agricultural households mostly in Karimganj district, taken from professional moneylenders. In fact, larger farmers reported no loans against the highest 3 interest slabs. Among the marginal farmers and small farmers, altogether 7 households borrowed low to nominal amount at 37 – 99 per cent rate of interest.

Table 3.16 shows social group wise percentage distribution of principal amount of borrowings, repayment and outstanding debt by interest groups. It can be mentioned that the total amount of borrowings (current year borrowings plus principal amount of old loans yet to be repaid) made by the SC households was Rs. 1 49 000; repayment made against the prevailing loans was Rs. 15700, while the outstanding debt was Rs. 176300. It would be relevant to note that while making any comparison between principal amount of borrowings and outstanding debt of the loanees, it should be kept in mind that a few general category households made full repayment of loans in the current year only taken in the previous year against KCCs. Such loans were not included in the borrowings column or debt-outstanding column, although they are included in the repayment column.

SC households borrowed 6.38 per cent of the total debt at nil rate of interest, while borrowings against mortgage of land accounted for 25.50 per cent. These two groups constituted less than 27 per cent of the total outstanding debt. No repayment was made against these borrowings. The poor repayment registered against 'with interest' loans and subsequently, accumulating burden of that portion of debt which carried interest burden can be attributed to the slightly lower share of the above loan categories in total debt-outstanding (as compared to their share in principal amount of borrowings). In terms of incidence of loans, 11 – 15 per cent interest slab registered highest share in total indebted households (42.86 %), followed

Table 3.16

Percentage distribution of principal amount of borrowings (PAB), repayments (R) and outstanding debts (OD) by interest groups across the social groups.

Attributes	*Nil*	*1 - 10*	*11-15*	*Rate of Interest (%)* *16-20*	*21-36*	*37-50*	*51 & Above*	*Mortgage of land*
SC :								
PAB	6.38	4.7	56.04	-	-	-	7.38	25.50
R	-	12.74	55.41	-	-	-	31.85	-
OD	5.39	6.24	61.60	-	-	-	5.22	21.55
ST :								
PAB	3.38	9.27	57.21	2.11	0.74	-	3.69	23.60
R	0.06	15.95	73.13	2.45	-	-	6.87	1.53
OD	3.93	6.30	54.26	2.46	1.03	-	5.07	26.95
Others :								
PAB	6.48	2.95	60.20	8.59	2.84	1.39	1.81	15.75
R	1.72	5.44	79.17	8.35	2.02	2.35	0.95	-
OD	5.78	1.99	60.64	10.21	2.92	1.33	2.04	15.09

* Percentages were shown against the respective totals of each village group.

by nil interest category (23.81 %) and '51 and above' interest slab (14.29 %). There was no incidence of loans in 16 – 20, 21 – 36 and 37 – 50 interest slabs; while 1 – 10 per cent interest group and loan against mortgaged of land recorded two loan incidence each.

SC households made 56.04 per cent of their total borrowings at 11 – 15 per cent rate of interest. This component of loan registered 55.41 per cent of the total amount of repayment and yet, the outstanding debt constituted 61.60 per cent of the total.

The borrowings made at concessional/lower interest rate of 1 – 10 per cent had also shown the tendencies of accumulation of old debt. The percentage of borrowings at 51 and above category constituted 7.38 per cent. This group also registered some repayment (31.85 % of the total repayment made by the SC people). Consequently, the percentage share of outstanding debt accounted for 5.22 per cent in this group.

The ST group of households reveals a different picture. In terms of incidence of loans, the prominent group was loan against mortgage of land (32 %), followed by 11 – 15 per cent interest slab (30 %), interest free (18 %) and '51 and above' (10 %) categories. Borrowings in the rest of the interest groups were not significant. Of the total borrowings of Rs. 474550, about 57 per cent was borrowed at 11 – 15 per cent rate of interest. This group also recorded as high as 73.13 per cent of the total repayment (Rs. 163000) made by the ST households. A couple of big loans (monthly loan instalment to be deducted directly from the salary income) was recorded in this group for which the size of debt was found much higher than that portion of loans taken against mortgage of land.

Of the total debt outstanding of Rs. 406350, ST households borrowed as high as 54.26 per cent in 11 – 15 per cent interest category, followed by mortgage of land with 26.95 per cent, 1 – 10 per cent interest group with 6.30 per cent and 51 and above group with 5.07 per cent. All other interest slabs including interest free group recorded low to very low volume of debt. As compared to the initial amount of borrowings, ST households recorded higher volume of outstanding debt in 51 and above interest category, in spite of recording some amount of repayment.

It would be relevant to note that among the 'non-SC and non-ST' other households, the highest incidence of debt was registered in 11 – 15 per cent interest group (37.35 %), followed by few other prominent groups viz interest free group (19.28), loan against mortgage of land (14.46) and 21 – 36 interest group (13.86). In all other interest groups, much lower incidence of debt was recorded ranging from 6.02 per cent in 16 – 20 per cent to 1.81 per cent in 37 – 50 interest slab.

Among the general (i.e., non-SC and non-ST) households, interest free loans constituted nearly 6 per cent of the total outstanding debt, although incidence of interest free loans to total was found much higher at 19.28 per cent. These households, like SC and ST households, borrowed highest amount of loan at 11 – 15 per cent interest. Nearly four-fifths of the total repayment made by these households were registered against the loans incurred at 11 – 15 per cent interest rate. Some amount of repayment against KCC loans were also recorded in this group. Quite surprisingly, in spite of recording considerable amount of repayment, outstanding debt was found much higher than the principal amount of borrowings. The reasons were: (i) Some amount of repayment reported in the current year against the previous year's KCC loans helped in showing healthier repayment ratio. (ii) Higher incidence of current year loans/KCC loans, and (iii) Accumulation of old directed institutional loans against which repayment was not significant.

Borrowings against mortgage of land accounted for 15 per cent of the total outstanding debt. This was lower than the corresponding shares registered by the SC and ST households. The interest group, 16 – 20 per cent, constituted above 10 per cent of total debt. It is also significant to note that higher interest group, viz 16 – 20 per cent, 21 – 36 per cent and 51 and above registered higher amount of debt outstanding compared to the initial amount of borrowings, in spite of recording some amount of repayment.

Few important observations:

- It is observed from the above discussion that in all the three major social groups the high incidence of loans was recorded only in three groups viz 11 – 15 per cent interest slab, loan against mortgage of land and interest free categories.

- On the basis of the volume of debt, the importance of different interest slabs was not found in the same order as revealed by the incidence of debt. The highest amount of outstanding debt was recorded in 11 – 15 per cent interest category, followed by 'loan against mortgage of land', 16 – 20 per cent interest category, 21 and above interest category (when all the high interest categories are merged) and interest free category. In terms of volume of loan, however, interest free category looses much of its weight.

- A large number of small loans were recorded in interest free category particularly from friends and shop keepers. It is still an important category of loan. Its high incidence bears the testimony.

- ST households were seen more inclined to borrowings against mortgage of land. In remote villages (STs were taken mainly from remote villages), loan options were limited. This was also supported by the fact that SCs were mainly taken from nearby villages where land was relatively scarce (and more particularly among the SC communities). Consequently, incidence of loans against mortgage of land was negligible (only 2 households were registered) among the SC households which was partially responsible for lower overall debt-incidence recorded by these people.

Table 3.17 presents income group wise distribution of the principal amount of loan and outstanding debt by interest groups. In the lowest income group, more than two-fifths of the debt outstanding was incurred against mortgage of land, although only one indebted household was found in this group (incidence of debt not shown in the table).

In terms of incidence, interest free loan category was found to be fairly dominant, constituting over two-fifths of all loan incidence. However, this group constituted slightly more than 13 per cent of the total debt-outstanding. All the other interest slabs (except 16 – 24 % where no loan was recorded) registered one loan-incidence each and in all these groups, debt outstanding was found higher than the original amount of borrowings.

In the 11001 – 22000 income category, the debt scenario was equally dismal. As much as 41.36 per cent of the total outstanding debt was incurred against mortgage of land. Interest free loans, although constituted below one-tenth of the total debt, registered highest incidence of loans. Two-fifths of the total outstanding debt was recorded in the 11 – 15 per cent interest group. The higher 3 interest groups recorded 4 per cent of the total debt, while the lowest positive interest group, i.e., 1 – 10 per cent contributed below 5 per cent to total debt. These households show clear signs of increasing burden of 'with interest' debt.

Table 3.17

Percentage distribution of principal amount of borrowings (PAB) and outstanding debts (OD) by interest groups over the income groups.

Income Groups ('000)	*Rate of interest (%)*						
	Nil	*1 - 10*	*11-15*	*16-24*	*25-50*	*51 & Above*	*Mortgage of land*
≤ 11 PAB	15.46	7.93	13.21	-	13.21	2.64	47.56
OD	13.40	10.31	18.33	-	13.75	2.98	41.24
11 – 22 PAB	11.69	3.55	30.55	1.71	2.20	0.21	50.09
OD	9.59	4.81	40.19	1.41	2.41	0.23	41.36
22 – 26 PAB	6.83	-	21.14	9.59	41.79	3.25	17.40
OD	6.0	-	28.57	8.43	36.71	5.0	15.29
26 – 30 PAB	4.07	26.49	34.82	5.87	1.14	1.14	26.49

(Contd.)

(Contd. Table 3.17)

Income Groups ('000)	*Nil*	*1 - 10*	*11-15*	*16-24*	*25-50*	*51 & Above*	*Mortgage of land*
			Rate of interest (%)				
OD	3.43	15.49	49.57	5.83	0.91	1.05	23.71
30 – 36 PAB	9.49	-	38.10	23.16	2.37	9.49	17.39
OD	4.92	-	39.38	25.68	2.46	9.52	18.05
36 – 75 PAB	4.69	7.30	50.64	4.53	1.33	7.52	23.99
OD	4.51	4.68	55.60	4.0	0.89	7.25	23.07
75 - 200 PAB	3.56	-	75.96	3.62	-	1.54	15.31
OD	3.52	-	75.27	2.57	-	2.41	16.22
> 200 PAB	7.76	-	69.54	15.04	1.95	-	5.72
OD	7.58	-	62.82	21.50	2.51	-	5.58

*** Percentages were shown against the respective totals of each village group.**

It is evident from the table that among the lower income groups, interest free loans constituted higher percentage share of debt than the higher income groups. The highest income bracket also registered some amount of interest free loans (which were either loans from traders with hidden interest or CPF account loan). The higher income groups (above poverty line households) recorded much higher incidence as well as amount of loans in 11 – 15 per cent interest category, as compared to the lower income groups.

As percentage of the total debt-outstanding, 11 – 15 per cent interest category recorded 55.60, 75.27 and 62.82 in the successively three highest income groups. In the two successively highest income brackets, debt outstanding against mortgage of land was also found much lower at 16.22 per cent and 5.58 per cent.

Borrowings at higher rates of interest of 16 and above constituted 37.66 per cent (as percentage of the total outstanding debt) among the households in 30001 – 36000 income bracket. The corresponding percentages were 12.14, 4.98 and 24.01 in the successively three higher income groups. Amongst the lower income group people, this percentage was 16.73 in the lowest income bracket, and 4.05, 50.14 and 7.79 in the successively three higher income brackets. The amount of borrowings at the lowest interest group, 1—10 per cent, was on the lower side and mostly concentrated in the lower income groups.

Table 3.18 (also, 3.18a which was derived from Table 3.18) presents asset group wise percentage distribution of borrowings, repayment and outstanding debt by interest groups. The table reveals certain interesting features not exactly similar to that of the income distribution.

It is observed from the table that household group with asset value of Rs. 50000 or less, borrowed high percentage share of debt in 1 – 10 per cent category.

Table 3.18

Percentage distribution of principal amount of borrowings (PAB), repayments (R) and outstanding debts (OD) by interest groups over the asset value groups.

Asset Groups (Rs. '000)	*Nil*	*Mortgage of land*	*Rate of interest (%)* 1 - 10	*11-15*	*16-24*	*25-50*	*51 & Above*
≤ 50	15.12	2.14	54.21	12.84	3.14	12.55	-
PAB							
R	-	-	87.5	8.33	1.67	2.5	-
OD	17.94	2.54	41.46	16.07	3.72	18.27	-
50 - 100	8.30	16.16	5.88	44.09	4.01	6.61	14.92
PAB							
R	-	-	3.18	14.01	28.66	22.29	31.85
OD	5.87	11.43	7.38	55.90	3.43	4.47	11.53
100 - 200	6.23	21.91	7.75	54.22	2.52	-	7.37
PAB							
R	6.20	-	15.73	63.21	0.70	-	14.16
OD	4.44	21.80	4.38	60.04	2.51	-	6.84
200 - 300	5.02	29.49	-	51.41	14.07	-	-
PAB							

(Contd.)

(Contd. Table 3.18)

Asset Groups (Rs. '000)	Rate of interest (%)						
	Nil	Mortgage of land	1 - 10	11-15	16-24	25-50	51 & Above
R	-	4.70	-	65.41	29.89	-	-
OD	4.99	28.29	-	56.31	10.41	-	-
300 - 400	2.17	7.14	10.55	53.13	16.14	10.86	-
PAB							
R	-	-	20.41	36.37	31.21	12.00	-
OD	2.04	6.70	6.56	53.76	19.58	11.36	-
400 - 700	0.54	3.89	-	87.86	4.35	0.54	2.81
PAB							
R	0.63	-	-	94.05	3.88	1.44	-
OD	0.50	3.58	-	88.04	3.78	0.20	3.90
700 - 1100	20.14	35.01	-	44.39	0.46	-	-
PAB							
R	1.68	-	-	98.16	0.17	-	-
OD	23.56	41.92	-	33.97	0.55	-	-
> 1100	-	17.89	-	64.25	16.98	0.87	-
PAB							
R	-	-	-	99.77	-	0.23	-
OD	-	17.85	-	56.81	24.35	0.99	-

* Percentages were shown against the respective totals of each village group.

In terms of incidence of debt (not given in the table), interest free category was found fairly dominant (52.17%), followed by 25 – 50 per cent category (17.39 %), while the other groups including 1 – 10 per cent category recorded low debt incidence (i.e., below 9 per cent each).

As much as 17.94 per cent of the outstanding debt incurred by the lowest asset holding group falls in the interest free category. Above two-fifths of total debt were registered in the 1 – 10 per cent category, while 25 – 50 per cent and 11 – 15 per cent categories recorded 18.27 per cent and 16.07 per cent respectively. Other groups were insignificant or shown nil account.

It is an interesting finding that all the asset groups registered some amount of debt against mortgage of land. It was lowest at 2.54 per cent in the lowest asset value group, which steadily increased in the successive three higher asset groups (11.43 % in 50001- 1lakh; 21.80 % in above 1 lakh – 2 lakh and 28.29 % in above 2 lakh – 3 lakh group), than recorded

Table 3.18a

Percentage distribution of outstanding debt by two broad interest groups over the asset value groups.

Asset groups (Rs.)	*Interest groups (%)*	
	Interest free, 1 – 10 & 11 -- 15	*'16 plus' & mortgage of land*
Up to 50000	75.47	24.53
50001 – 1 lakh	69.15	30.86
> 1 lakh – 2 lakh	68.86	31.15
> 2 lakh – 3 lakh	61.30	38.70
> 3 lakh – 4 lakh	62.36	37.64
> 4 lakh – 7 lakh	88.54	11.46
> 7 lakh – 11 lakh	57.53	42.47
Above 11 lakh	56.81	43.19

a sharp fall to 6.70 per cent and 3.58 per cent in above 3 – 4 lakh and above 4 – 7 lakh groups, only to rise once again to 41.92 per cent in above 7 – 11 lakh and 17.85 per cent in the highest asset value group.

Incidence of borrowings at 51 per cent and above interest group was seen only in asset group of Rs. 2 lakh and less (apart from above 4 – 7 lakh category, which recorded small amount of loan). No borrowings was recorded in 1 – 10 per cent interest group by the highest 3 asset value categories.

It is also interesting to note that incidence of interest free loan was less in higher asset value groups with the only exception of above 7 – 11 lakh group, where one loan from CPF account and one sizeable amount of loan from a trader were recorded.

The 11 – 15 per cent interest slab, which contains mostly institutional loans, was seen dominant through the asset value groups, except the lowest asset value group. In the lower asset value groups, quite a few institutional loans were recorded in this group. Some repayment efforts can be seen in all the groups. However, all these groups recorded swelling debt burden due to poor repayment of these loans over the years. Incidence of institutional loans was very high in above 4 – 7 asset value group and also in the highest asset value group.

Easy availability of institutional loans /high share of institutional loans (plus interest free loans which were fast drying up) and low share of loans against mortgage of land to informal sources can be considered as signs of lower interest burden on the shoulders of the borrowers. It is true that the share of institutional loans are on the rise, but mostly among the better off class, while the incidence of loans against mortgage of land across the different asset groups has not decreased at all.

Quite a few IRDP loans had been registered among the weaker sections, which remained overdue for quite some times. This has resulted in accumulation of interest burden on the principal amount of borrowings. Similarly, a couple of PMRY loans (also, IRDP loans) were recorded by the rich households, a large part of these loans remained unpaid at the time of survey. It is evident from table 3.18a which is estimated from the previous table that, there is a tendency on the part of the richer households to take more loans at higher interest rate than their weaker counterparts, with the exception of above 4 – 7 lakh group. However, the actual fact is that in the lower asset value groups, (relatively) considerable amount of directed institutional loans got accumulated over the years, due to poor repayment. Among these people, the incidence of institutional loans was very low in recent times. It is because of the swelling size of the old institutional debt (accumulating interest amount plus principal amount) on the one hand and considerable amount of borrowings already made against mortgage of land on the other, which reduces their scope to raise fresh loans from the market, these households apparently recorded lower borrowings at higher interest rates.

The relatively high share of the high interest loans among the two successive top asset-value groups was reported mainly because of the concentration of big loans – two direct loans from commercial banks and one from private bank for consumer durables – which carried 16 to 18 per cent rate of interest. Also, among these groups, higher incidence of loans from group funds which carried high interest was recorded.

References

1. EPW Research Foundation, (2003), 'New Credit Policy', EPW, November 22.
2. Gogoi, J K, (2004), ed. 'Rural Indebtedness in North East India', Department of Economics, Dibrugarh University.

3. Y. Jacob, et at (1997), 'Rural Finance', Monograph Series 14, The World Bank.
4. Yunus, M. (1997), 'Towards Creating a Poverty-Free World', Institute of Social Sciences, New Delhi.

4

Purpose, Source, Repayment and Overdue Position of Debt

One of the vital aspects of the study of indebtedness is the purpose for which it was taken. When a large number of borrowings are made for productive purposes – for agricultural, allied and non-agricultural activities – it helps in revival of the economy by directly contributing to the socio-economic health of the borrowers. On the other hand, the large amount of borrowings for meeting the unproductive household expenditures like consumer durables, marriage and ceremonials, etc. constrained concerned borrowers' productive economic activities which sometimes push them into a debt-trap.

It can be mentioned that loans for health care, house building and education stand in between productive and unproductive loans. Illness, besides reducing the efficiency of the workers also reduces the number of days worked. This is woefully true for those who are engaged in unorganized sector or working as wage earners. However, a large part of the private nursing home bill, in absence of faith in government hospitals or its unavailability, has become a matter of concern in recent times particularly for the landed households.

Similarly, small educational loans for payment of examination fees, admission fees, etc from unorganized sector can only ensure the continuation of education for some more times in the traditional rural educational institutions devoid of professionalism, definite purpose and mission.

House building loans, apart from generating income, also add health to the concerned borrowers by improving overall hygiene. In flood affected villages, any permanent building structure proves extremely beneficial (also to the neighbours) in terms of safe storage of grains and livestock; and reduced repairing costs which stem from recurring floods in the state. However, the construction of a large underused building with costly decorative materials often shows the impact of consumerism even in the countryside.

It is very significant to note that, at the aggregate level, household consumption was found to be the single most important reason for taking loans in rural Assam. However, it is because of the smallness of the per unit consumption loan, its percentage share in total debt was quite low. Sometimes, fewer loans of a particular purpose (such as housing loans, PMRY loans) may get more importance in total debt because of much higher per unit loans. In other words, the percentage shares of debt to total debt by purposes may give us a better measure of the relative importance of various reasons for borrowings.

It is evident from Table 4.1 that as many as 35 households had borrowed for the purpose of food consumption. In addition, 11 households had also borrowed largely for food consumption during floods/natural calamities. Thus little less than one-fifth of the total incidence of loans was incurred for consumption.

Table 4.1
Purpose wise distribution of incidence, extent, repayment and overdues of debt (all households)

Purpose of borrowings	*Incidence of loans*	*Average debt per unit (in Rs.)*	*Average repayment per unit*	*Overdues as % of total outstanding debt*
Farm Business:				
Capital Expenditure	10	21600	5700	25.00
Current Expenditure	32	10530	2366	3.56
Allied Sector:				
Purchase of land (/MI)	4	12000	6500	-
Fishery	6	7433	1117	88.57
Livestock (/Poultry)	25	9904	926	92.33
Non-farm business:				
Capital Expenditure	31	17871	8745	73.19
Current Expenditure	19	7289	874	12.56
Sub-Total:	127	12485	3750	47.74
		(1585650)	(476240)	(757000)
Household Expenditure:				
Food consumption	35	1677	57	1.36
Health care	26	6921	850	5.00
Marriage	9	11361	1889	-

(Contd.)

(Contd. Table 4.1)

Purpose of borrowings	*Incidence of loans*	*Average debt per unit (in Rs.)*	*Average repayment per unit*	*Overdues as % of total outstanding debt*
Education	5	1560	520	6.41
House building	8	56000	18875	-
House repairing	5	12000	2260	-
Funeral	5	4660	460	-
Other household durables	11	10355	1091	-
Floods/storms	11	5645	591	5.48
Litigation	2	7000	-	7.14
Repayment of old debt	2	7000	-	-
Electricity dues	8	1875	-	100.0
Others	5	4700	-	-
Sub-Total	132	8504	1718	2.65
		(1122500)	(226800)	29700
Grand Total	259*	10456	2714	29.05
		(2708150)	(703040)	(786700)

Notes: *Quite a few households reported loans against two or more purposes.

**Outstanding/Extent of Debt: (principal amount + interest calculated there on) – any repayment. Overdues : That part of debt incurred for any specific purpose which has remained unpaid ('principal + loan' instalments in default) by the date the entire debt liability was expected to have been cleared.

*** Figures in brackets show the total volume of outstanding debt/repayment/overdues.

Incidence of loans for health care constituted one-tenth of the total loans. Housing loans (and repairing) constituted 5 per cent of the total loan-incidence. 'Household durables' and 'marriage' were the other two important purposes for which quite a few loans were taken. In all, 50.97 per cent of the total incidence of loan were incurred for different purposes under household expenditure group.

In the directly productive sector, the purposes for borrowing money according to their importance were capital expenditure in agricultural sector and allied activities (17.37 % of the total incidence), followed by current expenditure in farm business (12.36 %), capital expenditure in non-farm business (11.97 %) and current expenditure in non-farm business (7.34 %). Of the productive purposes loans, farm business loans constituted one-third of the total productive loan-incidence, allied sector constituted 27.56 per cent, while the non-farm loans constituted nearly two-fifths of all productive loan-incidence.

The average per unit debt by different purposes reveals certain important facts (Table 4.1). Although food consumption was found the most familiar reason for indebtedness, per unit loan was very low (1677) along with the educational loan (1560). The highest amount was borrowed (per unit) for house building (56000), distantly followed by capital expenditure in agriculture (21600) and capital expenditure in non-farm business (17871). The other important purposes of borrowings according to their volumes were house repairing (12000), purchase/mortgaged-in land (12000), marriage (11361), current expenditure in agriculture (10530), other household durables (10355), livestock (9904) and current expenditure in non-farm business (7289). All others, in terms of volume of debt, were much less important causes of borrowings.

The repayment column shows the highest per unit repayment against house building loan (18875). It was mainly because of the fact that these loans were provided mostly to the salaried people with the provision of recovery of monthly instalments directly from the salary account. The other important purposes against which some amount of repayment was recorded were capital expenditure in non-farm business (8745), purchase of land (6500), capital expenditure in agricultural sector (5700), current expenditure in agriculture (2366), house repairing (2260) and marriage (1889).

At the aggregate level, overdues as percentage of total outstanding debt constituted 29 per cent. Apparently, it looks surprising that productive purposes of loans accounted for high amount of overdues (47.74 %), while the unproductive purposes together recorded merely 2.65 per cent of the respective total as overdues.

It can be noted that overdues as percentage of the total debt was found very low at 3.56 against the head 'current expenditure in agriculture'. This was mainly due to the fact that a considerable amount of borrowings made against KCCs was recorded in this group, where default rate was negligible. Also, most of the KCC loans were taken only during the current year.

The highest amount of overdues (92.33 % of the respective total) was registered against livestock loan, closely followed by fishery loan (88.57 %). These loans were taken from banks, under directed loan schemes. Capital expenditure in non-farm business (73.19) and capital expenditure in agriculture (25.00) also recorded substantial amount of overdues.

No amount was found overdue against house building and house repairing loans, although mostly taken from banks. Funeral, household durables, repayment of old debt and 'others' also reported no overdues. Food consumption loan account reported lowest positive overdues (1.36), while health care (5.0),

Table 4.2

Social group wise distribution of debt, repayment and overdues by purposes.

Social Groups	*Purposes of indebtedness (% of the respective totals)*					
	Agricultural activities	*Allied activities*	*Non-farm business*	*House building*	*Other household Expen diture*	*All Total (in Rs.)*
Principal amount of loan taken:						
SC	14.43	13.42	22.82	20.13	29.19	149000
ST	2.05	18.02	28.87	21.07	29.99	474550
Others	24.18	7.34	27.38	20.14	20.96	2036800
Repayment made:						
SC	-	10.83	63.69	19.11	6.37	15700
ST	0.06	7.48	43.56	36.81	12.09	163000
Others	25.29	8.0	39.42	18.94	8.35	524340

(Contd.)

(Contd. Table 4.2)

Social Groups	*Purposes of indebtedness (% of the respective totals)*					*All Total (in Rs.)*
	Agricultural activities	*Allied activities*	*Non-farm business*	*House building*	*Other household Expen diture*	
Size of outstanding debt:						
SC	12.54	22.97	19.97	19.85	24.67	176300
ST	2.37	24.02	21.53	17.23	34.85	406350
Others	24.52	9.51	26.81	18.96	20.20	2125500
Overdues as % of respective total outstanding debt						
SC	-	100.0	31.25	-	-	29.21 (51500)
ST	-	85.66	25.14	-	9.04	29.14 (118400)
Others	12.66	71.25	68.43	-	3.94	29.02 (616800)

Figures in brackets show the total amount of overdues.

education (6.41), floods/storms (5.48) and litigation (7.14) also reported low to insignificant amount of overdues.

Apparently, it looks surprising that loan taken for unproductive purposes like food consumption, health care and house repairing during natural calamities shown low overdues. These loans were largely taken against mortgage of land for an unspecified period.

The reasons for high overdues of productive purpose debt (or low overdues of unproductive debt) were many:

- **Productive purpose loans were largely taken from banks (institutional sources). Institutional source generally lack any personal relationship (vital information about the borrowers' socio-economic conditions, borrowers' past record) with the loanees/potential borrowers. Once the loan amount was released, almost all contacts between bank officials and loanees virtually come to an end because of weak monitoring or loan recovery system.**

- **Productive loans were mostly advanced against government sponsored schemes. These loans (with anti-poverty tag) extended by the bankers were often treated as government grants which may not be returned. Even many bank officials implement these schemes very casually thinking it simply as doles to the poor and cause sometimes much inconveniences to the beneficiaries by delaying the release of funds.**

- **Wilful default was also found considerably responsible for growing overdues of productive loans.**

- **The presence of speed money in many banks (in the range of 50 % to 80 % of the subsidy amount in the case of PMRY and IRDP /now SGSY loans) also hampers bankers' image and the borrowers' willingness to return the loan.**

- In the case of unproductive components of debt, quite a few small loans were taken during the current year.

- Quite a few loans were taken from SHGs, where chances of accumulation of debt was less because of SHGs in-built system of monitoring, guidance in time of need and repayment in small instalments at a short regular interval.

- Quite a few loans from moneylenders (shopkeepers and friends) were taken for unspecified period, against mortgage of land.

Table 4.2 presents social group wise percentage distribution of initial amount of loan taken, repayment, outstanding debt and overdues by purpose. The table was constituted to find out the relative position of the different social groups in rural debt scenario by purposes. To have a clear idea about the major features of borrowings by purposes, the reasons for borrowings were rearranged in five groups in the table. All unproductive purposes of borrowings (house building and repairing shown separately) were grouped as 'other household expenditure'.

It appears from the table that among the SC households, above 29 per cent of the total borrowings were made for unproductive purposes (house repairing/building loan was considered as unproductive purpose in the NSS 48th Round). House building constituted another 20.13 per cent, while the share of productive loans constituted above one-half of the total. ST households reported one percentage point higher in the share of unproductive loans, as compared to the SC households. The 'non-SC and non-ST' other households recorded nearly two-fifths of the total borrowings for productive purposes.

Some important differences can be seen between the columns showing the percentage shares of productive and unproductive debt to total debt-outstanding and also their percentages to initial amount of borrowings. It is very clear from the table that the share of first three productive purposes, as percentage of outstanding debt, increases to 55.48 per cent (from 50.67 per cent registered in the initial amount of borrowings) for the SC households and 60.84 per cent for general households (from 58.9 %), while ST households recorded a marginal fall to 47.92 per cent (48.94 % recorded in the initial amount of borrowings head).

The share of productive loan as percentage of outstanding debt was found higher mainly due to accumulation of old institutional loans (i.e., the growing size of overdues)

- It can also be partly attributed to drying up of the concessional loans. In this case, the burden of accumulation of interest, in the case of non-repayment was less.

- Lower percentage share of interest free loans (CPF account, Government loans, etc).

- A sizeable amount of unproductive purposes loans was taken against mortgage of land. Also, loans from traders (trade credit) were reported as interest free. Consequently, any delay in repayment of such loans was not associated with the problem of accumulation of interest burden with the principal amount of borrowings (in all these cases, 'hidden interests' were paid in kind which did not reflect in total outstanding debt).

It can be seen from the table that considerable amount of repayment was recorded by all the three 'major' social groups against non-farm loans. However, save ST households, the other two household categories registered increase in the size of outstanding debt, as compared to their original amount of borrowings on this head. It seems that these two household groups had a large share of borrowings made in the past years. This is substantiated by high percentage share of overdues recorded by SC (31.25 %) and general households (68.43 %) against the loans for non-farm business.

High amount of overdues was also recorded in the 'allied activities' category. This was found true in the case of all the three major categories of households. Consequently, its share in total outstanding debt was found much higher than the initial amount of borrowings.

'Other household expenditure' recorded much lower amount of borrowings. In this category of loan, repayment was also low. However, since most of these loans had a hidden component of interest and taken for long/unspecified period, the problem of overdues was found nil in the case of SC households, very low at 3.94 per cent for general households and a modest 9.04 per cent for ST households.

It appears from Table 4.3, which shows the percentage distribution of debt by purposes over the three occupational groups with land status, that landless household (wage earners) in agricultural sector borrowed higher amount for different household expenditures (52.76 %) than that of the productive loans (47.24%). Landless households registered blank account on the heads viz agricultural activities, non-farm business and house building. These households only borrowed for 'livestock', among the productive components of loans. The entire amount of livestock loan was found as overdues, while nearly 17 per cent of the household expenditure was in default. The overdues as percentage of the total outstanding debt of agricultural landless households stood at 56.17, which was considerably higher in comparison to marginal farmers (43.23), small farmers (18.17) and bigger farmers (14.32). Landless agricultural households' position was also found more bleak compared to tertiary or industrial workers. The percentage share of productive debt in total debt will be much lower had we not been incorporated the IRDP loans taken by these households (also, by other households categories) which was in default and where even loan-asset was missing.

Landless agricultural households and industrial households were placed at the lowest economic standing at the time of survey and many of them seemed to be trapped in debt for quite some time. However, as it appears from the table, it cannot be safe to conclude that the problem of overdues (or the incidence of defaults) gets reduced as one move to the higher income levels.

It is very interesting to note that marginal farmers, small farmers, bigger farmers and landless as well as landed households engaged in the tertiary sector had recorded much higher absolute size of overdues than that of the agricultural households without land.

Amount of overdues was found very high against allied sector loans across the occupational groups. Allied sector loans mainly constituted livestock loans which were taken from the banks under the anti-poverty schemes. On this head, as percentage of the respective outstanding debt, overdues accounted for 100.0 among the agricultural households without land and also, the tertiary households without land, closely followed by marginal farmers — 96.02, small farmers – 62.04, bigger farmers – 61.04, landed industrial households – 50.72 and landed households whose most of the income came from the services – 52.0.

Non-farm business account had also shown extremely high percentage share of overdues for some household groups, viz

Table 4.3

Occupation and land status wise percentage distribution of outstanding debt and overdues by purposes.

Occupation / Land status	*Size of debt and overdues as % of the outstanding debt in the respective head.*					
	Agricultural activities	*Allied activities*	*Non-farm business*	*House building*	*Other household Expen diture*	*All Total (in Rs.)*
Primary Sector:						
Landless	-	47.24	-	-	52.76	38100
		(100.0)			(16.92)	(56.17)
MF	17.73	28.31	9.29	0.31	44.36	355300
	(20.63)	(96.02)	(100.0)	(-)	(6.98)	(43.23)
SF	29.62	16.99	2.61	11.64	39.13	398500
	(21.18)	(62.04)	(3.85)	(-)	(4.60)	(18.75)
SMF	32.64	7.98	11.29	16.06	32.03	482600
	(-)	(61.04)	(82.57)	(-)	(0.39)	(14.32)

(Contd.)

(Contd. Table 4.3)

Occupation / Land status	Size of debt and overdues as % of the outstanding debt in the respective head.					
	Agricultural activities	Allied activities	Non-farm business	House building	Other household Expen diture	All Total (in Rs.)
Tertiary Sector:						
Landless	-	23.81 (100.0)	49.66 (28.28)	17.50 (-)	9.02 (9.48)	245650 (38.71)
Others	17.62 (13.94)	4.39 (52.0)	39.63 (64.88)	29.84 (-)	8.51 (5.46)	1139400 (30.92)
Industrial Sector:						
Landless	-	-	-	-	100.0 (-)	200 (-)
Others	28.10 (-)	14.26 (50.72)	43.39 (80.95)	-	14.26 (-)	48400 (42.36)

***MF: Marginal farmers; SF : Small farmers and SMF : Semi-medium farmers and large farmers.**

***Figures in brackets indicate overdue position.**

marginal farmers – 100.0, bigger farmers – 82.57, 'others' in industrial sector – 80.95 and 'others' in tertiary sector – 65.88. This column included a few PMRY loans and also few other institutional loans extended under the government sponsored schemes.

The above facts bear testimony to the belief that richer households are not necessarily a good borrower, particularly when they borrow from the institutional sources under the directed loan schemes.

The head 'agricultural activities' comprises KCC loans, a few STW loans, a couple of power tiller loans, etc. A substantial proportion of these loans were taken during the current year and mainly by the richer households. All the household groups with positive account, thus, recorded very low overdues against agricultural loans. Similarly, house building and repairing loans were also mainly taken by the better off households, mainly from the banks. These fresh loans were borrowed mostly against the 'salary security', i.e., recovery of monthly loan instalment directly from the salary bill (In a few cases, borrowers salary was deposited in the same bank where from such loans were taken).

Better off households got relatively lower amount of loans under the directed loan schemes with a provision of subsidy amount, compared to their personal loan component for consumer durables. This has also helped in showing relatively lower level of overdues among the better off section at the overall level.

The above factors had also contributed to the relatively lower level of overdues shown by the better off households.

Table 4.4 presents percentage distribution of outstanding debt and overdues as percentage of outstanding debt by 5 broad purposes of borrowings. In this table, (also, the following table), the totals of the different sub-heads may not tally with the earlier tables, since in this table, smaller loans were merged with the bigger loans, where borrowers were reported to have incurred debt for more than one purposes.

It appears from the table that the bottom asset value group (Rs. 50000 or less) had registered no debt against agricultural business and house building. Some amount of debt was recorded in the head 'allied activities', the entire amount of which was in default. Nearly, 46 per cent of the outstanding debt was raised for non-agricultural business, while unproductive purposes loans constituted above 42 per cent of the total.

The percentage share of 'household expenditure' was found relatively less at 26.23 per cent and 26.20 per cent in the subsequent two higher asset groups. However, in 2 – 3 lakh and 7 – 11 lakh asset groups, the above share was found quite high at 39.62 per cent and 40.55 per cent respectively. In the former group, considerable amount of borrowings was reported for consumer durables, health care and funeral, while in the later group, relatively high amount of loan was taken for marriage and health care. In 4 – 7 lakh group and the highest asset group, very low percentage shares of unproductive purposes of borrowings were registered (8.54 % and 7.79 % respectively).

It can be mentioned that the 48th Round of NSS (1998) found that poorer households borrow mostly for unproductive purposes like incurring household expenditure and other similar needs whereas the better off households borrow mainly for productive purposes like operating and expanding their household enterprises. 'The percentage share of debt for productive purposes is seen to increase from 11.4 per cent in the bottom asset class to 27 per cent in the top asset class.

Further, the percentage share of debt against 'household expenditure' is seen to decrease from about 58 per cent in the bottom asset holding class to about 23 per cent in the top asset holding class.

Among the sample households, the trend was not very clear, although two of the three highest asset value groups had recorded very low percentage share of unproductive debt (However, the trend was found more clear when the households were classified according to their income or land holdings). It shows that 'other than land' factors have played a role in some of the asset holding groups in determining their demand for loans for various purposes.

One important factor is of course the increasing incidence of government services (and also trade activities) among the people in the higher asset value groups. Another important factor is the location of the village. For example, in Begenati village under Nagaon district, I bigha land was valued at Rs. 2 lakh (in Rangmohal, market value of 1 bigha land was also equally high), while in Bamungaon, Eraligul, Powaimukh, etc market value of one bigha land was much less than Rs. 50000. The annual yield also varied widely between villages from above Rs. 20000 in Begenati to Rs. 3000 in Rangmohal, to further down to Rs. 2000 in Eraligul and Powaimukh and very low and still uncertain of Rs. 1500 to Rs. 1800 in Bamungaon and Punjabari villages.

It seems that different assets value group might not have represented expected pattern of the income flow which was more true in the case of distribution of households according to their land holding status. Last but not the least, access to the credit agencies differed widely from village to village, between weaker sections and relatively richer households and even within the better off communities.

Table 4.4

Asset group wise percentage distribution of outstanding debt and overdues by purposes

Asset Groups (in Rs.)	*Size of debt and overdues as % of the outstanding debt in the respective head.*					
	Agricultural activities	*Allied activities*	*Non-farm business*	*House building*	*Other household Expenditure*	*All Total (in Rs.)*
Up to 50000	-	11.84	45.69	-	42.47	59100
		(100.0)	(90.74)		(17.53)	(60.74)
50001 – 1 lakh	7.06	46.44	16.10	4.16	26.23	192500
	(-)	(99.55)	(70.97)	(-)	(6.73)	(59.43)
> 1 lakh – 2 lakh	2.40	16.56	9.57	45.27	26.20	402250
	(-)	(65.47)	(37.66)	(-)	(2.85)	(15.19)
> 2 lakh – 3 lakh	12.03	6.89	26.32	15.16	39.62	252700
	(32.89)	(68.97)	(55.64)	(-)	(6.99)	(26.12)
> 3 lakh – 4 lakh	8.89	18.07	6.56	36.71	29.78	343200
	(9.84)	(53.23)	(64.44)	(-)	(9.78)	(17.63)
> 4 lakh – 7 lakh	19.15	14.04	50.82	7.44	8.54	600500
	(10.43)	(74.85)	(87.91)	(-)	(8.38)	(57.90)
> 7 lakh – 11 lakh	10.27	11.10	29.04	9.04	40.55	365000
	(-)	(92.59)	(6.60)	(-)	(1.35)	(12.74)
Above 11 lakh	47.27	4.06	20.90	19.98	7.79	492900
	(2.15)	(-)	(47.57)	(-)	(1.56)	(11.08)

Notes: * In this table, smaller loans were merged with the bigger ones, where a borrower borrowed for more than one purposes (i.e., one household, one loan). * Figures in brackets indicate overdue position.

It is also seen from Table 4.4 that among the bottom two asset holding groups, the overall level of overdues was much higher (60.74 % and 59.43 % respectively) than that of the highest two asset holding groups (12.74 % and 11.08 % respectively). However, 4 – 7 lakh asset holding group with very high percentage share of productive loans of above 91 per cent had reported nearly 58 per cent of the total outstanding debt as overdues. The table once again establishes the fact that the size of overdues against different purposes of loans depend more on habitual factors of the borrowers and less on the strengths of asset holding or income flow. Only in the case of a small section fall in the 'marginalised class', accumulating overdues stem from (extreme) poverty, flood ravages or recurrent floods led uncertainties about the continuity of the current activities and, above all, the absence of vital infrastructural linkages which turns incremental income yielded by the loan assets often insufficient to meet the loan obligation, after meeting the deficits in the family budget.

The table also shows no overdue amount against house building/ repairing loans across the asset holding groups. Both the agricultural activities and household expenditure heads registered low amount of overdues over the asset holding groups with a few minor exceptions. The bottom asset holding class recorded 17.53 per cent of the total borrowings as overdues in the household expenditure column, while 2 – 3 lakh asset holding class recorded one-third of the total debt as in default in the agricultural loan account.

Allied activities and non-farm business columns recorded extremely high to high overdue amounts across the asset groups. For instance, all the asset holding classes (save the top asset group) recorded much more than half of the total borrowings made in the 'allied activities' head as overdues. It was as high as 100.0 per cent in lowest asset value group, 99.55 per cent in 50001 – 1 lakh group and 92.59 per cent in 7 – 11 lakh group.

Similarly, in the non-farm business head, it was as high as 90.74 per cent in the bottom asset holding class, 87.91 per cent in 4 – 7 lakh group and 70.97 per cent in 50001 – 1 lakh group.

The percentage distribution of outstanding debt and overdues by purposes over the income groups is presented in table 4.5. It appears from the table that more than 71 per cent of the debts of the poorest households were contracted for household expenditure. In Rs. 11001 – 22000 group, considerable amount of productive purposes debt were also recorded for which unproductive purposes borrowings constituted below 45 per cent. Unproductive purposes debt was much higher in the next higher income group of 22001 – 26000 (64.14 %). In the next three successive higher income groups, the above share was found around 30 per cent, while the highest two successive income groups' corresponding shares were 15.96 per cent and 9.69 per cent. The overdue position shows some interesting features, although not much different from the expectations.

The size of overdues was less than one-third of the total outstanding debt in the bottom income group, while it was highest at 53.29 per cent in 26001 – 30000 group, followed by 11001 – 22000 group with 45.12 per cent, 37.63 per cent in 75001 – 2 lakh group and 35.0 per cent in 22001 – 26000 group. All other income groups registered much lower overdue amount, viz 26.34 per cent in 36001 – 75000, 22.23 per cent in 30001 – 36000 and 9.25 per cent in the top income group. It is clear from the table that in the lower 4 income groups, overdue amounts as percentage of the total debt was higher than the higher 4 income groups with the exception of 75001 – 2 lakh group. Much similar to the earlier tables, productive purposes borrowings other than agricultural activities had registered very high shares of overdues, irrespective of the income status of the households. For instance, in the head 'allied activities' both the bottom and the top income groups had shown the entire amount of debt as overdues. The overdue amount was also very high in 26001 –

Table 4.5

Income group wise percentage distribution of outstanding debt and overdues by purposes

Income Groups ('000)	*Size of debt and overdues as % of the outstanding debt in the respective head.*					
	Agricultural activities	*Allied activities*	*Non-farm business*	*House building*	*Other household Expenditure*	*All Total (in Rs.)*
≤ 11	-	18.33 (100.0)	10.31 (100.0)	-	71.36 (4.17)	43650 (31.62)
11 – 22	0.09 (-)	48.34 (75.24)	6.75 (52.17)	-	44.82 (11.65)	170450 (45.12)
22 – 26	20.0 (71.43)	-	14.29 (100.0)	1.57 (-)	64.14 (10.02)	70000 (35.0)
26 – 30	9.70 (-)	43.42 (88.67)	16.69 (86.32)	-	30.19 (1.28)	284650 (53.29)
30 – 36	22.56 (-)	24.20 (38.98)	20.51 (56.0)	2.71 (-)	30.02 (4.37)	121900 (22.23)

(Contd.)

(Contd. Table 4.5)

Income Groups ('000)	*Size of debt and overdues as % of the outstanding debt in the respective head.*					
	Agricultural activities	*Allied activities*	*Non-farm business*	*House building*	*Other household Expenditure*	*All Total (in Rs.)*
36 – 75	13.59	18.33	24.45	12.55	31.09	470300
	(4.69)	(73.78)	(42.87)	(-)	(5.47)	(26.34)
75 - 200	14.02	6.35	36.88	26.79	15.96	795100
	(10.76)	(46.53)	(89.70)	(-)	(0.55)	(37.63)
> 200	29.92	0.93	25.66	33.80	9.69	752100
	(2.22)	(100.0)	(25.39)	(-)	(11.80)	(9.25)

Notes: * In this table, smaller loans were merged with the bigger ones, where a borrower borrowed for more than one purposes (i.e., one household, one loan).

*Figures in brackets indicate overdue position.

30000 (88.67 %), 11001 – 22000 (75.24 %), and 36001 – 75000 (73.78 %) income groups.

In the 'non-farm business' head, bottom income group and 22001 – 26000 income group recorded the entire amount of debt in default, while 75001 – 2 lakh income group (89.70 %) and 26001 – 30000 income group (86.32 %) recorded very high percentage share of overdues. The agricultural activities head registered low overdues. The reasons were already explained in the above section. The table once again extends support to the fact that wilful default is the serious problem in this region which also encourages diversion of productive purposes loans to unproductive use.

The Report of the Expert Committee on Rural Credit (2001) reported woefully poor recovery performance of rural financial institutions under agricultural credit for the state of Assam, compared to the rest of India. As on 30 June, 1999, the recovery performance of the State Cooperative banks (1%), State Cooperative Agriculture and Rural Development Banks (1%), Commercial Banks (13 %) and Regional Rural banks (29 %) was found 'poor to extremely poor' in the state of Assam. The corresponding percentages for the state of Haryana were 99, 94, 69 and 72; Karnataka – 95, 33, 63 and 70; West Bengal – 78, 64, 47 and 38, while the all India averages were respectively 81, 62, not available and 61 per cent.

It is a harsh truth that repayment culture is still seriously missing even though in some parts KCCs and SHGs are coming up as a movement. The imperfections in credit market, agricultural market and other vital infrastructures were not really helping the situations to improve. Most unfortunately, credit is still playing far below the optimum as a major factor in boosting economic development in the region.

Important observations:

- Above three-fifths of the total debt incurred by the poor was for unproductive purposes.

- The actual share of the unproductive loans in total debt may go up further if we take into consideration the fact that their productive purposes loans were mostly taken under the IRDP schemes long back, the entire amount of which was in default. These 'old debts' accumulated over the years as neither the principal nor the interest accrued was paid back. In many cases, even the loan-asset was found missing.

- High rate of defaults under the directed loan schemes has made the banks reluctant to extend productive credit to rural poor. Needless to mention that the entire amount of unproductive credit and personal loans extended by the banks in recent times went to the better off households.

- Non availability of productive purposes credit under the government sponsored schemes and moneylenders' direct or indirect pursuance for security of land put the weaker sections once again in disadvantage, — as was the case before nationalization of banks. To get rid of this crisis, some households were motivated to form SHGs in some pockets mainly to increase their access to institutional credit.

Sources of Credit

Easy access to different sources of credit is the most desired aspect of rural credit business which would mean so much for the needy borrowers. As already mentioned, credit is an important input for rural development. However, its timely availability, adequate supply and distribution at reasonable terms and conditions are very important aspects having lasting impact on the effectiveness of credit.

The institutional credit agencies have an impact on the cost of borrowing. When institutional loans are made available at regulated low rate of interest, to that extent it makes it difficult for the moneylenders to charge a very high rate of interest, for those who have access to institutional credits.

The loans taken from the informal sector are often associated with the obligations like high interest, hidden interest, low paid contractual labour bondages, under-pricing of mortgaged properties, etc. During emergency like situations, i.e., when floods or storms destroy the living house/shelter, standing crops, or the only earning member falls sick, etc the affected people needs money immediately for which they cannot wait for the 'most uncertain' government relief. Friends, shop keepers, even moneylenders play a very useful role in such situations. There is no doubt that taking the full advantage of the adverse situation, a few moneylenders takes temporary hold of the borrowers' land for the period of loan which sometimes ends in alienation of land from the weaker sections. Many times poor borrowers face double exploitation when they borrow from informal sector. They have to pay interest on the borrowed amount and sell the field produces at pre-determined prices (the price which was prevailing at the time of loan transaction) or had to sale labour during the sowing and harvesting seasons at normal wage rates, — though during the peak seasons, market wage rates go up by around 10 – 20 per cent. The increase in the share of institutional credit simultaneously leads to a fall in the household's burden of high interest borrowings (check the chances of land alienation, low paid contractual labour, loss of right to use mortgaged land as sometimes happen in the case of loans from moneylenders) besides boasting productive economic activities for the needy households. Thus, the formal credit institutions, or any institution with a back up of formal institutions, are supposed to play the catalytic role in resurgence of rural economy.

Table 4.6
Village wise percentage distribution of outstanding debt by source (Part I).

Source	*Kamrup*			*Nagaon*		
	VNT	*IV*	*All*	*VNT*	*IV*	*All*
Banks (directed loans)	22.41	88.08	35.95 (20)	72.83	6.66	51.48 (30)
Banks (Other loans)	47.48	-	37.69 (6)	16.92	-	11.46 (3)
O I A	1.22	10.60	3.16 (3)	-	-	-
A I A	71.11	98.68	76.79 (29)	89.76	6.66	62.94 (33)
Agricultural moneylender	7.28	-	5.78 (7)	9.07	80.24	32.03 (19)
Professional moneylender	3.06	-	2.43 (3)	1.06	6.28	2.74 (6)
Shopkeeper	0.66	0.38	0.60 (15)	-	-	-
Traders	-	-	-	-	0.95	0.31 (2)

(*Contd.*)

(Contd. Table 4.6)

Source	Kamrup VNT	Kamrup IV	Kamrup All	Nagaon VNT	Nagaon IV	Nagaon All
Friends & Relatives	1.28	-	1.02 (4)	0.03	5.87	1.91 (6)
SHGs	7.77	0.94	6.36 (25)	0.09	-	0.06 (1)
Village societies	0.64	-	0.51 (2)	-	-	-
School benefit fund	2.20	-	1.75 (1)	-	-	-
Private bank	4.89	-	3.89 (1)	-	-	-
Others	1.10	-	0.87 (4)	-	-	-
A N I A	28.89	1.32	23.21 (62)	10.24	93.34	37.06 (34)
All-Total	100.0	100.0	100.0 (91)	100.0	100.0	100.0 (67)

O I A: Other Institutional Agencies. A I A : All-Institutional Agencies.
A N I A : All Non-Institutional Agencies.
Note: * Figures in brackets indicate incidence of loans.
** Quite a few households had taken loans both from institutional and non-institutional sources at the time of survey. The incidence would have increased further had we included **separately two or three loans sometimes taken from moneylenders** for different purposes.

Table 4.6

Village wise percentage distribution of outstanding debt by source (Part II).

Source	Tinsukia			Karimganj			*All- Total*
	VNT	*IV*	*All*	*VNT*	*IV*	*All*	
Bank(directed loans)	32.11	15.11	24.96 (12)	31.10	74.20	49.24 (16)	40.90 (78)
Bank (Other loans)	43.45	9.90	29.34 (2)	-	-	-	23.41 (11)
O I A	10.58	2.60	7.23 (2)	-	-	-	2.42 (5)
A I A	86.14	27.61	61.54 (16)	31.10	74.20	49.24 (16)	66.73 (94)
Agricultural moneylender	-	67.15	28.23 (21)	14.10	25.51	18.91 (3)	20.22 (50)
Professional moneylender	2.27	1.88	2.10 (2)	13.40	-	7.76 (3)	2.97 (14)
Shopkeeper	2.15	-	1.25 (2)	-	0.29	0.12 (1)	0.45 (18)
Traders	-	2.08	0.88 (2)	38.79	-	22.46 (1)	2.29 (5)

(Contd.)

(Contd. Table 4.6)

Source	*Tinsukia*			*Karimganj*			*All- Total*
	VNT	*IV*	*All*	*VNT*	*IV*	*All*	
Friends & Relatives	-	1.28	0.54 (5)	-	-	-	1.17 (15)
SHGs	1.13	-	0.66 (1)	-	-	-	2.55 (27)
Village societies	-	-	-	-	-	-	0.19 (2)
School benefit fund	6.04	-	3.50 (1)	2.47	-	1.43 (1)	1.38 (3)
Private bank	-	-	-	-	-	-	1.48 (1)
Others	2.27	-	1.31 (4)	0.14	-	0.08 (1)	0.56 (9)
A N I A	13.86	72.39	38.46 (38)	68.90	25.80	50.76 (10)	33.27 (144)
All-Total	100.0	100.0	100.0 (54)	100.0	100.0	100.0 (26)	100.0 (238)

One positive finding of the present study was the appreciable increase in the incidence of institutional loans in recent times. Banks constituted the single most important source of loans both in terms of incidence as well as extent of loans.

As it appears from Table 4.6 bank constituted above one-third (37.39 %) of all loan-incidence. Bank and other institutional loans accounted for nearly two-fifths of all loan incidence. The second most important source was found to be moneylenders, which constituted above one-fourth (26.89%) of all loan-incidence. It is a matter of great concern that moneylenders and traders and shop keepers together constituted nearly 37 per cent of all loan-incidence. It seems that although banking facilities have been expanded substantially over the years, it has not yet been successful to loosen the grip of the moneylenders. In fact, the moneylenders importance has increased substantially in recent times in the region as is evident by its higher-incidence recorded in the table.

Although at the very initial stage, it is good to see that savings backed borrowings have made some impacts in rural credit scenario, at least in some of the villages in the state. The incidence of loans from SHGs (which have not yet accessed institutional credit) constituted above 11 per cent. The percentage will increase a little further had bank loans to SHGs been included (which were shown against the source 'bank'). The incidence of loans from SHGs, village societies and school welfare/benefit fund together accounted for above 13 per cent. Apart from the banks, moneylenders, shop-keepers, SHGs and friends and relatives all other sources were found of marginal significance.

Areas of Concern

- At the aggregate level, informal credit agencies still serve the highest number of borrowers, i.e., above three-fifths of all loan incidence.

- Moneylender is still very dominant in rural credit business. It is playing a more dominant role in the remote villages.

- During the last decade (i.e., in the 1990s) moneylenders' importance has increased in terms of its share in total debt-incidence and size of loans.

- A lion's share of loans from the moneylenders was against mortgage of land. However, the growth of SHGs has definitely reduced the incidence of loans from moneylenders against mortgage of land at least among the members. During the last year or so (/in the beginning of the 21st century) fewer cases of such loans were recorded.

- SHG movement has failed to reduce the cost of borrowings in the informal market. It is a matter of concern that SHG loans were extended at a moderately high (to members) to very high rates of interest (to non-members).

- The growth of SHGs has led to drying up of the interest free sources like 'friend and relatives', since groups were mostly formed by the closely related members (affinity group).

The source wise incidence of indebtedness widely differed across the villages/districts. In the green revolution belt, i.e., vegetable belt of Nagaon, one-half (33 numbers) of the total loan incidence (67) was constituted by the institutional sources. In Karimganj district, although total incidence of loan was found quite low at 26, the institutional sources constituted about three-fifths of the total. In absolute terms, the incidence of institutional loans was found quite low in Tinsukia and Karimganj district, while Kamrup and Nagaon districts recorded high-incidence of institutional loans. In the remote villages of Nagaon, only a couple of institutional loans were recorded, despite higher level of agricultural diversification (one village falls in the rain shadow area). Equally dismal picture was seen in the remote villages under Tinsukia district where only 5 cases of institutional loans were reported. Only Karimganj district (and to some extent, Kamrup district) reported relatively higher incidence of institutional loans in the remote villages. The incidence of SHG-bank linkages (under the supervision of an NGO) and the distribution of a few KCC loans to the farmers can be identified as the reasons for showing this encouraging feature against the trend.

It can be noted that in two of the 4 remote village groups – one in Kamrup and the other in Karimganj – where many people participated in group movement, not a single incidence of loan from friends and relatives was reported. This source was found of some importance in the other two remote village groups of Tinsukia and Nagaon where SHG movement is about to start or just a couple of groups were formed at the time of survey.

Except Kamrup district, relatively very high incidence of loan from moneylenders was recorded in villages where access to institutional loans was found absent or very limited. These village groups were remote villages in Nagaon district (20 numbers), remote villages in Tinsukia (22 numbers) and advanced village group (4 numbers) under Karimganj district. Bank-SHG linkages and KCC distribution under the supervision of NGOs/FMCs/PRIs etc. can go a long way in making institutional loans accessible to the so far deprived lots viz marginal farmers, landless and other asset less poor particularly living in the remote villages (as was the case in Eraligul and also, in Begenati).

In the remote villages where a large number of SHGs were seen operating, the incidence of loans from moneylenders was reported much less (in the advanced villages of Kamrup, as much as 10 numbers of loans from moneylenders were reported. Most of these loans were borrowed in the past years). In the remote villages under Kamrup district, the incidence was found 'nil', while in Karimganj, only a couple of such loans were reported.

Incidence of debt to moneylenders was found high in villages affected by natural calamities viz. Dwigunpar (10 numbers, flood affected), Punjabari (20 numbers, drought affected) and Powaimukh (22 numbers, storm and flood affected).

From the above discussion, it can be said that moneylenders' grip is still much stronger in villages where institutional agencies are absent or their presence is at best thin. SHGs are yet to come up in a big way and to discourage any loans by the borrowers against mortgage of land. Natural calamities are occurring at regular intervals which has posed a serious challenge for many villagers whether to invest on permanent assets in a traditional way.

The percentage distribution of outstanding debt by sources shows that the institutional loans were of much larger size and constituted much larger percentage share in total debt. The institutional sources constituted less than two-fifths of all loan-incidence, but their share in outstanding debt was estimated at 66.73 per cent. All the non-institutional sources together extended nearly one-third of the total outstanding debt, although very high loan-incidence (above three-fifths) was recorded in the informal credit market.

Among the institutional sources, commercial banks and RRBs constituted the lion's share. The sources like government, cooperative banks, PF and insurance together contributed merely 2.42 per cent in total debt outstanding. In the last decade or so, institutional credit agencies other than commercial banks and RRBs, have dried up considerably. This partially supports our second hypothesis that government's supportive role for poverty eradication (in this case anti-poverty loan schemes) in the era of globalization may get thinner.

It is quite interesting to note that of the total outstanding debt to banks of Rs. 17,41,700, nearly 64 per cent was 'directed loans' comprising IRDP (SGSY and SHG-bank linkages), KCCs and PMRY loans. About 36 per cent of the bank loans were extended mainly for house building and consumer durables.

Among the districts, institutional loans constituted above three-fourths of the total debt in Kamrup district. In this district along with Tinsukia, banks' other category of loans (37.69 % in former district and 29.34 % in the later) constituted higher percentage share in total debt than that of the 'directed loans' (35.95 % and 24.96 % respectively). In Karimganj district, loans from banks for consumer durables (including housing loan) were not recorded at all, while Nagaon district recorded relatively a low percentage share (11.46 %).

Institutional sources constituted 76.79 per cent in total debt in the district of Kamrup, followed by Nagaon (62.94) and Tinsukia (61.54), while it was considerably low at 49.24 per cent in Karimganj district.

Other than banks the only important source in terms of total volume of loans extended was the agricultural moneylenders. Agricultural moneylenders constituted one-fifth of the total outstanding debt. The percentage rises up to 23 per cent when clubbed with the professional moneylenders.

It is significant to note that traditional moneylenders (agricultural moneylender plus professional moneylender) had registered a much thinner presence in Kamrup district with little above 8 per cent share in total debt. Savings backed sources viz SHGs (6.36 %), school welfare fund (2.26 %) and private banks with 3.89 per cent share in total outstanding debt were (along with the institutional sources) seen co-existing with moneylenders. However, there is a possibility of gradual substitution of moneylenders by SHGs (and KCCs to some extent) if the movement gains momentum in near future.

The role of moneylenders was found very strong in the other three districts nullifying all institutional efforts to liquidate the stranglehold of the unscrupulous moneylenders who were seen extending loans mainly against land security, which often ends up with alienation of land from the borrowers.

Moneylenders' share in total debt outstanding stood at 34.77 per cent in Nagaon, 30.33 per cent in Tinsukia and 26.67 per cent in Karimganj district. Only in Karimganj district, traders constituted 22.46 per cent in total debt outstanding. The share of all other non-institutional sources in the above districts was found insignificant.

It seems that the exploitative role of the moneylenders can be further diluted if concerted efforts are made to make the institutional loans frequently available against land possessed by the borrowers (like KCCs or group loans to the landless). The only extra provision that has to be incorporated is to extend loan even for unproductive purposes including consumption loans during lean season and natural calamities. To make such loans workable and economically viable and also, to ensure that a larger part of such loans are used for productive purposes, FMCs or SHGs or at least PRIs' intermediation has to be compulsorily facilitated with. The land records need to be up dated and in quick time. Single window services (at the Panchayat office) with the active involvement of the PRI members can be arranged for up dating land records so as to facilitate the KCCs to take the shape of a movement.

The relative position of the institutional and non-institutional sources varied across the state. In remote villages of Kamrup, where relatively very low incidence of debt was recorded and where a large number of savings and credit groups were found in operation, institutional sources were pre-dominant contributing 98.68 per cent in total debt. This has virtually wiped out moneylenders from the credit business. This was also the case with the advantageous villages in Tinsukia district, where institutional advances constituted above 86 per cent, while the share of moneylenders was merely 2.27 per cent.

In the advantageous village groups in Kamrup and Nagaon, and also in remote villages under Karimganj district, institutional loans accounted for very high percentage share ranging from 71 per cent in Kamrup to 74 per cent in Karimganj to even higher at 89.76 per cent in Nagaon. However, in all these villages, moneylenders also existed side by side.

In six villages, institutional loans were found either much less frequent or yet to open their account. In the remote villages of Nagaon, in sharp contrast to their (advantageously placed) counterparts, institutional loans constituted just 6.66 per cent in total debt. Also, in remote villages in Tinsukia, the corresponding share was below 28 per cent, while in the villages located near urban centres in Karimganj, it was just above 31 per cent.

In remote villages under Nagaon district, moneylenders constituted about 87 per cent in total debt. The corresponding share in Tinsukia district was above 69 per cent, while in Karimganj district, moneylenders contribution was above one-fourth of the total.

It is evident from the table that in six out of the 16 villages, institutional agencies have failed to make any dent in the credit market. In these villages, borrowers had to depend considerably on moneylenders, sometimes they have to pay high price for borrowing from the moneylenders during natural calamities, health care, food consumption or marriages which are explained in the next chapter. Only in 4 villages (where institutional agencies were found active) moneylenders was found ineffective or at best, their presence was very thin.

The conspicuous absence of institutional credit agencies in remote villages and much stronger grip of the moneylenders in these villages can also be seen from the following facts:

- At the aggregate level, in remote villages, institutional credit agencies constituted less than 44 per cent in total debt outstanding (Rs. 822650), while the share of moneylenders was found above 52 per cent. Friends and relatives constituted 2.55 per cent, while the rest credit agencies were insignificant.

- In sharp contrast, in 8 villages located near urban centres, nearly 77 per cent of all borrowings were made from institutional agencies, while the share of moneylenders was 10.42 per cent. Other informal sources like shop keepers (3.51), SHGs (3.56) and private banks, school benefit fund, etc (5.19) also contributed some amount of loan.

- It is a matter of concern that of the total outstanding loans of Rs. 18,07,200 to institutional agencies, the shares of VNT and IV groups were 80.08 and 19.92 per cent respectively. This speaks volumes about the poor reach of the institutional credit agencies in interior villages. It also indicates that almost 50 per cent of the villages placed in interior region or lacking access to all weather roads are still very much at the mercy of the moneylenders. The growth of SHGs in these villages and building up of the informal institutional set up for intermediation can only facilitate the access of these people to institutional credit agencies.

Even in advantageous villages, the increasing tendency of the banks to extend credit for house building or consumer durables, may further dry up the 'critical productive components of loans' required by the weaker sections of the society.

Infrastructural encouragement to the institution of SHGs and judicious application of KCCs under the supervision of rejuvenated FMCs/PRIs/teachers units/women organizations (NGOs) can only give a much desired impetus to the dismal rural credit delivery and recovery system in the region, which can ultimately ensure regular and sufficient quantum of credit flow to the rural sector.

As mentioned in the previous chapter, the size of indebtedness in rural Assam has gone up substantially in recent times. The much increased availability of personal loans of bigger size from banks has helped in its sharp increase. Since all these big loans were concentrated in the hands of better off communities, larger volume of debt/much higher average size of debt reported in the sample needs special treatment from different angles so as to correctly assess its impact on the poor. With this objective in mind, quite a few tables were included in the following sections emphasizing on different aspects.

Table 4.7 presents the district wise percentage distribution of principal amount of borrowings, repayment, outstanding debt and overdues by source of loans. It is evident from the table that in Kamrup district, in spite of recording considerable amount of repayment, i.e., 32.56 per cent of the initial amount of borrowings, the size of outstanding debt was higher than the principal amount by one and a half percentage points. The overdues which constituted 38.35 per cent of the outstanding debt was the main reason for this dismal picture. Another factor which can be partially attributed to higher size of outstanding debt was the higher incidence of fresh loans during the current year.

Table 4.7
District wise percentage distribution of principal amount of borrowings, repayment, outstanding debt and overdues by source.

Attributes	*Bank+*	*Money lenders*	*Shop Keepers / Traders*	*Friends & relatives*	*SHGs*	*Others*	*All*
Kamrup:							
Borrowings	77.09	8.72	0.61	1.63	6.13	5.82	100.0
Repayment	36.53	15.82	-	36.36	32.80	.7.12	32.56
Outstanding	101.10	95.48	100.0	63.64	105.31	122.37	101.49
Overdues	46.81	7.10	-	-	14.05	13.16	38.35
Nagaon:							
Borrowings	59.88	37.55	0.33	2.19	0.06	-	100.0
Repayment	29.21	3.78	-	5.08	-	-	19.02
Outstanding	113.99	100.44	100.0	94.92	120.0	-	108.45
Overdues	39.92	-	-	-	16.67	-	25.14

(Contd.)

(Contd. Table 4.7)

Attributes	*Bank+*	*Money lenders*	*Shop Keepers/ Traders*	*Friends & relatives*	*SHGs*	*Others*	*All*
Tinsukia:							
Borrowings	62.68	27.11	1.93	0.51	0.60	7.17	100.0
Repayment	33.54	19.49	10.31	3.92	16.67	44.44	29.82
Outstanding	89.35	101.84	100.0	96.08	100.0	61.11	91.01
Overdues	36.30	3.61	-	-	-	27.27	24.75
Karimganj:							
Borrowings	47.57	27.55	22.74	-	-	2.14	100.0
Repayment	29.21	23.88	-	-	-	38.46	21.30
Outstanding	104.24	97.46	100.0	-	-	71.15	100.70
Overdues	27.36	0.46	-	-	-	-	13.60

* Borrowings in different columns indicate percentage of the total amount of borrowings

* Repayment is shown as percentage of the principal amount of borrowings in the respective column.

* Outstanding debt as percentage of the principal amount of borrowings in the respective column.

* Overdues as percentage of the outstanding debt.

Also, in Nagaon and Karimganj districts, outstanding debt was found higher than the initial amount of borrowings. In Nagaon, apparently lower amount of repayment was registered (19 % of the total borrowings at the aggregate level) against almost all categories of loans. However, overdues were found lower both in Nagaon (25.14) and Karimganj (13.60) districts. One important reason for higher percentage shares of outstanding debt (108.45 % and 100.70 % respectively in the above two districts) and lower percentage of overdues was due to much higher incidence of current year borrowings from banks (KCCs and SHG-bank linkages) in these districts. In Karimganj district, very low incidence of institutional loans in the past years was registered. Institutional loans – be it extended in advanced district or backward, — had registered poor repayments particularly in the cases of IRDP (and DRI) loans. This was the most important reason for which overdues as percentage of outstanding debt was recorded at the lower side in Karimganj district.

In Tinsukia district, outstanding debt as percentage of the total amount of initial borrowings was found lower (91 %). This was the only district where institutional loans were found lower than the initial amount of borrowings (89.35 %). The overdue as percentage of the outstanding debt stood at 24.75 per cent, while the repayment constituted nearly 30 per cent of the principal amount of borrowings.

Very interestingly, Tinsukia district had registered lower percentage share of overdues in the institutional loan categories compared to Nagaon and Kamrup districts.

The repayment as percentage of initial amount of borrowings was found nearly 34 per cent in the case of institutional loans, while it was little less than 20 per cent in the case of moneylenders. All other sources also recorded moderate to substantial amount of repayment in the range of 3.92 per cent in the case of friends and relatives to 44.44 per cent against 'others' source.

Table 4.8 presents the social group wise distribution of principal amount of borrowings, repayment, outstanding debt and overdues by source. It is very interesting to note that all the three social groups – SC, ST and 'non-SC and non-ST' other households – had reported 29 per cent of their outstanding debt as overdues. Among the three groups, SC households reported low amount of repayment and much higher amount of outstanding debt as percentage of the principal amount of borrowings. Repayment as percentage of borrowings constituted merely 10.54 per cent, while outstanding debt accounted for above 118 per cent of the original amount of borrowings. Low repayment ratio and mounting overdues in the case of institutional loans were responsible for relatively higher amount of outstanding debt among these people.

The overall repayment ratio (below 26 %) was found relatively better among the non-SC and non-ST other households, although outstanding debt as percentage of initial borrowings still constituted above 104 per cent. These households had registered moderate to substantial amount of repayment (as percentage of the initial amount of borrowings): nearly 32 per cent against institutional loans, less than 25 per cent against loans from friends and relatives, 23.81 per cent against school welfare fund/village societies, nearly 20 per cent against SHG loans, and about 13 per cent against moneylenders (where a large chunk of loans contracted against mortgage of land). However, overdues as percentage of the outstanding debt was found as high as 41 per cent in the case of institutional agencies and 16 per cent in the case of group loans, followed by less than 8 per cent recorded in the 'others' category. Poor repayment led accumulation of principal and interest amounts in the case of institutional loans and also, considerable amount of overdues

Table 4.8

Social group wise percentage distribution of principal amount of borrowings, repayment, outstanding debt and overdues by source.

Attributes	*Bank+*	*Money lenders*	*Shop Keepers/ Traders*	*Friends & relatives*	*SHGs*	*Others*	*All*
SC:							
Borrowings	60.74	32.89	0.87	5.50	-	-	100.0
Repayment	11.82	10.20	-	-	-	-	10.54
Outstanding	132.15	96.33	100.0	100.0	-	-	118.32
Overdues	43.06	-	-	-	-	-	29.21
ST:							
Borrowings	67.54	27.18	-	0.43	2.32	2.53	100.0
Repayment	45.30	5.04	-	4.88	90.91	10.0	34.35
Outstanding	78.35	100.93	-	95.12	100.91	100.0	85.63
Overdues	42.05	2.84	-	-	0.90	75.0	29.14

(Contd.)

(Contd. Table 4.8)

Attributes	*Bank+*	***Money lenders***	*Shop Keepers/ Traders*	*Friends & relatives*	*SHGs*	*Others*	*All*
General:							
Borrowings	65.82	22.18	3.58	1.40	2.69	4.33	100.0
Repayment	31.82	12.79	1.37	24.56	19.93	23.81	25.74
Outstanding	107.15	99.76	100.0	75.44	106.03	97.39	104.35
Overdues	41.32	1.69	-	-	15.86	7.57	29.02
All hhs.:							
Borrowings	65.84	23.67	2.79	1.46	2.47	3.77	100.0
Repayment	33.26	11.00	1.35	18.32	31.81	22.16	26.43
Outstanding	103.17	99.73	100.0	81.68	105.18	97.70	101.80
Overdues	41.53	1.80	-	-	13.46	15.83	29.05

* Borrowings in different columns indicate percentage of the total amount of borrowings.

* Repayment as percentage of the principal amount of borrowings in the respective column.

* Outstanding debt as percentage of the principal amount of borrowings in the respective column.

* Overdues as percentage of the outstanding debt.

reported in the case of SHGs and 'others' categories were responsible for much higher amount of outstanding debt as compared to the initial amount of borrowings.

In sharp contrast, only among the ST households, outstanding debt as percentage of principal amount of borrowings was registered at 85.63, the repayment rate being 34.35 per cent. Nevertheless, much similar to the SC and other household groups, these households also reported above two-fifths of the institutional loans as overdues. The Relatively much higher repayment ratio reported in institutional loan categories (particularly against 'other' category of loans from banks) has definitely helped in keeping down the size of outstanding debt lower than that of the initial amount of borrowings.

The source moneylender was found more familiar among the SC households, followed by ST and other households. The SC households borrowed one-third of the total loans from moneylenders. The loanee households were mostly from villages under Karimganj district and fewer numbers from Nagaon. These people (other than Nagaon district) were relatively land constrained and were engaged in non-agricultural activities.

The ST households also borrowed a considerable amount of loans from moneylenders (27.18). A considerable percentage of the ST households were from remote villages. The households placed in villages near urban centres had much better access to institutional loans. The people of remote villages were relatively better placed in terms of per capita availability of agricultural land, while in the remote villages, the access of the institutional agencies was limited. The socio-economic peculiarities of these households were responsible for higher percentage share of moneylenders despite the fact that institutional agencies registered highest percentage share among these people.

Among the general households too, moneylenders contributed above 22 per cent of the total loans. The growth of

SHGs in some villages has helped in reducing the incidence of loans from moneylenders among the general households. This was also partially true in the case of ST households.

It is very interesting to note that overdues against the source moneylenders was found negligible (below 2 %). There is no doubt that moneylenders particularly agricultural moneylenders prefer lending against mortgage of land. They had also extended a considerable amount of credit which carried moderate to high interest rate. These loans were mostly for unproductive purposes — health care, consumption (including emergency loans during the floods/storms) and marriages, etc. In spite of the fact that moneylenders sometimes provided loans in adverse conditions, on most occasions, they were successful to recover accrued interest regularly.

Shop keepers and traders reported no overdues. It is more because of the recurring nature of these loans. In other words, the incidence of incurring debt and subsequently its repayment was seen as a continuous relay process. Retailers undertakes trade credit during busy season (for instance, during festival), repay the entire amount or a lion's part of it after a few months when the peak business season is over, and then, undertakes fresh credit purchase. Similarly, few households reported small amount of balance with the shop keepers for grocery items. Sometimes for limited income flow and again sometimes for habitual reasons, some amount remains unpaid. The repayment process was, once again a relay one i.e., clearing old dues but making fresh purchase on credit, or at least a part of the fresh purchase was made on credit.

It is interesting to note that SHG account (without access to the revolving fund/bank loans) had recorded 13.46 per cent of the advances as overdues. This may be high in comparison to the performance shown by a few southern states or the neighbouring country, Bangladesh. Nevertheless, the repayment records against SHG loans may be considered quite satisfactory in the state because of the following reasons:

- Till date, the overall repayment scenario in the state has been quite dismal.
- Even today, the repayment against SGSY was found quite unsatisfactory.
- A few SHG loans were extended to the non-members. The overdue amount against the SHG loans to the non-members was relatively higher.
- A good percentage of SHG loans were made at moderate to very high rate of interest. In spite of high interest burden that the recovery ratio was above 86 per cent at the time of interrogation, was really creditable. However, as mentioned elsewhere, high interest culture adopted by most of the SHGs in the region is not a good sign and definitely not going to serve the cause of the society appropriately, more particularly for the weaker section of the society.

Table 4.9 presents occupation wise and broad land status wise percentage distribution of outstanding debt and overdue position by source. It appears from the table that landless agricultural households (mostly wage earners, a few of them owned a pair of bullocks and incurred debt to institutional sources for livestock) had registered the entire amount of institutional loans as overdues. The poor flow of income from loan assets, absence of any planning either at the borrowers level or bankers/block level how to make loan-assets economically effective and viable, window dressing made by some banks on and off to show some amount of recovery, presence of speed money, flood havoc, complete absence of any professional/ inspirational organization to assist the loanees in different

Table 4.9
Occupation and broad land status wise percentage distribution of outstanding debt and overdues by source.

Attributes	*Bank+*	*Money lenders*	*Shop Keeper / Trader*	*Friends & relatives*	*SHGs*	*Others*	*All*
A.H.:landless							
Outstanding	47.24	19.69	6.82	11.81	14.44	-	100.0
Overdues	100.0	13.33	-	-	43.64	-	56.17
MF							
Outstanding	54.77	23.78	0.20	1.21	6.47	13.57	100.0
Overdues	73.28	1.78	-	-	26.09	7.26	43.23
SF							
Outstanding	42.79	41.63	0.79	4.55	4.47	5.77	100.0
Overdues	39.30	1.15	-	-	4.49	21.74	18.75
SMF							
Outstanding	59.99	39.60	0.21	0.21	-	-	100.0
Overdues	23.66	0.31	-	-	-	-	14.32
All A H:							
Outstanding	52.77	35.23	0.58	2.19	3.63	5.59	100.0
Overdues	44.02	1.11	-	-	19.87	11.94	25.01
TH: landless							
Outstanding	58.42	12.62	25.02	0.08	2.97	0.90	100.0

(Contd.)

(Contd. Table 4.9)

Attributes	*Bank+*	*Money lenders*	*Shop Keeper / Trader*	*Friends & relatives*	*SHGs*	*Others*	*All*
Overdues	64.81	-	-	-	1.37	90.91	38.71
Others:							
Outstanding	83.82	11.98	0.43	0.26	1.36	2.15	100.0
Overdues	35.71	4.62	-	-	-	20.41	30.92
All T H:							
Outstanding	79.31	12.09	4.79	0.23	1.65	1.93	100.0
Overdues	39.51	3.76	-	-	0.44	26.22	32.30
IH:landless							
Outstanding	-	-	100.0	-	-	-	100.0
Overdues	-	-	-	-	-	-	-
Others:					-		
Outstanding	74.59	23.97	0.41	1.03		-	100.0
Overdues	56.79	-	-	-	-	-	42.36
All I H							
Outstanding	74.28	23.87	0.82	1.03	-	-	100.0
Overdues	56.79	-	-	-	-	-	42.18
All hhs.							
Outstanding	66.73	23.19	2.74	1.17	2.55	3.62	100.0
Overdues	41.53	1.80	-	-	13.46	15.83	29.05

A H: Agricultural Household; T H: Tertiary Household and I H: Industrial Household.

* Overdues as percentage of the outstanding debt in the respective head.

adverse conditions, etc were responsible for frequent defaults among the weaker section.

It was observed that commercial banks had extended two small loans each (Rs. 12000 to Rs. 25000) to two economically sound village shop keepers under the anti-poverty schemes in Kamrup district. The second loan was released almost immediately after the full repayment of the first loan. These APL borrowers' sole interest was in Rs. 6000 subsidy component of the loan. Of the total subsidy amount of Rs. 6000 per loan, Rs. 3000 was distributed between bank and block officials for getting a share in 'government distribution'.

The overdues as percentage of the outstanding debt decreases substantially as one moves upward among the landed household categories. At the overall level, among the landless agricultural households, overdues was 56.17 per cent of the outstanding debt, which was 43.23 per cent among marginal farmers, 18.75 per cent among small farmers and 14.32 per cent in the case of bigger farmers. The level of overdues at the aggregate was dictated by the volume of institutional loans and period/time of loans and also, by the nature of loan taken from moneylenders. Other sources were found to be of much less significant.

Among the marginal farmers, nearly three-fourths of the total institutional loan was found in default, followed by small farmer with 39.30 per cent and bigger farmers with 23.66 per cent. Almost no amount was lying overdue against the loans from moneylenders, except the agricultural landless households (13.33 %). Among landless households and marginal farmers, high amount of overdues was registered even against SHG loans (43.64 % and 26.09 % respectively). These two household groups along with the industrial household group registered the highest incidence of poverty in the sample.

Among the tertiary households, at the aggregate level, overdues as percentage of outstanding debt was found higher at 30.92 as against 25 per cent recorded by the agricultural households; but above10 percentage points lower than that of the industrial households (42 % of the outstanding debt was in default). However, overdues (as percentage of the outstanding debt) was found lower against institutional loans in the case of tertiary households (39.51 %), as compared to industrial households (56.79%) and agricultural households (44.02 %). Landless category, even among the tertiary households, registered much higher amount of overdues (64.81 %) in the above category of loans.

Tertiary households borrowed much higher amount from institutional credit agencies (Rs. 10,98,500) which constituted about four-fifths of their outstanding debt. On the other hand, agricultural households borrowed the sum of Rs. 6,72,600 from institutional agencies which constituted nearly 53 per cent of their outstanding debt. Much contrary to the general belief, incidence of institutional loans was found higher among the tertiary households due to larger presence of personal loans (comprising housing loans and loans for consumer durables) from banks. A large number of salaried people including government services were reported among the tertiary households. It can be mentioned that as much as 36.43 per cent of the institutional loans of the tertiary households were incurred by the government employees only, which was found to be little less than the total institutional loans taken by the agricultural households together.

Better off loanee households were not necessarily a good repayer. Rather the very nature of loans was hugely responsible for registering lower or higher level of overdues. All the personal loans were contracted by the better off households. Repayment of most of these loans was made on small monthly instalment basis, which was often deducted straightway from the salary account of the borrowers.

For instance, among the broad 8 income groups, the first five groups registered 'nil' personal loans from the banks. The higher 3 income brackets recorded quite a few personal loans amounting excess of Rs. 6, 64,000 (one household, one loan basis). Even among the better off households, the distribution of personal loans was much skewed. Of the total personal loans, the percentage shares of the highest three income groups were respectively 9.94, 28.46 and 61.61 (top income group). The incidence of default in such cases was negligible. This is one of the main reasons for recording low overdues by the better off households. Poorer households recorded higher overdues against institutional loans which have had its impact on their overall overdue position. The small amount of per unit anti-poverty loans which failed to generate adequate flow of income, misuse of these loans, distribution of such loans as doles and presence of speed money at the time of release of loans, etc have affected the overall performance of these loans.

At least two rich households (above Rs. 75,000 annual income groups in the sample) did manage tractor/power tiller loans from banks under the group loan scheme. The other group members were mostly inactive and belonged to the relatively land-poor farming community. Right from the submission of application form, the rich borrower dominated the whole proceedings and took hold of the loan-asset immediately after acquiring it through bank loans and high amount of government subsidy valued as high as 40 – 50 per cent of the price of the loan-asset. Needless to mention that the burden of group loan was shouldered by the opportunistic and financially very sound member of the group and to avoid any controversy a lion's share of the loan was repaid by the concerned households who have tactfully made the group assets as their personal property and swallowed the entire amount of subsidy meant for the group. In one case, one such member dared to dispose of the tractor received under the group scheme (Nagaon district) even when a part of the loan amount was still due to bank.

The misuse of subsidy based scheme is rampant. Even when government is trying to restructure its subsidy scheme – i.e., instead of providing subsidy to individual beneficiaries, groups have been receiving more importance in recent times – the wrong use of such money is still high. This is where the role of catalytic agencies are extremely important in checking the development funds (meant for the revival of the rural economy) presently swallowed by a section of the unscrupulous people.

Table 4.10 presents income group wise percentage distribution of outstanding debt and overdues by source. The table is prepared to see the access of different income groups to the different credit agencies and also, each group's repayment habit judged by the respective groups' overdue position. In this table, each loanee household was recorded according to their main borrowing source.

It is evident from the table that the extremely poor households incurred less than 29 per cent of their debt from institutional sources. A few poor households were given livestock and raw materials for cottage industries under the different anti-poverty (loan-assets for self-employment) schemes of the government. The flow of income from these loan-assets was mostly inadequate which also affected the repayment of these loans.

The lower income brackets had registered high incidence of borrowings from moneylenders. This is partly because small institutional loans to weaker sections have dried up considerably (other than KCCs in some pockets) in recent times. In contrast, three higher income groups, had borrowed much larger amounts than their weaker counterparts. Three successive higher income groups respectively incurred nearly 59 per cent, 78 per cent and 77 per cent of their outstanding debt from institutional sources, while the share of moneylenders was found lower at 33 per cent, 18 per cent and 8 per cent respectively.

Table 4.10

Income group wise percentage distribution of outstanding debt and overdues by source.

Income group ('000)	*OD & O**	*Bank+*	*Money lenders*	*Shop Keeper/ Trader*	*Friends & relatives*	*SHGs*	*Others*	*All*
≤ 11	OD	28.64	57.96	0.34	12.60	-	0.46	100.0
	O	100.0	5.14	-	-	-	-	31.62
11 – 22	OD	39.60	49.87	3.64	3.31	2.29	1.29	100.0
	O	94.81	11.76	-	-	61.54	22.73	45.12
22 – 26	OD	32.86	59.29	2.71	0.43	4.71	-	100.0
	O	100.0	3.61	-	-	-	-	35.0
26 – 30	OD	62.25	32.90	1.97	2.46	0.42	-	100.0
	O	85.55	-	-	-	8.33	-	53.29
30 – 36	OD	40.20	50.53	-	-	9.27	-	100.0
	O	52.04	2.60	-	-	-	-	22.23
36 – 75	OD	58.71	33.06	0.85	1.70	2.28	3.40	100.0
	O	44.77	0.19	-	-	-	-	26.34
75 - 200	OD	77.60	18.41	-	-	1.28	2.70	100.0
	O	47.41	4.10	-	-	6.86	-	37.63
> 200	OD	77.41	7.92	7.31	-	0.17	7.18	100.0
	O	8.42	24.50	-	-	-	11.11	9.25

OD: Outstanding debt; O: Overdues.

* Overdues as percentage of the outstanding debt in the respective head.

* One household, one loan. Smaller loans are clubbed with the bigger ones where more than one loans incurred by the loanees.

Shop keepers (traders) and friends and relatives, as the two important informal sources of credit, lost much of their popularity in recent times. These sources only provided few small loans to the weaker sections. One trade credit of substantial amount was recorded in the highest income bracket. Other than this, contrary to general belief, loans from friends and relatives and traders were found almost absent among the higher income groups. To some extent, by substituting the source 'friends and relatives', SHGs are coming up in some pockets to distribute emergency loans to the people in need, while the insurgency led uncertainties may be responsible, at least partially, for lower availability of trade credits (from the wholesalers to the retailers) in certain areas.

It is very interesting to note that moneylenders and banks (institutional agencies) contributed moderate to much higher amount to the total outstanding debt of all income groups. This reflects one good thing that institutional agencies had been successful to reach more or less to all the economic classes, although they are yet to make credit frequently available, in time and in adequate amount. This has facilitated none other than moneylenders who had rather dominated the credit business in interior villages.

The loan overdue column shows very high percentage share of defaulted institutional loans particularly among the lower income brackets. The magnitude of the problem was so serious that it had also been reflected at the overall level in each income bracket. In three of the four higher income brackets, the overdue as percentage of outstanding debt was found considerably low. This is mainly because of the lower overdue amount registered against institutional loan-outstanding. These households recorded high proportion of personal loans from banks for house buildings and other consumer durables. The problem of overdues which is getting worse with every passing year needs a fresh look without which institutional credit agencies' role in rural development in the North Eastern region will be further diminished.

Table 4.11 presents asset-group wise percentage distribution of outstanding debt and overdues by source. The table shows, as percentage of total outstanding debt, almost equal access of institutional loans to all asset value groups with a sharp rise, then fall and once again rise in the shares in the highest three asset value groups. The share of moneylenders was also found almost equally high in all the groups except the lowest asset group (less than 13 %) and the third top asset value group (less than 10 %) where debt to moneylenders was considerably low. Friends and relatives as a source of credit was found somewhat present only in the lower 4 asset value groups.

Similarly, shopkeepers and traders were also relatively more familiar in the lower asset groups. The source SHGs was present in all the asset groups, although their share in total debt outstanding was only low to moderate amount.

The incidence of loan overdue was found relatively higher among the lower asset groups as compared to the higher asset value groups. However, the trend was not very smooth. The presence of fixed income earners (salaried people) in different asset groups and the higher incidence of loans among these people definitely have had its influence felt on the overall distribution of loans across the different asset groups.

The asset group wise distribution of loans by two broad sources reveals certain interesting features. The asset groups were condensed to four for better comparison between different groups.

It is evident from Table 4.12 that much higher incidence of institutional loans were recorded in all the asset value

Table 4.11

Asset group wise percentage distribution of outstanding debt and overdues by source.

Asset Groups (in Rs.)	*OD & O**	*Bank+*	*Money lenders*	*Shop Keeper/ Trader*	*Friends & relatives*	*SHGs*	*Others*	*All*
Up to 50000	OD	59.22	12.69	6.77	10.66	10.32	0.34	100.0
	O	92.86	13.33	-	-	39.34	-	60.74
50001 – 1 lakh	OD	63.17	26.31	3.45	3.74	2.18	1.14	100.0
	O	92.11	3.55	-	-	2.38	22.73	59.43
> 1 lakh – 2 lakh	OD	60.68	33.81	0.72	1.90	2.88	-	100.0
	O	22.98	3.68	-	-	-	-	15.19
> 2 lakh – 3 lakh	OD	60.66	35.02	0.12	2.1	2.1	-	100.0
	O	39.79	5.65	-	-	-	-	26.12
> 3 lakh – 4 lakh	OD	57.11	20.45	0.87	-	1.17	20.40	100.0
	O	27.81	-	-	-	-	8.57	17.63
> 4 lakh – 7 lakh	OD	85.76	9.84	0.17	-	1.23	3.0	100.0
	O	65.84	13.37	-	-	9.46	-	57.90
> 7 lakh – 11 lakh	OD	43.01	41.37	15.07	-	0.55	-	100.0
	O	29.62	-	-	-	-	-	12.74
Above 11 lakh	OD	77.60	21.42	-	-	0.26	0.71	100.0
	O	10.46	13.83	-	-	-	-	11.08

OD: Outstanding debt; O: Overdues.

* Overdues as percentage of the outstanding debt in the respective head.

* One household, one loan. Smaller loans are clubbed with the bigger ones where more than one loans had been raised by the loanees.

brackets in the nearby village group as compared to their remote counterparts. Higher asset value groups also recorded relatively higher incidence of loan and incurred much larger volume of debt. In the lower two asset brackets (in the nearby village group), non-institutional debt was found higher, although in the higher two asset groups, the opposite picture was found true (i.e., remote village group had registered higher amount of debt to non-institutional sources compared to their 'nearby' counterparts). Among the 4 groups, the bottom asset group had registered highest number of loans from non-institutional sources. Most of these loans were of very small amount.

The bottom asset value group constituted exactly one-fourth of the total loan incidence, while their share in total borrowings was less than 8 per cent. In the remote villages, both institutional and non-institutional sources of credit had registered 3 per cent each of the respective total borrowings in the lowest asset value group. The corresponding percentages in VNT group were 3.51 and 7.2 respectively. The situation has changed or rather reversed in the higher asset-value brackets.

In 1.1 – 3 lakh asset group, both in the IV and VNT groups, non-institutional sources recorded much higher amount of debt (8.23 % and 21.55 %), although the absolute size of non-institutional loan in VNT group was found far lower than that of the institutional borrowings.

In the top two asset brackets, remote villages recorded much higher amount of loans from non-institutional sources (12.87 % and 27.64 % of the total non-institutional borrowings) as compared to the institutional sources (8.22 % and 4.02 % of the total institutional borrowings). In sharp contrast, nearby village group accounted for much lower shares of non-institutional borrowings (12.64 % and 6.86 %) as compared to the institutional borrowings (28.36 % and 31.10 %) both in percentage terms as well as in the absolute size of borrowings.

Table 4.12

Asset group and village status wise percentage distribution of principal amount of borrowings, repayment, outstanding debt and overdues by two broad sources.

Attribute	*Up to 1 lakh*		*1 – 3 lakh*		*3 – 7 lakh*		*Above 7 lakh*	
	IV	*VNT*	*IV*	*VNT*	*IV*	*VNT*	*IV*	*VNT*
B IL	3.0	3.51	3.45	18.34	8.22	28.36	4.02	31.10
	(5)	(12)	(8)	(18)	(9)	(29)	(7)	(13)
BNIL	3.01	7.2	8.23	21.55	12.87	12.64	27.64	6.86
	(11)	(28)	(18)	(18)	(18)	(12)	(15)	(3)
All	3.0	4.75	5.06	19.42	9.78	23.08	11.95	22.96
	(16)	(40)	(26)	(36)	(27)	(41)	(22)	(16)
R IL	3.86	0.55	3.69	18.31	9.15	21.49	2.52	40.43
R NIL	3.32	8.3	3.65	29.13	32.37	21.16	0.17	1.91
All	3.77	1.88	3.68	20.16	13.13	21.44	2.12	33.82
OD IL	2.72	5.82	3.28	19.13	9.67	29.17	4.08	26.12

(Contd.)

(Contd. Table 4.12)

Attribute	*Up to 1 lakh*		*1 – 3 lakh*		*3 – 7 lakh*		*Above 7 lakh*	
	IV	*VNT*	*IV*	*VNT*	*IV*	*VNT*	*IV*	*VNT*
OD NIL	3.36	7.47	7.90	19.93	13.01	13.62	27.95	6.75
All	2.93	6.36	4.79	19.39	10.76	24.08	11.89	19.78
O IL	6.14	12.74	2.16	14.45	18.94	32.46	6.33	6.79
ONIL	8.53	18.96	-	-	9.0	60.66	2.84	-
All	6.20	12.90	2.10	14.06	18.67	33.21	6.24	6.61

IL: Institutional Loan. NIL : Non-institutional Loan.

BIL : Borrowings as % of total institutional loans (principal amount).

BNIL: Borrowings as % of total non-institutional borrowings (principal amount) .

R IL: Repayment as % of total institutional repayments.

R N IL: Repayment as % of total non-institutional repayments

OD IL: Outstanding debt as % of total debt to institutional sources

OD NIL: Outstanding debt as % of total debt to non- institutional sources

O IL: Overdues as % of total institutional overdues.

ONIL: Overdues as % of total non- institutional overdues

*Figures in brackets show incidence of debt.

The asset value group, 1.1 – 3 lakh, constituted less than 28 per cent of all loan-incidence, while these households borrowed nearly one-fourth of the total borrowings made by all households. The corresponding percentages stood at 30.35 and 32.86 in the immediate higher asset value group and 16.96 per cent and 34.91 per cent in the top asset value group.

The repayment column shows some form of uniformity in the repayment culture only in the VNT group. In thc nearby villages, highest amount of repayment (33.82 %) was recorded by the top asset value group (the group which had recorded very high amount of borrowings) followed by the immediate lower asset-value group with 21.44 per cent (the group which had recorded highest amount of borrowings). The bottom asset group recorded nominal amount of repayment, while the 1.1 – 3 lakh group recorded (20.16 % of the total repayment) considerable amount of repayment. No such uniformity can be seen in IV group.

In the remote villages, non-institutional loan constituted higher percentage share in total debt where repayment was apparently far less. The very nature of non-institutional loan (a high percentage of loan was taken from moneylenders against mortgage of land) was responsible for low and uneven repayment performance recorded across the asset groups.

Asset group wise estimation of overdues, as percentage of total institutional loan overdues, shows some very interesting features. Nearly 19 per cent of the total institutional overdues fall in the bottom asset group, although these households owe less than 9 per cent of the total outstanding debt to institutional credit agencies. The subsequent higher asset group, 1.1 – 3 lakh, registered less than 17 per cent of the total institutional overdues, although they constituted above 22 per cent of the total outstanding debt to institutional sources. The corresponding shares were more than 51 per cent and less than

39 per cent in the 3.1 – 7 lakh group and above 13 per cent and 30.20 per cent in the top asset group.

It appears from the table that the population groups in 1.1 – 3 lakh and 3.1 – 7 lakh asset groups recorded very high amount of overdues against institutional borrowings. The households in the assets value of 3.1 – 7 lakh also registered considerable amount of overdues at the aggregate level. The above facts sufficiently support the statement made earlier that the rich households need not necessarily be a good borrower/ repayer. The nature of loan, the type of security offered and the mode of repayment, etc were also very important determinants of the overall repayment performances recorded by the households in the region.

Table 4.13 shows the percentage distribution of both institutional and non-institutional loans by the year of loan taken. It is expected that it will help in understanding the broad nature of the loans taken over the years which remained partly or fully unpaid. It may also give some lights to the relative position of the institutional and non-institutional sources over the years. The problem of overdues and the severity of the problem of non-repayment /debt-trap, if any, may also be gauged from the table.

Since the year 1990-91, when a few small borrowers were relieved from repayment burden of institutional loans up to Rs. 10000 and which subsequently created great confusion among the rural borrowers and also, among a section of the bank officials, the recovery ratio in the state of Assam has further worsened. With the objective of making the small loans working both for the poor borrowers and also, for the credit agencies, expert committees were formed from time to time and different schemes were implemented. The most important schemes (strategies) were micro credit through MFIs/SHGs, extension of KCCs to farming population as well as artisans, etc. The

Table 4.13

The percentage distribution of both the institutional and non-institutional loans (principal and outstanding debt) by the year of loan taken.

Attribute			*Year of loan*					
			2001-03	*1998-2000*	*1995-97*	*1992-94*	*Others (old and unspecified)*	*All*
Institutional loan		P	46.08	22.81	20.92	9.11	1.08	100.0
		OD	49.20	14.80	25.26	8.86	1.88	100.0
Non-institutional loan	With interest	P	60.53	33.17	1.66	3.65	1.0	100.0
		OD	70.14	24.23	1.64	3.60	0.39	100.0
	Mortgage of land	P	20.22	25.01	22.80	20.84	11.14	100.0
		OD	20.41	24.82	23.01	20.51	11.25	100.0
	Others*	P	77.91	5.27	-	-	16.82	100.0
		OD	76.55	5.59	-	-	17.86	100.0

P: Principal amount of borrowings. OD: Outstanding debt.

* Includes interest free loans, current liabilities, etc.

introduction of these schemes have significantly contributed to employment generation and rural production in certain pockets of the country. In the sample state, these schemes were found working at the time of survey. The impact of these schemes can be partially felt against the growing popularity of personal loans as can be seen in the Table 4.13.

It appears from the table that the frequency and size of institutional loans was higher during 1995 – 97 (20.92 %) over the immediate past three years, i.e., 1992 – 94 (9.11 %). Since the recovery ratio in the state of Assam was very low, particularly against directed loans (while the incidence of personal loans from banks in rural Assam, was a recent phenomenon), the above comparison bears significance. During 1998 – 2000 (22.81 %), there seems to be no real increase in banking activities. However, during the recent times (2001 – 03, less than 3 years time), a substantial increase in the institutional loans (also in non-institutional loans) was recorded which constituted 46 per cent of the total borrowings. (The details of the institutional loans taken since 1980 – 81 also included in Table 4.14, which compares well with the Table 4.13).

Institutional loans constituted two-thirds of the total loan outstanding. However, active institutional loans constituted around three-fifths of the total outstanding debt to institutional sources. It appears from the table that 49 per cent of the total institutional loans outstanding were taken in recent times. The loan taken during 2001 – 03 comprises KCC loans, personal loans and a few loans from banks to SHGs (including loan under SGSY scheme). The loans taken during 1998 – 2000 also registered a couple of personal loans, IRDP/SGSY loans and one PMRY loan. This period recorded considerable amount of repayment partly because of the sizeable share of the personal loans where monthly instalment was paid directly from the salary account. However, a good percentage of these loans particularly under the IRDP/SGSY scheme was found in default. The old and unspecified category (where the year of loan could not be recalled), and also loans incurred during 1992 – 94 and 1995 – 97 had registered no repayment at all or at least where no repayment was made during the last five years constituted a high percentage share. These bad advances (together constituted 36 %) along with that part of the loans distributed during 1998 – 2000, against which no repayment was recorded, accounted for two-fifths of the total outstanding debt. In other words, around 40 per cent of the total institutional loans in Assam were simply accumulated as bad loans. The presence of such a large share of 'dead loans' have a considerable negative effect on the rural economy. It also gives wrong signal about the composition of the rural credit which needs immediate attention of the policy makers.

When bad debts are not written off, reported loan recovery performance may be highly distorted. In Assam (as per field data), 'dead loans' constituted as high as two-fifths of the total institutional loans, the presence of which has considerably been responsible for state's poor recovery scenario. The dismal recovery ratio, in turn, affects the willingness (and also, the confidence) of the bankers to extend fresh loans, while borrowers' confidence level and seriousness about the end use of loans receive a setback because of the 'missing' repayment culture. This dismal situation can be explained with an example.

In the case of informal loans which carried moderate to high interest rates (taken from sources like moneylenders, SHGs and village societies/school welfare fund), the incidence of default was found quite low. As much as 70 per cent of such loans were taken in recent times. Another one-quarter debt was incurred during 1998 – 2000. Such loans which were taken before 1998 and remained unpaid partly or the full amount at the time of interrogation constituted only nominal amount. Since in these cases borrowers cannot easily escape from repayment, and the accrued interests on the principal amount has to be cleared

'Assume that rural financial institutions lend 100 crores every year of which 10 crores are never collected and never written off. The denominator (demand) consequently increases by 10 crores annually, resulting in a misleading deterioration of the recovery ratio while actual performance has remained constant – at a 90 per cent annual collection ratio.

Year — **1st**: $\frac{\text{Collection}}{\text{Demand}} \times 100\% \quad \frac{90}{100} \times 100 = 90\%$

2nd: $\frac{90}{10 + 100} \times 100 = 82\%$

3rd: $\frac{90}{(10 \times 2) + 100} \times 100 = 75\% \ldots$

10th: $\ldots \frac{90}{(10 \times 9) + 100} \times 100 = 47\%$

Source : Jacob Yaron, et. al. (1997),

annually, repayment was found, as expected, much better. Very cleverly, moneylenders insisted on timely recovery of that portion of loans which carries interest charges, while in the cases of loans extended against security of land, they often discouraged borrowers to make part payment and thereby try to delaying the process of repayment. Moneylenders bad intensions accompanied by borrowers' weak economic standing were largely responsible for poor repayment of such loans taken against mortgage of land. It appears from the table that these loans were taken in considerable amounts during the last decade. Contrary to the 'with interest' loans from moneylenders, loans taken against mortgage of land recorded extremely poor repayment. Of the total loans of Rs. 4,80,200 taken against mortgage of land, '2001 and after' category constituted around one-fifth, 1998 – 2000 period accounted for one quarter, 1995 – 97 recorded 2 percentage points less than one quarter, while 1992 – 94 period registered little above one-fifth of the total and the unspecified category (i.e., the period that 'can not be recalled') constituted the lowest amount of 11.25 per cent.

There was a sharp erosion of the interest free component of loans in the state. These loans were mostly taken for the short period except a small segment of loans taken from friends and relatives for emergency needs. This category of loans also included trade credit which often bears hidden interest. It appears from the table that nearly 77 per cent of such loans were taken in 2001 and after, while others and unspecified category which also included electricity bill dues constituted just less than 18 per cent.

It is observed that interest free loans constituted a low percentage share in total debt outstanding. The source friends and relatives, in terms of volume of loans, reduced to a much less important source in recent times. As mentioned earlier, the growth of SHGs might be responsible at least partially for steady erosion of this source. Another important factor might be the rise of moneylenders who had extended quite a few loans against mortgage of property.

On one hand, interest free sources and bank's concessional loans have dried up to a considerable extent. On the other hand, moneylenders and SHGs contributed a considerable amount of high interest loans. Even bank was reported to have extended credit at 12.5 per cent to 18 per cent rate of interest (save a few KCC loans). In addition, high proportion of loan was borrowed against mortgage of land which contains high hidden interest. It appears that during the liberalization of the economy, rural borrowings have become dearer and scarce for the weaker section.

A large proportion of the fresh institutional loans fall in the 'personal loan' category which were taken by the higher income / higher asset value groups. The KCCs were concentrated mostly in villages located near urban centres while the incidence of SHG-bank linkages is yet to get a momentum. The remote villages were largely bypassed by the institutional credit. The recent development in the nationalized banking sector to emphasize on extending bigger loans for economic viability (often at the cost of social goal) has definitely constrained the small and cheap loans meant for the rural poor in Assam, remote villages in particular.

It can also be noted that the amount of subsidy constituted nearly one-third of the total directed loans incurred by the sample households. It was above 30 per cent in the case of IRDP loans, less than 10 per cent in PMRY scheme, above 40 per cent in the case of group loans for power tiller, tractor, pumpsets, etc. The group subsidy in the case of SGSY scheme sometimes went up to 50 per cent of the project costs. There is no gainsaying that subsidy amount reduces the burden of repayment, but, at the same time, this also attracts unscrupulous borrowers who takes a good share in the subsidy amount. These people often pay (/ compelled to pay) some amount to the concerned loan sanctioning officials and thereby vitiate the overall loan delivery and recovery system.

The statement of institutional loans taken between 1980 and mid 2003 (i.e., till the date of survey) which were fully repaid or waived or partly repaid and the rest amount waived is given in Table 4.14. The exercise was very difficult. Chances of memory lapses were high. In 3 cases, the concerned beneficiaries were found dead, where the rest of the family members expressed their inability to say anything about the current status of the loan. In a couple of cases, the beneficiaries received one hybrid cow in first instalment. However, soon after the possession of the insured loan assets, devastating flood was responsible for the death of the milking cow. In these cases, the second and final instalment was not released. The beneficiaries could not say anything about their loan obligation, if any. All these five cases were not included in the table.

It is also very important to note that waived amount shown in the two subsequent periods viz 1980–1985 and 1986–1991 had to be adjusted a little bit since the beneficiaries' recollected figures fall short of the principal amount of loan. As the beneficiaries reported the waived amount in lower side (waived amount plus repayment fall short of the principal amount), the difference between principal amount of borrowings and repayment was taken as the size of loan written off. There is no doubt that a few households might have reported higher amount of repayment (then the actual repayment) and lower amount of loan waived or just did not report about their previous loan which was waived.

In spite of all these shortcomings, the table was included in the report as it incorporated few important information about the institutional loans over the years. It also gives an idea about the incidence of institutional loans in the sample region over the years (along with the previous table).

It appears from the Table 4.14 that altogether 24 households got the benefit of loan waiver scheme in early 1990s. Another 3 households got the benefit under the repayment of old debt in easy instalments scheme (i.e., partially waived). In all these cases, getting fresh loans by the beneficiaries from institutional sources will be very difficult in future.

It is evident from the table that the benefits under the loan waiver scheme was not of very high magnitude – both in terms of the number of poor beneficiaries who were relieved from 'debt-trap' and the amount of benefit received. However, as many research studies revealed, this non-judiciously implemented scheme has vitiated the repayment culture in subsequent period so much so that almost all banks have lost their complete interests in directed loan schemes, more particularly in the eastern and north-eastern region.

The sample households recorded very poor repayment performance during the 1990s. Between 1992 and 2000, 14 IRDP loans were fully repaid. The one feature which was not visible in the table was the window dressing made by a couple of banks. Of the 14 cases of repayment of IRDP loans, more than 6 were taken by the opportunistic households who were not poor. For instance, two economically better off small traders took IRDP loans twice each. On either occasion, they took loans just for getting a share in the 'government doles' in the form of subsidy. On each occasion, traders gave away 50 per cent of the total subsidy as speed money to loan sanctioning authorities. Another beneficiary household could manage two IRDP loans and did clear the second loan only after getting elected to the PRIs.

It seems that the genuine borrowers under the anti-poverty schemes may not be more than two-thirds of the total.

Since the end use of loans were not monitored by any agency and sometimes, the presence of speed money eats into the critical subsidy component of loans, the incidence of defaults increases to that extent.

The presence of speed money has been a cause of much displeasure amongst a section of the borrowers. Whether it is a direct loan from commercial banks or industrial loan from Assam Financial Corporation, or DIC loan, a few beneficiaries hesitantly admitted that without greasing the palm of the concerned loan sanctioning authorities, no loan can be sanctioned in Assam.

It would be relevant to note that of the total 94 incidence of loans reported by the sample households to institutional sources, 22 households were compelled to concede speed money, largely for PMRY and IRDP loans. Contrary to general belief, the incidence was higher among the villagers living close to banks/block office. It was thought that beneficiaries from remote villages will be the main victims of greed of the bankers and other concerned officials, for they have to walk or ride long distances to reach bank/block office to get the loan proposal sanctioned. The amount of bribes varied from Rs. 1000 (mostly IRDP) to Rs. 5000 (mostly PMRY/ DIC) to maximum of Rs. 10000 (others, including AFC).

Of the 22 households who had paid bribes mainly to bank officials for getting their loan amount released, as many as 8 households were from the rich or very rich group (the highest two income groups), 5 were from the APL group (Rs. 36001 – 75000) and the rest belonged to the BPL households. In addition, 3 potential borrowers reported to have paid Rs. 5000 each to DIC officials in Karimganj district to get DIC loans sanctioned in their favour. One can not deny the possibility of even higher incidence of such cases, since many people confessed only after giving them full confidence that their names as well as the corrupt officials' identity will never appear in the report. The unfair means adopted by a section of the bank officials and other concerned government departments in sanctioning a loan (other than KCC loans and SHG-bank linkages) will definitely dampen the recovery scenario as it hampers the image of credit institutions, seriousness of loan repayment in time and in extreme cases, as if, it transforms the loan as government doles which can be shared between borrowers, bank officials and other concerned government departments. This bad practice needs to be checked forthwith; otherwise this may also vitiate the healthy growth of the SHG and KCC movement in the region.

It can be mentioned that in Kamrup and Nagaon districts, in the case of PMRY loan category (where no speed money was involved) overdues as percentage of outstanding debt was found at 79.75 per cent as compared to 100 per cent where borrowers had to surrender at least Rs. 5000 to the bank officials. In the case of IRDP (now SGSY) loans, the corresponding percentages were 91.38 and 91.75.

In Tinsukia and Karimganj districts, no PMRY loan was reported in the sample villages. In the case of IRDP (SGSY) loans, overdues was found at 100 per cent where beneficiaries had to pay some amount for tea and sweets at the time of receiving loan amount, while the other group reported overdues at 94 per cent.

The incidence of diversion of funds from productive to unproductive use was found much higher among the loanee households who had to pay bribes to get the loan amount released. However, one good thing was that the misuse of loan was found of nominal amount in the cases of KCC loans and bank loans to SHGs. No incidence of speed money was reported in the cases of loans to KCC holders or SHG-bank linkages.

It appears from the above discussion that irrespective of the fact whether or not the borrowers paid bribes to the loan sanctioning authorities, the overdue position was almost equally dismal in all cases (other than KCC/SHG loans).

One positive feature was that as many as 20 IRDP (DRI) beneficiaries reported their loan assets as fully or partially intact and yielding nominal to substantial proportion of their income. Very surprisingly, 15 such households were reported in the 1980s category, while only 5 households, out of the total 14 households who had received loans during 1990s, were able to make productive use of the loan assets. The above information, although insufficient in many respects, justifies the utility of these schemes.

High incidence of institutional loans (KCC loans in particular) in Begenati and also, to some extent, in Eraligul (and Kamrup district in general), has helped the growth of high-input based commercial agriculture and also added some health — directly or indirectly – to the allied sector. Higher availability of institutional loans has increased the irrigation coverage and cropping intensity to a significant extent in Begenati village which has helped in bringing about rural prosperity in quick time. Loans against KCCs, SHG-bank linkages, etc proved that (easy) finance is an important input for rural development. Debts for productive cause, adds health to the borrower's socio-economic standard. Quite a few households reported at least some amount of income from the loan-assets acquired as far as 10 – 15 years back (Table 4.14).

Important Observations:

- It is an interesting finding that the amount of overdues was found (relatively) very high among the people of higher asset value groups.

- Mounting overdues particularly in the case of loans taken from institutional sources put the formal credit agencies reluctant to extend small credit to the villagers.

Table 4.14

The statement of institutional loans taken between 1980 and 2003 (i.e., till the date of survey) which were fully paid back or waived.

Attribute	*Year of Loan*					
	1980-1985	*1986-1991*	*1992-1994*	*1995-1997*	*1998-2000*	*2001 & after*
IRDP (/DRI) loans:						
Amount (Rs.)	48500	119000	31000	39000	25000	-
(incidence)	(12)	(20)	(6)	(5)	(3)	
Repayment	5400	40100	32900	40700	28000	-
(in full/part)	(5)	(9)	(6)	(5)	(3)	
Waived	43100	78900	-	-	-	-
	(11)	(13)				
Loan assets present (part or full)	5	10	1	2	2	-
Other institutional loans (KCCs, personal loans, industrial loans from AFC, etc)						
Amount (Rs.)	24000	301000	170000	154000	53000	47400
(incidence)	(1)	(3)	(2)	(2)	(1)	(3)
Repayment	15000	235000	55000	160000	55000	50400
(in full/part)*	(1)	(2)	(2)	(2)	(1)	(3)
Loan assets present (part or full)	1	2	1	2	1	1**

* The remaining part is expected to have been waived/written off.

** Included two KCC loans.

- Loans taken against mortgage of land remained unpaid for long years. Since these loans were taken for emergency purposes or to meet social needs, it often eroded borrowers' flow of income in the subsequent period till the loan obligation was cleared completely.

- Loans against mortgage of land leads to transfer of right of using mortgaged land from borrowers to lenders. In a sense this reduces borrowers' flow of income from that part of his arable land which is under mortgage, from two-third to one-third of the crop yield, one-third being the cost of production (assuming that mortgaged land was taken back by the loanees on lease).

- Loans taken during the last two and a half years constituted less than half (47.62 %) of the total outstanding debt. Debt incurred before the year 1998 constituted over 35 per cent. This segment of loan shows that a section of the borrowers are still in debt-trap particularly to the moneylenders. A considerable numbers had also expressed their inability to repay loans taken against government sponsored schemes for their weak economic standing even after getting hold of productive loan-assets. Although a sizeable amount of willful defaults was recorded in this category, there was almost no sign of intentional delay in clearing debt to informal sources (with the exception of the dues with shopkeepers).

- One bright thing about bank/institutional credit agencies is that it has willy-nilly extended much larger amount of loans in recent times. Incidences of loans against KCCs and SHG-bank linkages have been recorded in some pockets. However, it is a matter of concern that the share of personal loans for house building and consumer durables constituted high proportional share. The increasing tendency of the banks to play safe will make the banking services further away from the reach of the common people where SHGs and KCC movement are yet to get acceptance among the mass people.

- Apparently, institutional loans constituted above three-fifths of the total loan outstanding. However, if all the directed institutional loans which were taken before 1997 and against whom not a single loan instalment was paid back since 1997 are omitted from the discussion (as dead loan), the share of institutional loan will look much thinner.

- The accumulation of institutional loan – old and a portion of the new ones – has been partially responsible for showing much healthy percentage share of institutional loan. In the case of non-institutional loans, generally annual interest on principal amount of loan is cleared regularly, while a larger part of the exploitative loan goes unnoticed as these were taken against mortgage of land which falls in hidden (kind) interest payment category.

- Apparently, it seems that a considerable amount of repayment was made against institutional loans. However, the unusual delay in clearing institutional loan due, accumulation of interest and higher percentage of loans carrying rate of interest in the range of 12.5 per cent to as high as 18 per cent (other than KCCs where the rate of interest was 11 – 12 per cent. In the case of bank loans to SHGs, actual interest was 14.5 per cent. It was at least 14 per cent in the case of PMRY loans) might have contributed a little bit to the growing burden of repayment. During the era of economic liberalisation, concessional loans have dried up, while the share of loans in the range of 12.5 per cent to 14.5 per cent has increased from the institutional sources.

- Non-institutional sources contributed some amount of production loan, while the institutional sources were responsible for much larger share of unproductive loans in recent times. Loans from SHGs and a couple of agricultural loans and trade credits were the main forms of productive loans in the informal market.

- Misuse of the IRDP (and a few SGSY) loans encouraged by the absence of proper supervision and monitoring of these loans after the release of fund was an equally important reason along with the high incidence of poverty for non-repayment of such loans by a section of the beneficiaries.

- The institutional credit agencies lack access to the remote villages even after the continuous pressure from the academics, social activists and media persons over the years. Neither banks nor governments have taken any concrete steps to make institutional credit agencies accessible to all villages. Neither the 'non-functioning' condition of the cooperatives is, helping the cause. To add insult to the injury, the SHG movement is still at its infant stage. With minor exception of Begenati village, only a few KCCs were distributed by banks not for assisting rural development (evolving a viable strategy to reach the maximum number of potential borrowers), but only to comply with the government's direction. Lack of involvement of the bank officials on one hand and lack of pressure from the genuine farmers on the other have facilitated the opportunist group to take the full advantage of the government sponsored loan schemes often by depriving the needy for which it means.

Needless to say that government's populist policies like loan mela, cheap credit/ subsidized credit and loan waiver schemes etc. proved ineffective and caused on many occasions, more harm than good. Unless and until government stops from dictating financial experts with an eye on the vote bank, 'aiming to serve the poor may end up giving poor service'.

It can be noted that nearly 20 per cent households had never applied for institutional loans. A majority of them believe it as an unnecessary harassment where the end result is zero. Bank loan is not accessible to all and without harassment and greasing the palm of the officials none can get it. These people rely solely on their own savings, whatever amount it be, and the informal credit market for contingency .

As many as 120 households had reported that they have submitted loan proposals to banks/ government offices during the current years or in the past 3 years. The highest number of such cases (45) were recorded in Tinsukia district (among the ST people), followed by Kamrup (40), Karimganj (26) and Nagaon (19). The numbers look impressive as the application for KCC or SHG loans were also incorporated.

In Nagaon district, quite a few households received KCC loans in the current year (while in the rain shadow area not a single household applied for or were distributed KCCs) for which applicants for fresh loan was found little less than our expectation, while in Tinsukia district as high as 20 applications were submitted for KCCs.

Of the 120 loan applications (including KCCs), 7 proposals were submitted for DIC loan of above Rs. 35 000. As many as three households reported to have spent some amount as speed money (together Rs. 18000) already to get the loan. This also indicates the pressing need of a section of the unemployed for funds to start their own enterprise or expand their tiny operation.

Altogether 18 households reported to have submitted their proposals for PMRY loans. Most of these proposals were of much higher value and for business like grocery stores, hardware stores, pharmacy, PCO, auto rickshaw, etc. About 11 households applied for fishery loans of moderate to high amount. Quite a few households wanted loan for livestock, i.e., milking cow, rickshaw, weaving, etc all of which were of smaller value.

The proposals for housing loans (6), car/scooter (3), power tillers/tractors (3), pumpsets (4), etc were the other important categories of loan proposals. Only two SHGs had submitted loan proposals for agro-service centres. Many other groups were either waiting for revolving fund or any schemes under the SGSY scheme. This is where (professional) NGOs can play an important role to make this movement effective. Experts' services are required for generating (sustaining) productive employment avenues, cooperative marketing / direct marketing of the SHG products to consumers, growing thrift habit and hundred per cent repayment performances, at least in normal times.

That the rural economy of Assam lacks investment opportunities, or that there is no demand for loans as such, as often claimed by the bank management to justify for the region's low credit-deposit ratio, is not correct. The present study amply shows that there were several loan proposals which remained unattended year after year. With the active involvement of the catalytic agencies, the merit of these proposals can be properly assessed and improved wherever necessary, and the process of viable loan transactions can be facilitated with even in this region.

As repayment culture is missing in the state, all efforts to increase institutional credit should be based on evolving a unique credit delivery and recovery system. This calls for a positive role of the rural traditional institutions in the rural credit market as intermediaries.

Incidence of institutional loans was found much higher among the better off households. It is also seen that households having members in PRIs/women organizations/FMCs/NGOs/SHGs got much higher amount of institutional loans. Needless to mention that among the better off households, the incidence of PRIs members or associationship with other village institutions was found more frequent. In other words, status of HRD is an important determinant of getting higher / lower amount of institutional loans. In the sample, more than 70 per cent of the households with access to institutional loans had one or two members reported in FMCs/PRIs/SHGs/women organizations, etc. Less than 30 per cent households with access to institutional loans had no members with any of the above institutions.

The problem of increasing reluctance of the bankers to extend credit to the small farmers, artisans and asset poor can be solved amicably (in a viable manner) if the following five things receives utmost importance from all concerns :

(i) Compulsory preliminary groundwork before initiating a loan proposal by the potential borrower/self-help group.

(ii) For skill development, for diffusion of market information, for development of the concept of cluster marketing, etc government may encourage development of good network of NGOs with professional acumen under the each PRIs/block/district.

(iii) The merit of the loan proposals to be submitted by the potential borrowers must be scrutinized thoroughly by an NGO and finally by the loan sanctioning banks wherever they feel it necessary.

(iv) Monitoring the usage of funds should be left to NGOs (women organizations, PRIs, FMCs or village youth clubs, etc). The time of collection of instalment i.e., loan recovery may also be left to NGOs, for which they should be allowed a fixed percentage of the recovery amount towards meeting their (NGOs) managerial costs and minimum amount of incentives for utilizing their professional services.

(v) The government should develop a transparent, quick and at the same time strictly accountable recovery cell under each district to assist NGOs whenever and wherever they need its services.

References

1. Government of India (1998), '48th Round of NSS', NSSO, Report No. 420. July 1998.
2. NABARD (2001), 'Report of the Expert Committee on Rural Credit', Mumbai. India.
3. Yaron, J, et. al. (1997), 'Rural Finance – Issues, Design and Best Practices', Environmentally and Socially Sustainable Development Studies and Monographs Series 14, The World Bank.

5

Image of Moneylenders in Rural Credit Scenario

In Assam the main problems being faced by the smaller farmers (also to some extent by the non-farming population) are economically non-viable size of operational holdings, acute shortage of irrigation network despite extremely high potentialities, recurring and devastating floods in almost every year necessitating a drastic change in the pattern of cropping in larger parts of the state and unavailability of operational credits from the institutional sources and as a consequence, villagers easily fall prey to the usurious moneylenders. It is needless to mention that the prospects of faster economic development of Assam squarely depend on vibrant agricultural (primary) sector which is, in turn, sustainable through capital investment through credit but which has so far, though unfortunately, failed to elicit adequate attention from the planners.

In the era of globalization and lower supportive role of the government for poverty eradication or inequalities reduction, there is every possibility that the informal credit regain its grip over the rural credit market which was primarily responsible for alienation of land from the poor farmers particularly during the pre-nationalisation of banks. In fact, in the previous chapter, it was found that moneylenders are still very much active and a dominant source of credit particularly in the remote villages in Assam. Its overall share, of late, has increased considerably in the region.

The persistence of the 'very influential' position of the moneylenders in the rural economy, high proportion of overdues, and poor borrowers' exposure to double exploitation as they take loans from moneylenders, shopkeepers, employers, etc. are known facts, but, in this chapter, a serious attempt has been made to explore the recent proof of some of these phenomena along with the relative position/image of the moneylenders in rural credit scenario of Assam/India.

Review of the literature

In ancient Indian literature, the institution of moneylender was recognized as an essential part of the society whose function was to extend credit to those people who need it for different purposes. Manu, the Vedic lawgiver, justified high interest rate on the ground that capital was essentially productive. Quite surprisingly, even in those days, the rate of interest varied from class to class, i.e., it was influenced by the caste of the borrower (2% per month from the Brahmin to as high as 5% per month from the Shudra), purpose for which money was borrowed, the likely advantage to be reaped, economic resources of the borrower, etc. Borrower's caste, economic condition and past relationship with the moneylenders, etc did play a role for charging or not charging a compound rate of interest (Thingalaya 2003 & Srivastava 1974).

Kautilya was in favour of the regulation of the interest rate and suggested, as a general rule, 15 per cent as the just rate of interest. No interest was allowed on mortgaged property (Paul 1979). He also proposed the public regulation of interest because, for him, the relationship between the capitalist and the productive borrower was of vital importance to the national economy. The situation has changed considerably since then, with the proliferation of money lending business in the rural areas. Several recent studies both at the official level and the academic exercises have shown the resurgence of informal finance in the countryside (Bhattacharjee 2003, Gogoi 2004, and Purkayastha 2004).

During the latter part of the 19th century, the problem of rural indebtedness became acute and the incidence of passing of agricultural land from the hands of the indebted farmers to the moneylenders took a serious proportion. The system of state loans (taccavi), the Deccan Agriculturists' Relief Act 1879, Land Improvement Loans Act 1883, Agriculturists Loans Act 1884, etc were some of the notable attempts to address rural indebtedness, but failed to make any inroads into the all pervasive informal credit market (Sankaran 2004).

According to Bottomley (1964 and 1975), 'there are four components of rural rates of interest which are sufficient to explain the reason for very high level of usurious rate of interest as compared to that of the organized financial institutions. These four components are: (i) the opportunity cost of the money involved, (ii) the premium for administering the loan, (iii) the premium for risk and (iv) monopoly profit'.

Highly publicized cases of high interest rates have very often prompted governments to outlaw informal money lending through the passing of usury laws which set the ceiling on interest rates. These actions of the governments have gone against the thought of Ohio School (Von Pischke 1991), which argued that the high rate of interest charged by the moneylender is understandable because of 'his high risk nature of the business'. Even they tried to justify their arguments by stating that high interest rate often included payment for a range of services such as storage facilities for the produce, payment of market taxes, etc. provided by the moneylenders (Mishra and Nayak, 2004).

In recent times, Sharma and Chamala (2003) expressed that 'the emphatic push towards a positive image of the moneylender which has become very visible internationally has not been so visible in Indian rural finance practice. The positive image of the moneylender has survived all through the centuries of Muslim and British domination in India and the push from negative to positive paradigm in development thought needs only to resuscitate a latent image which has been lying under the dominant negative one'. Financial sector reforms in India has resulted in very selective expansion of bank branches in the rural areas, while a considerable number of loss making branches in backward areas have already been liquidated or shifted to urban areas. This has, at least partially, created a vacuum in rural credit particularly in backward areas, which is to be filled up by the informal sector. In this regard, the moneylender's socio-economic image is very important in shaping rural finance policies.

There is substantial historical evidence of the exploitation of the peasantry by the moneylender during the 19th and early part of the 20th centuries across the Indian countryside (Royal Commission Report – 1928, Famine Commission Reports – 1880 and 1901, Deccan Riots Commission Report – 1875, etc.) The moneylender and his malpractices, such as compounding the interest, usury and confiscation of landed property from the debtor, were adding to the burden of indebtedness on the peasantry and were also responsible to a considerable degree for the backwardness of the Indian agriculture during the pre-nationalisation of Indian banking (Chavan 2003). One of the revelations of the All-India Rural Credit Survey conducted by the RBI in 1951-52 was the fact that the moneylender (and the trader) still reined supreme in the field of rural credit, supplying

70 per cent or more of the total credit requirements. The institutional sources (government and cooperative) supplied as little as 6 per cent. Out of this very little, the larger part went to the bigger agriculturist (RBI 1958). Till date, institutional sources are bias towards bigger farmers while the weaker section, landless, artisans and womenfolk left largely uncovered. The various poverty alleviation schemes launched by the government (directed credit programmes) from time to time tried to emphasise on the credit-worthiness of the project instead of credit-worthiness of borrowers, which was partially successful in correcting the maldistribution of the institutional loans. However, as the Committee to Review Arrangements for Institutional Credit for Agriculture and Rural Development, 1979 noted (RBI 1981) the credit-worthiness of the programme by itself is not sufficient unless the growth of income generated by the programme, over time, takes care of the initial non-productive indebtedness and puts the family on its feet. The ubiquitous moneylender absorbs the growth and the credit institution is faced with mounting overdues.

Bhaduri (1984) pointed out that the collateral offered by the poor peasants (e.g. already encumbered land, standing crop or his future labour service, etc.) has hardly any market value and therefore is not accepted by the organized institutions. But the local moneylender is willing to accept them as collateral because, he can make personal use of them or he can undervalue such collateral substantially in a loan arrangement. He also observed that in the case of organized credit institutions, default in the repayment of loans leads to a loss for the lending institutions, while in the case of moneylender the borrower runs the risk of losing his collateral to the lender at a price far below the market price. Similarly, Sarap (1991) also observed that a high interest rate coupled with a short repayment period induces default and thereby establishes control over the borrower's assets or labour.

Interestingly, the Banking Commission - 1972, had emphasized the responsibility of the banker to support his lending for production by also lending to the necessary infrastructure, supply structure and marketing structure without which credit for production by itself may be self-defeating. The Commission admitted that 'in the field, we have seen cases of the poorer sections making good with the application of modern technology but with the help of the moneylenders' loans. We cannot, therefore, lightly deny, on ideological grounds, the facility that the private sector may offer in certain circumstances' (RBI 1981).

However, like most of the official documents, the All India Debt and Investment Survey (AIDIS) 1992 reported that for long, the household sector, particularly in rural India, was exploited by the traditional credit agencies like moneylenders, landlords, traders etc. It seems that their stranglehold which was gradually loosening during the 1960s (as the share of institutional loans increased quickly to 17 % in 1961, from around 7 % in 1951), was very nearly broken during the 1970s (institutional loans constituted 61% in 1981), with the institutional agencies making steady inroads into the rural scene (64% in 1991). The combined share of all the non-institutional credit agencies in the outstanding cash dues of cultivator households recorded a sharp decline of more than 30 percentage points during 1970s but the decline got arrested in the 1980s – the fall being just of about 6 percentage points. In fact, the share of professional moneylenders has reported a rise to about 11 per cent in 1991, after registering a fall to 8 per cent in 1981 from about 13 per cent in 1971.

Moneylender's position in Assam/North East India

Indebtedness is very much rampant in the tribal societies in the NE-region (Purkayastha 1997 and 2004 and Gogoi 2004). In a study conducted by the Assam Tribal Research Institute, it was found that 43.75 per cent of the sample tribal families were indebted, of which only 12.61 per cent had accessed institutional credit and the rest 31.14 per cent borrowed from non-institutional sources (Das 2004).

In the *Char* (riverine) areas of the Brahmaputra, i.e., the most backward region of Assam and predominantly occupied by the immigrant Muslim peasants, the presence of exploitative money lenders can be felt very severely. Virtually speaking, these people have helped the state economy to attain self sufficiency in paddy/food grains production in recent times by dint of sheer courage (daring the fury of floods), hard work and experimenting temper. Marwari traders and even Assamese Mahajans provided a substantial part of the necessary finance to enable these peasants to bring virgin soil under the plough. 'While among the Assamese, the general rate of interest was 2 per cent, in case of the immigrants, money lent out at 1 anna, 1.25 anna and 2 annas for a rupee per month' (as narrated by Lalit Chandra Nayak before 'The Assam Provincial Banking Enquiry Committee: 1929-30, p 466). The very high interest regime in the *char* areas continues over the years, largely because these flood-hit people are deprived of institutional sources of credit. In a recent study (Chakraborty 2004) carried out among the people settled in *char* areas, 70 per cent households were found indebted to various sources. About 42 per cent of the indebted households borrowed money against mortgage of land, 38 per cent borrowed from professional moneylenders who charged high to very high interest rates ranging from 60 per cent to 170 per cent, while the rest fell upon the relatives and school benefit fund.

The situation is not very satisfactory in other parts of the state. In Barak valley of Assam, two recent case studies also reported very high percentage share of moneylender in total debt of the rural households (51% reported in Ghose, where the survey period was 2002 and 36 % reported in Sen Gupta, where the survey period was 2000-03). In another study conducted by the Agro-Economic Research Centre for North East India during 2000-02, high concern was expressed about moneylender's exploitative role in this part of the country stating 'for the borrowings of money the private moneylenders takes the land on mortgage as security. Since it is not possible to repay debt, their mortgaged land had to be handed over to the moneylender. Thus the indebtedness has given birth to a new class of tenants/ landless proletariat in the rural sector' (Saikia 2004).

Similar concern was also shown in some other academic studies (Ph.D thesis, Minor Research Projects, etc) and government reports covering different parts of the region and time periods (Ahmed 1987, Purkayastha 1997 and 2004, Dutta and Mitra 2004, Sharma 2004, NSS 8th Round 1962, NSS 18th Round 1969, Report of the All India Rural Credit Review Committee 1969, Review of Agricultural Development and Cooperative Credit in Assam 1961-76, etc.) Loans from cooperative societies (/institutional sources) at around 13 per cent to 15 per cent can hardly be considered more advantageous than moneylender's advances especially when we take into account the additional attraction that the latter offers to an agriculturist, such as adequate funds without delay, as and when required, absence of cumbrous procedure, deferring repayment when the farmer so desires, etc. It is, no wonder, therefore, that the cooperative movement in Assam which was expected to eliminate the unscrupulous moneylender and take over the function of supplying cheap credit failed in both these tasks ("Cooperation in Assam –A New Experiment", RBI, undated and Sarap 1991).

In another study recently carried out by the author under the UGC's MRP scheme, it was observed that the access of institutional sources was far from satisfactory in the interior villages in the region. The share of institutional credit (42%) to total indebtedness was found substantially lower compared to the national or state's standard (64% each) registered in the

AIDIS-1991. Friends and moneylenders together contributed half of the total rural borrowings. There is no denying the fact that these two sources often accord loans to the villagers – sometimes without caring much about the security of loans – during their hard time viz., ill-health, floods, etc. However, one-half of the total debt constituted by the informal source does matter because a considerable share of these loans either carried a high interest burden or had to be taken against mortgage of land thereby opening up the gate for further alienation of land from the already marginalized farmer class. It seems that in the post-liberalisation period, the frequency of institutional loans in rural areas of Assam has received a set back (Purkayastha 2004).

Important Findings of the Present Study

As mentioned earlier, one-third of the loanee households borrowed money either at 'high to very high' rate of interest or against mortgaged of land. There were quite a few households who had borrowed money from different sources for the same or different purposes at the same point of time/over a period of time. The total incidence of loan was recorded at 257, which included 28 cases of high interest borrowings (above 36 % annual interest rate) and 62 cases of loan drawn against mortgage of land. Altogether, 45 households borrowed against mortgage of land. None reported mortgage of ornaments, utensils or any other valuables other than land to moneylenders (/shop keepers). The share of loan drawn against mortgage of land and/or, at a high interest rate will go up further if we ignore those institutional loans taken at least 5 years back and where not a single instalment was paid back since then.

The extremely poor households reported low incidence of indebtedness, because they were treated as unbankable both by the formal as well as informal sources. The incidence of transfer of land utilization right from borrowers to land mortgagee was found alarming among the 'poor', 'nearly poor' and 'above poverty line' small farmers. As many as 7 poor households and 6 nearly poor loanee households had to mortgage some amount of arable land for drawing consumption loan particularly during floods and subsequently transformed into tenant households. Marriage and health care loans were the next two important causes of alienation of land from the poor farmers. It is because of the continuous increase in population and subsequently its direct proportionate pressure on agricultural land in the absence of alternative non-farm avenues, lending against land has become more attractive option for the moneylenders. A few rich families also borrowed substantial amount of money from the moneylenders to make up a part of the disproportionately high expenditure incurred in children's marriage or hefty nursing home bill. The nagging problem of insurgency has indirectly contributed to the growth of informal money lending against mortgage of land, by seriously hampering the growth of banking activities (movement of the bank officials in sensitive areas) in the rural areas.

Very interestingly, a few APL households reported consumption loans during floods, though the reason for such loans by the rich farmers was not very clear. It may be related to their socio-cultural peculiarities (in the case of tribal households) or the usual practice of keeping a part of the grocery bill uncleared (in a rare case, it may be a tactic adopted by the non-indigenous people to show different activist groups working in the region that they are running short of cash flow and is currently passing through a tough time).

It is also important to note that two rich households mortgaged 4 bigha land each for purchase of land suitable for the plantation of tea. One household each from the 'very rich' and 'rich' groups reported of mortgaging out 7 and 4 bigha of farm land respectively (all these plots of land fall in the rain shadow area under Hojai sub-division in Nagaon District) and invested the loan amount either for the purchase of or mortgaged

Table 5.1

Income group wise and purpose wise distribution of average amount of outstanding loan drawn against mortgage of land

Income group	*Cultivation*	*purchase of land / Business*	*Tea Plantation*	*House Repairing*	*Food consumption*	*Marriage / Funeral*	*Health Care*	*Others*
EP	*-	-	-	-	-	-	(1) 18000 3B	-
BPL	-	-	-	-	(7) 7457 2.6B	(1) 4000 1B	(2) 7000 2B	(1) 8000 2B
Poor & Nearly Poor	(2) 2750 1B	-	(1) 2000 0.5B	-	(6) 5917 1.5B	(5) 6300 1.5B	(5) 2500 1.1B	(3) 5833 1.5B
APL	-	(1) 7000 2B	(1) 5000 1B	(1) 12500 2.5B	(2) 8000 1.5B	(2) 10000 2B	(2) 8500 2B	(6) 5167 1.5B

(Contd.)

(Contd. Table 5.1)

Income group	*Cultivation*	*purchase of land / Business*	*Tea Plantation*	*House Repairing*	*Food consumption*	*Marriage / Funeral*	*Health Care*	*Others*
Rich	(1) 5000 1B	(1) 20000 4B	(1) 8000 4B	-	(2) 8000 1B	(2) 17500 3.5B	(3) 12667 2.6B	(1) 15000 2B
Very Rich	-	(2) 21000 7B	-	-	-	-	-	-

* In box: Ist figure : Number of loans.

2nd figure : Average size of loan.

3rd figure : Average amount of land mortgaged.

** 'B' stands for bigha (I bigha = 0.13 hectare).

Note: Extremely Poor – Annual income of a family less than Rs. 11000; Below Poverty Line – Rs. 11000 to 22000; Poor & Nearly Poor – 22001 to 36000; Above Poverty Line – 36001 to 75000; Rich – 75001 to 2 lakh and Very Rich – above 2 lakh.

in better quality farm land. Of the 62 cases of loan drawn against mortgage of land, only 11 were for productive purposes. The rest 51 cases were primarily unproductive in nature. The very nature of transfer of land utilization right seems to aggravate the burden of debt for the economically disadvantaged section, though this may not be the case at all for the better off communities.

Broad Terms and Conditions of Mortgaged Land

* In all the sample villages save the vegetable belt of Nagaon district, it was observed that in normal situation, against mortgage of one bigha land (1 bigha = 0.13 hectare) villagers can borrow maximum of Rs. 5000. The market value of land may be higher by 6 – 7 times the loan amount. When the productivity of land is low (flood affected, drought prone, etc) and the mortgaged land is only suitable for rice cultivation, the amount of loan available may be even less (Rs. 2500 – Rs. 3000).

* In all the villages viz. Powaimukh (Margherita Block in Tinsukia District), Bamungaon (Udali Block in Nagaon District) and Dwigunpar (Kamalpur Block in Kamrup District) where the current practice is mono-cropping (Sali rice), one bigha land yields crop value worth Rs. 2200. The cost of production was estimated at one-third of the total production. The moneylenders will get at least one-third of the total production from the land taken in mortgaged, even if he leased out the mortgaged land quite often to the borrower himself. In other words, he will go on receiving (approximately 20 – 40 % annual rate of interest in kind) Rs. 733 as interest in all the normal years till the borrowers fully repay the loan amount. Quite understandably, repayment in instalments is often discouraged by these moneylenders.

* Terms and conditions of such loans widely differed in villages like Begenati and Heeragaon under Nagaon sub-division. In the vegetable belt, one bigha land can yield crops worth Rs. 10000 (in flood affected land where jute and boro paddy is grown)

to as high as Rs. 28000 (where 3 – 5 cash crops are grown, for instance, potato (30 quintal) + brinjal (40 quintals) + ridge-gaurd (20 quintals) + one or two leafy vegetables for a short duration of 45 to 50 days each). In Begenati and Heeragaon, landed households borrowed up to Rs. 20000 against mortgage of one bigha land. In such cases, moneylenders often pursue the borrowers to make an informal agreement so that land can be released only after 5 years. The borrowers can release his land at any time after the completion of 5 years by paying back the principal amount of Rs. 20000.

* If the borrower borrows in the range of Rs. 5000 – Rs. 10000, or even less, in such a case, mortgaged land can be released at any point of time by making full repayment of the loan amount.

* In the flood free vegetable belt, if a borrower borrows in the range of Rs. 5000 to Rs. 10000, he will get back his land automatically after 5 years. In this case he need not repay the principal amount borrowed. The mortgaged land can be released even before the 5 years term. In that case, however, the borrower will have to pay back the entire loan amount.

It can be mentioned that 2 households, out of the 45 loanee households borrowed against mortgage of land, were also required to pay 10 per cent simple rate of interest on the principal amount borrowed. In both the cases, quality of land was poor and flood prone.

Table 5.2 reveals that the incidence of borrowing at high to very high rates of interest was more common among the higher income groups. This is contrary to the prevailing views (Sarap 1991 and Bhattacharjee 2003) that the poor are charged with higher rate of interest due to high risk involvement in such cases. 'Nil' interest group mainly incorporates sources like friends and relatives, shopkeepers and traders/wholesalers. The

Table 5.2

Income group wise distribution of average amount of loan outstanding over rate of interest.

Income group	*Nil*	*Interest in kind / Land Mortgaged*	*1—10%*	*11-15%*	*16-24%*	*25-50% ***	*51% & Above*
Extremely Poor	1462 (4)	18000 (1)	4500 (1)	8000 (1)	-	6000 (1)	1300 (1)
BPL	1028 (20)	7382 (11)	4100 (2)	9833 (9)	1660 (5)	7450 (4)	1950 (2)
Poor & Nearly Poor	1750 (9)	4068 (22)	11025 (4)	10506 (18)	5988 (8)	1867 (3)	3650 (4)
APL	2120 (10)	7233 (15)	11000 (2)	10896 (24)	4700 (4)	2100 (2)	5683 (6)

(Contd.)

(Contd. Table 5.2)

Income group	*Nil*	*Interest in kind / Land Mortgaged*	*1—10%*	*11-15%*	*16-24%*	*25-50% ***	*51% & Above*
Rich	28000 (1)	11727 (11)	-	27205 (22)	3400 (6)	-	9600 (2)
Very Rich	28500 (2)	21000 (2)	-	39375 (12)	48900* (3)	6300 (3)	-

Figures in brackets indicate incidence of loan.

* Includes a bank loan worth Rs. 1,20,000 at 16 per cent rate of interest (and another small business loan at 18 per cent interest rate was also recorded in 16 – 24 % category) .

** No loan was recorded in 25 – 35 per cent rate of interest.

Note: Extremely Poor – Annual income of a family less than Rs. 11000; Below Poverty Line – Rs. 11000 to 22000; Poor & Nearly Poor – 22001 to 36000; Above Poverty Line – 36001 to 75000; Rich – 75001 to 2 lakh and Very Rich – above 2 lakh.

institutional sources mainly constituted two successive lower interest groups of 1 – 10 per cent and 11 – 15 per cent.

Rich and 'APL' families drawn substantial amount of loan from moneylenders even though they are aware of the high rates of interest associated with such borrowings. For many households, either banking services were not available within a convenient distance or, as usual, bankers showed least interest to their loan proposals for daughter/son's marriage, health care, etc. Often official documents failed to adequately highlight the moneylender's role in these respects.

One extremely poor household (non-SHG member) borrowed money at 60 per cent annual rate of interest from a self-help group. Nearly two-fifths of the total high interest borrowings were made from SHGs (thrift and credit group). All the three loans, recorded in 25 – 50 per cent rate of interest by the very rich households, were taken by the female SHG-members from their respective groups for the purpose of marketing their weaving products in trade fairs. These people (particularly the better off members) seemed to be least bothered about high interest rate, because group's income will be shared between themselves at the end of the year. There is a hidden competition between different thrift and credit groups in the sphere of distribution of profits among the members at the end of the year/term of the group.

One very interesting observation was that SHGs used to extend small loans to the members at 2 – 5 per cent monthly rate of interest for contingent needs and also to assist household industries among the group members. Quite a few SHGs extended loans to non-members but only at higher rate of interest, i.e., 5 – 10 per cent monthly rate of interest. The increasing tendency of some of the SHGs to provide high interest loan to outsiders has been instrumental in promoting them to the club of moneylenders (minus any greed for land).

It is significant to note that during the past 3 years, 12 households (3 households in the current year) had borrowed money from moneylenders against mortgage of land. As reported by the households, the incidence of loan against mortgage of properties was much higher in the years prior to their membership with SHGs.

There is a clear indication that in the rural areas of Assam/ NER, the moneylender is regaining their lost ground slowly but steadily. It is partly because public sector banks have already started withdrawing from certain activities (including extension of small loans) particularly from lending to the agricultural sector in remote areas. In 2001, institutional credit to agriculture in Assam was only 9 per cent against the mandated 18 per cent for agriculture. The RRBs originally meant for rural lending (priority sector lending) have started to emphasise on lending to the salaried people for consumer loans. The cooperative credit infrastructure has been found to be miserably poor and almost on the verge of withering away. For instance, in the sample, only one household reported a loan from the cooperative bank drawn 10 years back. During the past 3 years, the sample households borrowed Rs. 8,07,200 from the nationalized banks (/institutional sources). In the total loan drawn from banks, the share of loans against KCCs constituted nearly 25 per cent. The loan under the SGSY (SHG – Bank linkage) scheme constituted less than 7 per cent. The housing loan (including major repairing) constituted above 49 per cent, while the other purposes including business loan, scooter loan, etc constituted above 19 per cent. Direct loans (from banks) were given to the better-off people with the provision of compulsory realization of monthly instalment from salary account (in the case of salaried people) or against savings certificates. The increasing tendency of the bankers to extend bigger loans against good security on the one hand and the limited access of KCCs and SHGs in Assam on the other, will definitely add to the miseries of the already marginalized class.

To add insult to the injury, the SHG movement in the region by maintaining high interest culture of the informal sector has made the moneylender's job easier and tolerable even to the eyes of the die-hard critics including NGOs in the region.

References

1. Ahmed, A. (1987) "The Anatomy of Rural Poverty in Assam" Mittal Publications Pvt. Ltd. New Delhi.
2. Bhaduri, A. (1984) "The Economic Structure of Backward Agriculture" Academic Press, London.
3. Bhattacharjee, S. (2003) "Rural Credit and Class-Differentiation" K P Bagchi & Company, Kolkata.
4. Bottomley, A. (1975), "Interest Rate Determination in Underdeveloped Rural Areas" American Journal of Agricultural Economics, Vol. 57, No. 2, May.
5. Bottomley, A. (1964) "The Determination of Pure Rates of Interest in Underdeveloped Rural Areas" Review of Economics and Statistics, Vol. 46.
6. Chakraborty, G. (2004) "Informal Credit or State's Discredit: The Saga of Char Areas in Assam" in J. K. Gogoi (ed.) "Rural Indebtedness in North East India", Dept. of Economics, Dibrugarh University.
7. Chavan, P. (2003) "Moneylender's Positive Image:Regression in Development Thought and Policy" Economic and Political Weekly, December 13.
8. Das, M N (2004) "Can We Free the Tribals From the Debt Trap: In Search of an Answer" in J. K. Gogoi (ed.) " Rural Indebtedness in North East India", Dept. of Economics, Dibrugarh University.
9. Dutta, B. M. and Mitra, A. (2003) "Indebtedness in Rural Assam: A Case Study of Dhemaji District" Paper presented in a national level Seminar on 24-25 September, 2003 at Dibrugarh University, Assam.
10. Ghosh, A. L. (2003) " A Survey of the Causes and Consequences of Rural Indebtedness: A Case Study" Paper presented in a

national level Seminar on 24-25 September, 2003 at Dibrugarh University, Assam.

11. Gogoi, J. K, (2004) " Rural Indebtedness in North East India", Seminar Volumes, Dept. of Economics, Dibrugarh University.
12. Government of India (1962) "Tables with Notes on Rural Indebtedness" The Cabinet Secretariat, NSS 8th Round, No. 68.
13. Government of India (1969) "Tables with Notes on Indebtedness of Scheduled Tribe Households" The Cabinet Secretariat, NSS 18th Round, No. 68.
14. Mishra,B. & Nayak, P.(2004) "Limits of Micro Credit for Rural Development: A Cursory Look" in J. K. Gogoi (ed.) " Rural Indebtedness in North East India", Dept. of Economics, Dibrugarh University.
15. NSSO (1998) "Debt and Investment Survey-1992" NSS 48th Round, Ministry of Planning & Programme Implementation.
16. Paul, R. R.(1979) "History of Economic Thought" Kalyani Publishers, Ludhiana.
17. Pischke, V. (1991) "Finance at the Frontier" World Bank, Washington.
18. Purkayastha, G. (1997) "Rural Labour Indebtedness in Assam" Mohit Publications, New Delhi.
19. Purkayastha, G. (2004) " Human Development and Rural Indebtedness in North East India", Anmol Publications Pvt. Ltd. New Delhi.
20. Reserve Bank of India (1958) "The Integrated Scheme of Rural Credit", (Pamphlet), Agricultural Credit Dept. Bombay.
21. Reserve Bank of India (1969) "Report of the all India Rural Credit Review Committee 1969", Agricultural Credit Dept. Bombay.
22. Reserve Bank of India (1978) "Review of Agricultural Development and Cooperative Credit in Assam (1961-1976)" Bombay.
23. Reserve Bank of India (1981) "Committee of Review Arrangement for Institutional Credit for Agriculture And Rural Development 1979" Bombay.

24. Reserve Bank of India (undated) "Cooperation in Assam(A New Experiment)", Agricultural Credit Dept. Bombay.
25. Saikia, T. N. (2004) "Dynamics of Rural Indebtedness: An Empirical Study in Four Districts of Assam" in J. K. Gogoi (ed.) " Rural Indebtedness in North East India", Dept. of Economics, Dibrugarh University.
26. Sankaran, P. N. (2004) "Indian Cooperative Movement: Retrospect and Prospect" Kurukshetra, October issue.
27. Sarap, K. (1991) "Interlinked Agrarian Markets in Rural India" Sage Publications, New Delhi.
28. Sen Gupta, K. (2004) "Rural Indebtedness: A Case Study of Cachar District of South Assam" in J. K. Gogoi (ed.) " Rural Indebtedness in North East India", Dept. of Economics, Dibrugarh University.
29. Sharma, A.(2004) "SHG-Bank Linkage Programme in Assam – A Review" in J. K. Gogoi (ed.) " Rural Indebtedness in North East India", Dept. of Economics, Dibrugarh University.
30. Sharma, S. & Chamala, S. (2003) "Moneylender's Positive Image Paradigms and Rural Development" Economic and political Weekly, April 26.
31. Srivastava, S. K. (1974) "History of Economic Thought" S. Chand & Co. Pvt. Ltd., New Delhi.
32. Thingalaya, N K (2003) "Moneylender's Positive Image" Economic and Political Weekly, June 28.

6

Credit Deepening in Assam Through SHGs and KCCs

The credit needs of the poor are very small. Perhaps a loan worth Rs. 100 is enough to transform the life of a beggar (representing the most humiliated section of the society i.e., the poorest of the poor). He/she can lead a respectable life as a newspaper hawker in a public place. Giving onetime hefty dole or occasional alms to the beggars may always prove misdirected, a purely temporary exercise to reduce their sufferings. Apart from their access to kick-start capital, it is very important that they are being provided with right kind of information and necessary motivation which generally comes from voluntary organizations with professional skills / self-help groups (SHGs).

As explained in the earlier chapters, credit is a major input in boosting economic development, only when it is effectively utilised. Its timely availability in the right quantity and at reasonable interest goes a long way in providing gainful economic activities in farm and non-farm sectors, particularly to the asset less poor. Hence, the two innovative schemes, i.e., micro credit through SHGs and entitlement to credit to all eligible people in the countryside through KCCs (Kisan Credit Cards), etc. launched in the late 1990s in Assam along with the rest of the country.

Since India attained her Independence, a large number of Committees such as All India Credit Survey Committee (1951), All India Credit Review Committee (1966), Agricultural Credit Review Committee (1986) etc, were set up by the Centre to analyze the arrangements for institutional credit delivery. These Committees were more sector-oriented rather than being people-centered. Consequently, the share of rural household borrowings from formal institutional sources increased from a negligible amount in 1951 to 64 per cent by 1991. Notwithstanding this shift in the dependence on institutional sources of credit, the dependence of non-cultivator households, who constituted the rural poor, on non-institutional sources of credit continued to be very high (41%) in 1991 (Jayaraman ,2001). As revealed by the All India Debt and Investment Survey (1991), rural households with assets less than Rs. 20000 could have access to institutional sources for their credit needs only to the extent of 35 to 37 per cent, the share of non- institutional agencies in their outstanding debt was as high as 52 per cent to 62 per cent. On the other hand, those having higher asset base had better access to institutional credit, up to 70 per cent or more of their outstanding debts. In a society where demand for credit is much more than its availability, credit gets rationed and landless and other asset poor applicants are screened out.

Policy makers are working on the second generation of reforms with focus on agriculture and strengthening our credit delivery mechanisms. Public sector banks have been formulating Special Agricultural Credit Plans (SACP) since 1994-95 with a purpose to give the most necessary boost to the flow of credit to agriculture. NABARD has formulated a model scheme for issue of Kisan Credit Cards (KCCs), an innovative scheme towards facilitating access to short term credit to all farmers. The KCCs are issued on the basis of farmers' land holdings so that the cards can be readily used to purchase agricultural inputs such as seeds, fertilizers, pesticides and draw cash for production needs (wage payment, hiring costs of power tiller, pumpset for irrigation, storage and marketing, etc.). To increase the reach of the scheme, banks were even advised to issue KCCs for limits even below Rs. 5000. The banks have also been advised to issue cards to even those farmers who were defaulters of institutional credit and where the outstanding amount was not very high. Nevertheless, the defaulter farmers must clear their old dues in convenient instalments while enjoying the benefits under the KCC scheme.

Till 2004, 41.4 million KCCs involving credit sanctions of Rs. 98000 crore were distributed across the nation. It is a matter of concern that when the national leaders were thinking of providing KCCs to all the eligible farmers in the next couple of years, the progress of Assam was quite tardy. Less than 2 lakh cards were distributed in the state till 2004. The government has set a target of issuing 2 lakh KCCs for the year 2004-05. However, till the end of December only about 40000 such cards had been issued. Lack of involvement of the FMCs, poor coordination among the agricultural extension officers, bankers and the farmers, incomplete land record and the exceptionally low recovery ratio (Table 6.1), etc. were responsible for such a poor performance.

At the time of interrogation, only 20 card holders were reported. Three rich farmers could manage 2 cards each. Two card holders were not given any loan even after two agricultural seasons passed off. Two ST households (Powaimukh - Margherita block – Tinsukia district) did not accept Cards because they were more interested in subsidy-based fat loan. They believe that acceptance of KCCs may reduce their chances of getting PMRY loans for which they have already applied. Almost all the

FMC President/Secretaries had KCC or were in the process of getting it.

Of the 20 households with KCCs, the share of big (medium) farmers, small farmers and marginal farmers were 5, 5 and 10 respectively. Distribution according to their economic status stands at 7 – rich, 10 – APL, and 3 – 'near poor and poor'. Nevertheless, that the marginal farmers are getting KCCs and repaying their loans in time is something special in Assam. Very interestingly, as many as 14 KCC holders were also the member of SHGs. The group movement has definitely contributed to the whatever little success achieved so far by the KCC movement in Assam. It is very important that multi-purpose KCCs (for short term as well as long term) are issued to the farm and non-farm sectors so as to impart the desired flexibility to the scheme. Small tea growers, etc should be covered under credit card scheme.

It can be mentioned that those who have received the KCCs, took it as if, it was a ration card or more appropriately, an entitlement to credit. That their entitlement to credit had to be applied judiciously and on a regular basis. It has become a matter of prestige to have a credit card. Three households had acquired two credit cards each. Also, a couple of KCC holders who did not require credit for agricultural operations in the current year, took loans against their cards only to lend the same to other needy farmers without KCCs, to whom the card holders leased out his arable land. One card holder in Karimganj district was seen to have invested the credit released against card in the non-agricultural activities (cloth stores) just before *Dushera*. The repayment rate was higher as farmers knew that they can raise even higher amount of loan once they clear the previous loan. However, involvement of the bank officials and other change agents in rural area are the pre-condition for the success of the schemes. For instance, in Tinsukia district, in sharp contrast to Nagaon, a couple of bank managers (one from

RRBs and the other, UBI rural branch) reported that only one, out of eight loans sanctioned against KCCs, returned the

Table 6.1
State wise Average Recovery of Agricultural Loans and Credit Flow

State	*Average rate of recovery*	*Agricultural credit per hectare of Net Sown Area (Rs.)*
Northern Region		
Haryana	80	8611
Punjab	88	10786
Rajasthan	74	1167
North- Eastern Region		
Arunachal Pradesh	29	132
Assam	10	276
Manipur	11	115
Meghalaya	36	328
Mizoram	51	338
Nagaland	9	316
Tripura	32	481
Sikkim	NA	253
Eastern Region		
Bihar	26	572
Orissa	45	1269
West Bengal	61	1734
Central Region		
Madhya Pradesh	61	1104
Uttar Pradesh	66	2172
Western Region		
Gujarat	74	2887
Maharashtra	61	2363
Southern Region		
Andhra Pradesh	66	5253
Karnataka	62	3253
Kerala	83	9948
Tamil Nadu	70	7640
All India	63	-

Source : ECRC – 2001, NABARD, Annexure 9.2

loan amount. The average size of loan was about Rs. 4000. For the recovery of loan no correspondence was made even after two agricultural seasons passed off. It seems that bankers have fulfilled his obligation simply by releasing some amount of loan. In fact, neither bank officials nor any representative from the local administration who were seen pressurizing the banks for issuing KCCs, had visited the defaulter households before or after the release of loans. Mounting work load was shown as the prime cause for such a big gap between bankers and loanees, which needs to be bridged urgently.

Quite surprisingly, no card was recorded among the sample households in Kamrup district. In Nagaon district, the average size of credit against KCCs was found substantially higher (above Rs. 20000) than that of the Karimganj district (little less than Rs. 8000). In Tinsukia district, although no KCC loan was recorded by the sample households (a couple of

---

* It is important to note that in one of the sample villages (Begenati), 52 households got KCCs (not all these households were included in the sample) at the time of survey. Another 10 – 12 households were in the process of getting KCCs. This is quite high in comparison to other villages in Assam. During the 2002 (Kharif + Rabi), SBI Khutikutia branch distributed crop loans worth Rs. 5 lakh to its 37 KCC holders, while the Assam Cooperative Apex Bank (11 KCCs) and Lakhimi Gaonlia Bank (4 KCCs) together advanced Rs. 1.5 lakh to the farmers of Begenati. Only a few years back this village was in the bank's defaulter list. However, the situation has changed dramatically in recent times, with the active involvement of SBI staff (manager in particular) and the village FMC. All the 34 KCC holders with the SBI branch repaid their loan instalments in time for the year 2001. In the year 2002, quite a few KCC holders were approached by the bank officials to take much higher amount of loans (for power tillers, tractors, etc). The credibility of the KCC holders has increased considerably because of the bumper production which was made possible by increasing mechanization and more use of manures, HYV seeds, irrigation, etc through credit.

households not accepted the card for the time being), bankers' interview schedule expressed very low incidence of issuing KCC loans.

Needless to say that KCCs by increasing the reach of the institutional credit in rural areas can contribute significantly to the revival of rural economy. The important precaution that is to be adopted with utmost sincerity is, however, the compulsory supervision of the scheme by the village FMCs / PRIs so as to make the scheme more effective (as was the case in Begenati village*), and chances of misuse of the entitlement right by a few unscrupulous persons or poor persons can be discouraged. This will save the poor farmers from spending extravagantly during the local festivities and subsequently, falling into the debt trap, as was found true in some cases of IRDP loans.

Self Help Groups

Extending credit in small doses to the rural borrowers is not cost effective for the bank. High transaction costs (from both ends) on the one hand and low margin (because of political intervention) on the other left the millions of rural enterprises starved of funds. Consequently, up to March 2001, only about 2 crore rural customers (out of the 74 crore rural population) were provided with credit facilities from the banks. Nearly 95 per cent of these rural borrowers borrowed less than Rs. 25000 from the banks. This has necessitated a shift of strategy from priority sector lending to self-help groups to micro credit and now to micro-finance. In this regard NABARD is playing an important role in evolving the concept of 'relationship banks'. Improvements in the existing relationship between the poor and the banks are attempted with intermediation by the NGOs, who either play the role of promoters of SHGs or financial intermediaries. A special feature of the linkage model is that the banks also directly act as SHPIs (i.e., lend directly to SHGs which they help come up). The unique feature of the above development is that the intermediation of the NGOs and SHGs helped banks to reduce transaction cost of loan by an extent ranging between 21 per cent and 41 per cent. Equally encouraging fact is that the intermediation of NGOs and SHGs contributed in reducing the transaction cost of borrowers by about 85 per cent (in all these estimates, the cost of capacity building has not been taken into consideration). The recovery rates improved up to 95 per cent or more when there was intermediation by NGOs, as compared to the much higher default risk of 22 per cent in case of direct lending by banks (Jayaraman, 2001).

The report of the Expert Committee on Rural Credit (2001) mentioned that the flow of credit to the non-farm sector in the NE-India is not commensurate with the potential available. The weak banking infrastructure, poor recovery levels, scarcity of sound bankable proposals, uncertain political climate, poor transport and communications, etc were the main obstacles on the way to greater flow of credit into the region. The Report also highlighted the fact that financial institutions in rural India have so far concentrated on agriculture and related activities. They will have to be prepared to play a much larger role in the establishment and growth of rural non-farm activities (NABARD, 2001). 'The rural non-farm sector covers a wide spectrum of activities, including handlooms, handicrafts, cottage and village industries, agro-processing units, service and transport activities which contributes about 30 per cent of the total income of rural households'. With land resources being limited, agriculture will not be able to absorb the additional workforce of the country. Here lies the importance of non-farm sector, which also serves as the safety net for many rural households in times of natural calamities.

Of late, formation of a large number of SHGs across the country and subsequently lending through SHGs/MFIs has improved repayment culture and recycle of credit significantly in certain states (apart from the availability of credit to all sectors). In fact, since the movement started in India, a large number of employment avenues were created in the non-farm sector apart from the production of high value crops and improved inputs based production. So far the SHG movement has proved more successful in providing gainful self-employment to the rural poor women both in the farm and non-farm activities thereby lending a great help in reducing the intensity and volume of rural poverty*.

However, like KCCs, the performance of the entire NER in group formation has been slow. Once again, southern states particularly Andhra Pradesh, dominates in this field, as it was in the case of KCCs. The southern region of India accounted for 67 per cent of SHGs and 78 per cent of SHG credit. The poorer regions like NER, eastern and central regions accounted for only 0.2, 4.1 and 6.9 per cent of SHG credit by March 2001**.

---

*Collateral-free lending, timely delivery, flexibility in loan transactions, regular savings and continuous learning through training and group meetings etc are some of the features for which micro credit movement has been proved remarkably successful among the people including very poor people. In Andhra Pradesh, 60 per cent of the women members were engaged in vegetable and flower cultivation, food crops and pulses, oil seeds cultivation on leased land. Similarly women agricultural labourers preferred rearing of calves, dairy, value addition to milk and milk products. Nearly 20 per cent of the SHG members are artisans and engaged in making handicrafts and handloom products.(Ramalakshmi, C. S, 2003).

* *It has been pointed out that the large, influential and well-funded NGOs may not be able to concentrate resources in regions and sectors that are most important for national development. This is born out by the fact that out of 12136 organizations receiving foreign funding and reporting to the Home Ministry in 1996-97, there were 5721 organizations in South India, while the number was only 1779 in BIMARU region. As a result, service delivery is taking place in the already better-off region while the poorer states are left out. (Kulshrestha, L. R. and Gupta, A. 2002)

Till March 2002, banks in India financed 4.61 lakh SHGs. Of them, 90 per cent were SHGs comprising only women. The most encouraging feature was that timely repayment of loans consistently remained at over 95 per cent, although nearly 85 per cent of the SHG members were first time borrowers. The SHG movement in the NE states started only during the late 1998-99. The cumulative number of credit-linked SHGs was 1490 (725 in Assam) in NER by March 2002. More than 60 per cent were women SHGs. However, the situation has just started to show the sign of improvement with the growth of number of small NGOs and also, because of the special efforts made by the government, NABARD, SIRD, etc. By March 2003, around 5000 SHGs were credit-linked in Assam (as against all India figure of 7.17 lakh). NABARD had formulated a medium term strategy so as to cover one-third rural poor of Assam through credit linkage of about 48000 SHGs by March 2007. This is quite a reasonable target. It (NABARD) has to move very cautiously in the initial years in the sphere of facilitating credit-linkages, so that the in-built mechanism can easily identify/reach the interest groups, while the user groups (only those which were formed just to get a share in the government distribution) and opportunistic groups are screened out.

Field Observations

Among the 500 sample households, 93 households (male – 47 and female – 55) reported to have at least one SHG member in the family. Quite interestingly, 86 households (including 9 SHG households) reported to have at least one member to 'savings and credit' groups. Savings and credit groups existed in certain pockets of Assam since early 1970s. In a sample village (Malukhatal under Bezera Block in North Guwahati—Kamrup district), a few ST people reported that they were the members of the savings and credit groups with a regular break for 2-3 months after every 2-5 years since Indo-Pak war in 1971. All-male or all-female these savings and credit groups were formed with 15 – 35 members (model group was 25 – 30) for a fixed period of 2 –5 years (normally for 3 years). Their (regular) monthly contribution depends on the weaker members' capacity to contribute. However, there was a provision for the better-off members to save more in the name of their wards. Normally, a fixed part of their regular monthly savings is kept in the bank in the form of fixed deposit (only a few groups kept the entire amount in fixed deposit). The remaining part is being used for lending among the members at 2 – 5 per cent monthly rate of interest, while the non-member borrowers need to pay much higher rate of interest (5 – 10 %). The non-member borrowers can borrow from the savings and credit groups only if any group member gives assurance of recovery of the loan in time. Savings and credit groups are explained separately because unlike SHGs, these groups were temporary in nature in the state of Assam. These groups automatically become dysfunctional after every 2 – 5 years as they distribute the entire amount of their savings and interest income among the members at the end of the fixed terms. After a while, they form similar groups once again with the provision of joining in new members and omission/exit of old members. A couple of ST groups reported that on completion of their first term of group savings, they did celebrate the occasion feasting the village communities. Few non-ST women members reported to have spent the entire amount in ornaments. The above features were inimical to the groups' sound capital build-up.

It is a matter of concern that SHGs were mostly concentrated among the better off families (Table 6.2). Agricultural and non-agricultural labourers, artisans, petty traders/vendors, etc the poorest of the poor remains yet largely unrepresented in this new movement. Of the total SHG members of 102 in the sample, 66 (65%) belonged to the better off communities. The poorest of the poor or those who really need to come under SHG umbrella constituted merely 15 per cent. It is mainly because of the fact that they have no idea about the socio-economic benefits implicit in group movement. Since SHG movement in the state is only 4 years old, only 20 per cent of them were reported to exist for more than 2 years. About 40 per cent were less than 6 months old. Only 11 per cent of all the SHGs received revolving fund. Banks have extended credit to 8 groups only. The poor presence of NGOs (SHPIs) as financial intermediaries in the state is posing a problem in fostering relationship banking in this region. Nearly 40 per cent of the SHG members were either illiterate or LP drop-out. Except a few cases, these members were not ready to work as President/ Secretary of the groups. High rate of illiteracy mostly belonging to '40 plus' age group is posing a problem in terms of 'crisis of self-confidence', which also affects moral of other members of the groups. However, one positive thing is that 'below 40' age group constituted over 70 per cent of all SHG members, and most of them can be taught accounting part a bit.

It is observed that 18 SHG members (including 15 BPL households) were saving Rs 20 per month. The most familiar situation, however, was saving at the rate of Rs 10 per week or monthly contribution of Rs. 40. The monthly contribution of about 31 per cent SHG members could not be confirmed. In the absence of SHG members at the time of interview, either their family members expressed their ignorance or the SHG member himself/herself was in confusion, particularly where groups were newly formed. Few new group members expressed that their friends paid their monthly contribution and so they were unaware about the exact contribution. This is indicative of the lack of total involvement of the group members in the movement and the existence of some groups which were constituted by a few better off people only to squeeze advantages through SHGs (e.g., power tiller can be managed through SHGs with Rs. 50000 government subsidy).

Table 6. 2

Details of the (households) members of the SHGs and Savings and Credit (S&C) groups

Attributes	*SHGs*	*Savings & Credit groups*
No. of households with SHG/ S&C member	93	86
Break-up of the households according to their income status		
a) Extremely Poor (Annual income of less than Rs. 11000 per family)	3	1
b) BPL (Rs. 11000 – Rs. 22000)	12	11
c) Poor & Nearly Poor (Rs. 22001 – Rs.36000)	21	16
d) APL (Rs. 36001 – Rs. 75000)	45	33
e) Rich (Above Rs. 75000)	12	25
Duration of the Groups		
Less than one year	53	*Ceases to function after a fixed term
More than one year	33	
Unspecified	16	
No. of Groups received Revolving Fund	11(F-4)	-
No. of Groups with credit linkages to banks	8 (F-2)	-
No. of Groups with nil assistance as on March'03	82	86
No. of Group members (total)	102	117
Male	47	38
Female	55	79

(Contd.)

(Contd. Table 6.2)

Attributes	*SHGs*	*Savings & Credit groups*
Educational attainment of the members		
Illiterate	17	18
Up to V	24	17
VI – X	42	38
Matric – undergraduate	16	27
Graduate (+ technical)	3	17
Distribution according to the Age groups		
15 – 25	25	24
26 – 40	47	59
41 & above	30	34
Distribution according to their monthly contribution		
Up to Rs 20	18	12
21 – 50	44	38
51 – 100	8	17
101 & above	1	9
**Unknown	31	41

Note: 9 households reported both 'SHG and S&C group' members at the same point of time, so entered on both sides.** In the absence of the member at the time of survey, other family members failed to provide relevant information or the member himself/herself could not tell the exact amount.

It is important to note that among the sample households, 5 respondents reported that their groups broken down immediately after getting the revolving fund (manipulation of fund by a few members and poisoning of the piggery feed by unidentified persons, etc. were shown as the main reasons of failure). Another 14 people reported that their respective SHGs were abandoned mainly because of two reasons: (i) irregular monthly contribution by some members and, (ii) even after 8 – 10 months of their existence they did not get any (big) subsidy-cum-loan scheme from the government.

It is a matter of concern that SHPIs (Self-help Promoting Institutions) were missing in large number of villages in Assam till date. In Kamrup district, only in 2 villages (out of 4 sample villages) under the Kamalpur and Bezera blocks, Block officials were found willy-nilly engaged in the promotion of only women-SHGs. Panchayat officials were not visibly involved in the process/promotional activities.

In Nagaon district, a couple of FMCs were found involved in group formation but was not ready to act as financial or non-financial intermediaries (one each in Nagaon and Hojai sub-divisions). The FMC of Begenati village (nearby Nagaon) was found actively involved in the selection of farmers for the issue of KCCs and (to some extent) timely recovery of the loan extended against the Cards.

In Tinsukia district, in a sample village (Ulup, under Margherita Development Block) one FMC worker (district level NGO) was involved in group formation and also on few cases motivated farmers to apply for KCCs. Interestingly, among the ex-tea communities, father of a Don Bosco school was seen advocating formation of groups particularly among the women. Income and education wise these people were lagging far behind in the state of Assam. Quite a few SHGs have come up during the last 2 years only because of the Father's spiritual influence in the society. These groups are yet to get revolving fund or critical credit component. But almost all the groups were running well (leaving their traditional low paid jobs like plucking of tea leaves or working as casual labourers and leased land by women SHGs to grow more remunerative ginger, turmeric, etc besides poultry) thereby reduced their dependence on usurious moneylenders and incidence of land mortgages significantly.

In South Karimganj Block, NAVARUN – a local NGO and ready to perform as financial intermediary between bank and groups formed under it – was seen receiving necessary training from NABARD for facilitating the necessary infrastructure for 'relationship banking'. Almost similar job (in a much smaller scale) was also performed by Pragati Self-help Group of SriDurgapur village but only under the supervision and guidance of SIRD. No such arrangement was found in the sample villages in North Karimganj block.

One good thing is that, of late, at least some local (small) NGOs are coming up in certain areas, which is an essential condition for the success of micro finance programme. Almost 50 per cent villages recorded the presence of NGO workers/ FMCs. However, a good percentage of existing NGOs were not honest to their task. Rather, it has become a lucrative platform for a few people to earn money, social status and fulfil their narrow political interest. All these local NGOs lack professional skills (expertise) to extend 'support services' to the SHGs.

As already mentioned, in Kamrup district (Dwigunpar under Kamalpur block and Malukhatal), a large number of women savings and credit groups were formed*. They used to extend small loans to the members at 2 to 5 per cent monthly rate of interest for contingent needs and also to assist household industries (weaving, handicrafts, knitting, agro service centers, poultry, piggery, etc) among the group members. Sometimes, such groups jointly make arrangements for the display of their products at/nearby important public gatherings, festival venues, etc. Many of these groups used to provide loans to outsiders but only at higher rate of interest, sometimes at 5—10 per cent monthly rate of interest. At the end of the year, each member earns Rs. 500 to 1000 (plus around Rs. 1000 from household industries) in the form of interest income on their own savings as well as income from the micro lending. The involvement of

---

*Also, in Bandarkuna Gram Panchayat under the South Karimganj Block, under NAVARUN as many as 156 SHGs each comprising of 10 members were formed between 1999 and December-end 2002 (18 such groups were included in the sample – Eraligul village). In sharp contrast to Kamrup district, all these were male SHGs mostly belonging to the minority community. Of them, 30 groups had already established credit linkages to banks. Another 45-50 SHGs were in the process of getting either revolving fund or bank credit with NAVARUN's intermediation. Three SHGs got dairy project (golden cow scheme) worth Rs. 2.50 lakh each with 50 per cent subsidy from UBI, Patherkandi branch. The rate of interest it carried was 14.5 per cent (including NGOs and SHGs' supervision charge of 1 % each). The rate of interest was on the higher side (if 'high subsidy' part is ignored) compared to the rates allowed on group deposits but on the lower side compared to the Grameen Bank of Bangladesh, next to its doorsteps. The rest 27 SHGs with linkages to bank credit got Rs. 25000-50000 (where subsidy amount was Rs. 10000 – 20000 respectively) for projects like poultry, goat rearing, fishery (fish let), agro service center, banana and ginger farming, petty trade, etc. Quite a few groups were doing business quite sincerely and creditably – either jointly or singly. Quite a few groups have raised their monthly contribution after receiving revolving fund. Moreover, under the IRDP schemes, projects were allotted to the BPL families by the government agencies. This undesirable situation has changed considerably with the formation of SHGs in recent times, where group members submits loan proposals (in consultation with NGOs, wherever possible) according to their aptitude, skill and market potentialities.

the NGOs having linkages to the SIRD / NABARD's 'research, training and promotional programmes directed to SHGs', may extend the necessary infrastructure to these women groups to expand their activities and give their present part time occupation a permanent shape. Already quite a few SHG Marketing Complexes were established in important places across the states with the active participation from NGOs, SHG-members and government, etc. Of late, SIRD, NEDFi, etc. were seen making special efforts to display the products of SHGs by organizing trade fairs, etc.

Also, in the sample villages, not a single SHG or KCC holder reported to have paid any speed money either to government officials or to banks for getting their loans sanctioned. This is no mean achievement.

Areas of concern

- Almost all FMC Secretary/President's wives formed SHGs, although they sometimes possessed above 50 bighas of land. In the sample ST villages like Mosoka, a Dimasa village nearby Lanka town, and two Bodo villages in Kamrup district, all SHG members were women.

- Another area of concern is that a large number of SHGs were controlled by one or two members, either by secretary or president or both, for their personal benefit. A couple of SHG members (each of them having above 3 hectares of irrigated land) took power tillers for personal use by depositing Rs.35,000 each to the bank against their respective SHG accounts (Rs.50,000 subsidy per power tiller). In the case of 3 SHGs (Nagaon district), their earlier secretary or president or both swallowed the entire amount of the government subsidy/ revolving fund (Rs.10,000 each) and then quit the group to form a new one. In the absence of NGOs, which is not yet widespread in Assam, Panchayats/FMCs must have to play a role in timely detection of such an erring person and be appropriately punished by imposing penalty or social boycott.

- At the time of interview, many SHG members could not remember the exact amount of their savings, rate of interest in case of bank credit linkages, exact number of members in the group, and above all, the name of the SHG he or she belongs to. This frustrating scenario was at least partially due to the target-oriented approach of the different government agencies, which has undermined the actual purpose of forming SHGs among the landless labourers and other asset-poor people. The different change agents cannot ignore the fact that SHGs are much more than just financial mechanisms for extending micro credit to the poor for micro enterprises. Governments and NABARD's enthusiasm (target oriented approach) to promote and support a large number of SHGs always run the risk of transforming these groups into 'state-helped groups', thereby ruining their very foundation of self-help and autonomy of grassroots democratic organizations.

- 'Micro financing' has become the prime business of a few SHGs — a new class of moneylenders belonging to the not-so-poor communities. These groups charge 2 – 5 per cent monthly rate of interest on any advances to the members and sometimes, as high as 5 – 10 per cent (monthly interest) from the borrowers who are not members of the group. Such a high rate of interest from the members and co-villagers can not be justified as one important objective of organizing the poor into small thrift and credit groups was to make the credit readily available to them and at reasonable rate of interest as well. The use of revolving fund as well as common fund of the group should be facilitated in such a way that it keeps all the group members away from raising usurious loans from moneylenders, which often ends in alienation of land from the smallholders.

- Many banks were not cooperating with the new/potential SHGs, lest it should increase their volume of works. Shortages of staff were their main concern, sometimes genuine. Restructuring of the banking staff (between urban and rural branches) may be the short-term solution to the problem. Quite a few bankers in the sample districts were found awfully apprehensive of loan recovery. A few prospective borrowers among the SHG members were 'IRDP' defaulters, which allowed the reluctant bankers to justify their cause of indifference.

- It is observed that bank managers are transferred frequently, particularly in rural branches. In fact, no manager seems to be mentally prepared to work in rural branches. They often try to somehow manage their short stay in rural branches from the nearest or sometimes far-flung urban areas. One bank manager sanctions a loan and then, after some time, gets transferred to another place. It becomes very difficult for the new managers to establish individual contact with all the loanees in short time, being pre-occupied with lots of work and crippled by shortages of staff and procedural inefficiencies. Shortages of staff, non cooperation from the local administration in any recovery drives and exaggerated stories of 'arms threat' from a section of loanees, are the main excuses for many manager who performs badly in the sphere of debt- recovery.

- Frequent shifting of rural branches of nationalized banks (sometimes to liquidate the loss making rural branches) to the nearest urban centres on security ground (threat posed by the ultras to its working capital) have affected the banking habits of the villagers. This has badly affected the growth of SHGs in the interior villages, women SHGs in particular, who have to depend mostly on the male members for depositing their monthly group savings in banks. Sanction of loans in time also gets delayed where banks are located in 10-20 km distance and where all-weather road linkage is missing. Looking into the ground level realities and the high cost of extending banking services in the underdeveloped areas, the FMCs/ Panchayats/women organizations/teachers associations and even religious institutions (e.g., *Namghar* / Cristian father / *Maulabi*) may be considered as financial intermediaries (or at least non-financial intermediaries) between the banks and the needy villagers in remote areas of Assam in particular, and sparsely populated entire North East India in general.

There is no denying the fact that under privileged people working in a group are now gradually gaining confidence that they can save some amount even from their meager income and that they can also procure a loan if their group savings fall short of the requirement to launch any productive ventures. This is no mean achievement. Moreover, seeing the high success rate in repayment against micro credit, a few banks are now developing interest in lending to SHGs (and KCCs to SHG members) even if these were formed by the downtrodden. This will go a long way in ameliorating the plight of the rural poor, so long as NGOs, FMCs, Panchayats and banks work in tandem.

References

1. Jayaraman, B. (2001), 'Micro-Finance Retrospect and Prospects', Occasional Paper – 20, NABARD, Mumbai.
2. Joshi, D P, (2003). 'Managing the Finance to Meet the Goals' Yojana, January, Vol. 47.
3. Kulshrestha, L. R. and Gupta, A. (2002), 'NGOs in Micro Financing' Kurukshetra, February.

4. NABARD, (2001), 'Expert Committee on Rural Credit', Mumbai.
5. NEDFi, (2003), 'NEDFi Data Bank Quarterly', Vol. 2, Issue 1, January 2003. Guwahati.
6. Ramalakshmi, C. S (2003), 'Empowerment Through SHGs', EPW, March 22 – 29.
7. The Assam Tribune, July 7, 2003.
8. Vatta, K (2003), 'Micro finance & Poverty Alleviation', EPW, Feb 1.

7

Poverty-free Assam Through Micro Credit: Vision 2020

This chapter was incorporated after the submission of the Report. Some of the facts in this chapter may be repeated, from the earlier discussion. The importance of the chapter lies in the fact that here an attempt has been made to project the minimum credit requirements of the poor which can effectively contribute in any exercise towards eradication of poverty from the rural Assam.

Assam's Overall Economic Performance

As per Centre for Policy Alternative's recent report, 'Assam experienced growth rate of only 2.46 per cent annually during the last decade as against 4.46 per cent for NER and 5.98 per cent for India. The credit-deposit ratio was merely 28.95 per cent in the state as compared to the national average of 59.37 per cent as on March 31, 2003. All India Financial Institutions and Investment Companies are operating in the state, but there presence can be felt least in the region. Consequently, centre's special economic packages could generate only a little response in the economy.

Till recently, merely 2208 habitations out of the eligible 13144 habitations in the state have been connected under the schemes like PMGSY. Nearly 60 per cent villages still lack all-weather connectivity. Most of the villages remain cut off from all marketing linkages during the long monsoon period of 4 to 6 months.

The Planning Commission's latest estimate shows that the incidence of poverty was very high in Assam, particularly in rural areas. Poverty estimates for the state of Assam in 1999-2000, on the basis of consumption expenditure data collected by NSSO (55th Round), indicate that 40.04 per cent of rural population (over all – 36.09 %) was living under the poverty line. The corresponding national figures were 27.09 and 26.10 respectively. In absolute terms, nearly 10 million people constituting 3.63 per cent of the poor Indians were living in Assam. The open unemployment in Assam accounted for 2 millions of which nearly 70 per cent were educated unemployed youths. Another 3 millions of the total work force were disguised unemployed, primarily engaged in the agricultural sector.

Providing employment to such a huge army of unemployed is a herculean task for the government. The possibility of absorbing a sizeable proportion of unemployed in different government departments/defence sector is remote, because of the contractionist policy of the government around the globe. Traditional agriculture cannot offer any additional (gainful) employment. The options left to the unemployed are in the modernization of the agricultural sector (diversification, mechanization, intensive use of the small holdings) and exploiting the untapped self-employment opportunities in the non-farm sectors including services (transport, health, education, etc). One important solution to the above dismal picture surely lies in fostering SHGs among the disadvantaged people and involving NGOs (through a systematic institutional encouragement to them) in guidance and support services (viz.

finance management, enterprise development, packaging and pricing of products in consultation with expert teams studded with industrialists/industry managers) to the SHGs. The government role should be restricted simply to a facilitator.

The current economic growth rate in the state is unsatisfactory. Population growth rate is still high. Moreover, there is a persistent threat of occasional spurts in infiltration of poverty ridden people from the neighbouring countries. Insurgencies are at large. Under such conditions, reduction of poverty in the state to half by next 10 years and below 10 per cent level by 2020 warrants an all out efforts from all sections of the society in the areas of capacity building among the poor / in backward areas.

Micro Finance

Micro finance comprises micro credit as well as savings products, pensions, payment services, housing loans, insurance, emergency and other private loans, etc. to poor and low income people and / or the enterprises they own. To bridge the wide gap between demand and supply of funds in the lower rungs of the rural economy, the formal sector took the initiative to develop a supplementary credit delivery mechanism by encouraging institutional arrangements outside the financial system. The above credit products can not be provided cost effectively by the banking system in isolation, in absence of NGOs / SHGs' cooperation and support. At the all India level, 80 per cent (even higher at 86% till March 2002 – Table 7.2) of the total SHGs with linkages to banks received credit with NGOs' intermediation — financial or non-financial (Table 7.1). In Assam, merely 6 per cent of the total SHGs got credit from banks till March 2003. The role of NGOs in fostering SHG-bank linkages is still very much wanting in the state. The present dismal scenario of Assam can be changed substantially within a time bound period by facilitating the growth of competent NGOs and empowering the other agents of change in the society.

The conference of CEOs of Zila Parishads, BDOs and DRDA Project Directors, held at the Assam Administrative Staff College (Ist week of September, 2003) made an assessment of the SHGs, especially the factors retarding their growth. Lack of access to skill training, absence of market facilities, infrastructural bottlenecks, etc were cited as the problem areas

Table 7.1

SHG – Bank Linkage Patterns — All-India (March 2003)

	No. of SHGs	*% share*
Model – 1: SHGs formed and financed by banks-	142667	20
Model –11 : SHGs formed by NGOs & directly financed by Banks-	513005	72
Model –111: SHGs financed by banks through NGOs (on-lending)-	61688	8

Cumulative as on March 31, 2003.

Source: Progress of SHG-Bank Linkage in India: 2002-03, NABARD, Mumbai, 2003.

Table 7.2

SHG – Bank Linkage Patterns — All-India (March 2002)

Model – 1 SHGs formed and financed by banks	–14 % SHGs
Model – 11 : SHGs formed by NGOs & directly financed by Banks	– 70 % SHGs
Model – 111: SHGs financed by banks through NGOs (on-lending)	– 16 % SHGs.

Source : Financing Agriculture- Inhouse Journal of Agricultural Finance corporation Ltd., April – June 2002.

for the SHGs. It was also discussed with a note of concern that except those in Sonitpur district, none of the SHGs have received any sort of support from any NGO·

Micro Credit in Assam

Individually poor households are considered as unbankable. However, in groups, poor households' credibility increases substantially to 'economically viable level'. In Assam, during the last 6 years or so (since 1999) nearly 1 lakh SHGs have been formed which covered roughly 60 lakh population. The state accommodates above 129 lakh population living at the subsistence level (including 'nearly poor' population). Moreover, above one-half of the total SHGs were formed by the better off population and these groups constituted at least two-thirds of the state's SHG-bank linkages.

It seems that a mere 1/6th to 1/5th of the downtrodden in the state have come under group movement, which is a pre-requisite for the success of micro finance business and subsequently, eradication of poverty. The future task is very big. Still about 10 million people are needed to be motivated to pursue certain group activities for their socio-economic development. This demands, among others, large scale participation of PRIs and NGOs for capacity building particularly in rural areas.

The growth in SHGs linked to banks in the NE-region was very low till the end of 2002. However, during 2003-04, SHG-bank linkages recorded an impressive 200 per cent growth over the previous year as against the national average of 50 per cent. Till March'04, in Assam, nearly 11000 SHGs got bank loans worth Rs. 16.86 crores.

NABARD had formulated a medium term strategy so as to cover one-third rural poor of Assam through credit linkage of about 48000 SHGs by March 2007. This is quite a reasonable target. It (NABARD) has to move very cautiously in the initial years in the sphere of facilitating credit-linkages, so that the in-built mechanism can easily identify/reach the target (interest) groups, while the opportunistic groups are screened out.

An all out effort is warranted from PRIs, NGOs and other catalyst agencies to change the dismal scenario in the state. When the state is reeling under poverty, unemployment and insurgencies, the poor involvement of banks in the rural market is a serious matter of concern. However, it is the responsibility of the catalyst agencies not to allow empowerment drive at the grassroots level goes waste like all other development drives of the past years by laying utmost priorities on capacity building of the SHG members, so that loan money can be circulated among an increasingly large number of SHGs. Most unfortunately, state's credit scenario is not yet as good as in the many other Indian states, even in the case of SHG and KCC loans.

Table 7.3
Performance of micro credit—1992-2004

Country / state	*SHG-bank linkage (cumulative progress)*	*Bank loan (crore)*	*Average loan per SHG (Rs.)*
All-India	10,79,091	3904.2	Rs. 3618
	6,11,043	2124.24 (Refinanced disbursed)	Rs. 3476
Assam	10706	16.85	Rs. 15747

Keeping in mind the fact that too small a loan can not generate sufficient income for a poor people to place him above the poverty line and also, fails to raise his repayment capacity, the total requirements of financial resources to allow access to

Table 7.4

Projected population, BPL population, SHGs and Micro Finance in Assam.

Current Population (2005): **2.86 crore** (by simple aggregative method)	**Poor population** (30%) – 85.8 lakh. Nearly poor (15%) – 42.9 lakh. **Total ----------------------128.7 lakh** Or, 26 lakh poor households (Av. Size of the family = 5)
Projected population (2020): **3.75 crore**	**Poor population** (10 %) – 37.5 Nearly poor (10 %) – 37.5 **Total ------------------------ 75 lakh** Or, 15 lakh poor households.
1. Cumulative Micro credit requirements (including refinanced by 2020) : • 2004 -- 10706 SHGs – 16.86 crore • 2007 – 48000 SHGs -- 96.00 crore (@ Rs. 20000 per group). • 2010—80000 SHGs – 160 crore • 2013 – 110000 SHGs- 220 crore • 2017 – 150000 SHGs – 300 crore • Refinanced disbursal -- 300 crore • Total cumulative MC requirements by 2017/2020: (300 + 300) = **600 crore**.	• Alternative estimate for micro credit (MC) needs of the State (when access to the institutional credit for the poor is total): Total poor hhs: 26 lakh. MC requirements: (@ Rs. 5000 per hh): Rs. 1300 crore. (@ Rs. 10000 per hh): Rs. **2600 crore**.

(Contd.)

(Contd. Table 7.4)

2. Capacity building (assistance in group formation and recovery and delivery system); skill development: **Rs. 130 crores** (5 % of the loan amount, alternative estimate).
3. Connectivity: *Around 14000 villages need connectivity/better roads : (a) **Rs. 7000 crores** (@ 50 lakh per village), and (b) Infrastructure for living with floods : Rs. **7000 crores.**
4. Integrated resource management and Marketing linkages : Warehousing, cold storage, linkage to processing unit, better market information network : **Rs. 260 crores** (10% of the loan amount)
5. Housing loans/assistance: **Rs. 400 crores** (33 % of the poor households @ Rs. 5000).

livelihood finance (at the current price index) to all the needy households in Assam are estimated below:

Role of NGOs and Panchayats

SHGs/NGOs constituted institutional arrangement outside formal financial system to make small credit workable. Micro credit cannot by itself eradicate poverty or assist in faster economic growth. 'Other financial and business services' must complement micro credits so as to make it work. Establishing connectivity/marketing linkages, proper identification of livelihood opportunities, upgradation of managerial and business skills and technical training of the poor, etc. are equally important issues which need to be looked into to foster microcredit as a strategy of poverty alleviation and development. The whole exercise may require an investment of Rs. 25000 – 30000 crores by 2020.

The impact assessment studies of micro-finance in India (MYRADA – NGO based in Bangalore; SHARE – NGO based in Hyderabad and BASIX – Non-Banking Financial Company based in Andhra Pradesh) reported substantial reduction (38 % — 50%) of poverty among the SHG members. Other positive changes noted were improved self-confidence of the members, decision making in family affairs by women, decline in domestic violence (reported by 37 %) and alcohol consumption.

In an important assessment study carried out at Basix six years after inception, it was reported that 'only 52 per cent of our three-year plus micro credit customers reported an increase in income, 23 per cent reported no change while another 25 per cent actually reported a decline'. The reasons behind the poor performance were identified as follows:

- un-managed risk
- low productivity in crop cultivation and livestock rearing, and

inability to get good prices from the input and output markets.

"Based on this study, Basix revised its strategy and now offers microcredit along with a whole suite of insurance products covering life, health, crop and livestock. For enhancing productivity, a whole range of agricultural and business development services are being offered to borrowers. For ensuring better prices, alternate market linkages are being facilitated both on the input and output side. Producers are encouraged to form groups and cooperatives, which are then given institutional development services to become more effective". Institutional development services covered : formation and strengthening of various producer organizations such as self-help groups, water users' associations, forest protection committees, credit and commodity cooperatives, panchayats, etc. (EPW, October 8, 2005).

It seems that the concept micro finance covers a wide range of services. In absence of any of these services by the NGOs/Panchayats, this relatively more effective poverty alleviation movement originated among the downtrodden may fail. This is more important in case of Assam where a large number of SHGs has come up under the government's effort only by luring them with revolving fund and easy loan facilities.

Recent studies by CGAP show that only about a 100 of the 10000 odd microfinance institutions round the world are financially self-sufficient. This indicates that the general belief that micro credit can adequately serve the poor and in an economically viable manner is not well-grounded (at least in the initial years).

According to NABARD data, by the end of the 1990s, about 800 NGOs were participating in its SHG-bank linkage programme. As regards emergence of NGOs as financial intermediaries (on-lending) or non-financial intermediaries (promoters of SHGs), the trend is positive.

A study of 16 NGOs in Karnataka concluded that there is a mismatch between objectives and activities of these NGOs and the situation and needs of the poor with whom they work, but influenced by donor's priorities and policies (Rajasekhar 1998).

In Assam, only a few NGOs are working in this area. Most of them suffer from weak institutional capacities. Moreover, only a few NGOs are working with the poorest of the poor. Consequently, ex-tea communities and Muslim women (in the Barak valley) remained largely uncovered by the current movement (Gautam Purkayastha, 2005).

Future Course of Action

- Attitude of the bankers needs to be changed on urgent basis. NGOs and PRIs' intermediation, pressure from other catalytic agencies, etc can help a lot in this regard.

- Culture of repayment needs to be improved. In author's one recent study it was found that as high as 48 per cent of the institutional loans accumulated as overdues. Even in the case of bank loans to SHGs, the performance was found lower (<70 %) than the national average of above 90 per cent.

- Rate of interest charged by many SHGs from the members (2% — 5% monthly) and non-members (3% -to sometimes as high as- 10%) was found quite high. Presently, many SHGs formed by the well-off members are engaged in usurious money lending business.

- Formation of the adequate number of NGOs in each district must receive due attention of the social institutions/ higher educational institutions and also, of the policy makers (government). Provision of the meaningful training for capacity building of the NGOs, women organizations, Panchayats, etc must receive utmost importance. In Assam, women organizations have a very large network which can be transformed into an effective and the largest NGO in the state by providing adequate amount of incentive, encouragement and training.

- It is estimated that if the Panchayats in Assam — with the help of women organizations and NGOs — take up the responsibility to motivate at least 1 million poor a year to form groups for better utilization of their resources, only then, by 2017/2020, the problem of mass poverty can be addressed appropriately.

- Commercial banks including RRBs, cooperative banks (which is presently in bad shape), NEDFi, SIRD, etc must go ahead with a lot of determination to make profit from lending to the poor. This demands putting considerable amount of energy for micro credit planning so that both ends gain and goals are achieved.

- Initially villages with better connectivity must be provided with micro credit services in adequate amount and only after improving basic infrastructures other villages should be brought under total coverage.

- SHGs and financial institutions must give priority to insurance of loan assets. This is very important as Concurrent Evaluation Study (July1995-June 1996) revealed that in Assam, 52 per cent IRDP beneficiaries were affected by natural calamities against all India average of 10 per cent.

8

Summary and Policy Implications

Summary of the Main Findings

Of the 500 sample households, 43 per cent were indebted (any household who had taken cash loan + kind loan + current liabilities of above Rs. 100 during the current year and /or earlier, and a part or the full amount of which remained unpaid at the time of interrogation was considered as indebted household). Remote villages reported much lower debt incidence (35.2 %) and lower volume of debt as compared to the villages located near urban centres (50.8%). Incidence of debt was recorded higher among the landed households and group of households represented by higher income and asset value groups, as compared to their asset-poor and income-poor counterparts. However, in terms of debt-income ratio and debt-asset ratio, income-poor and asset-poor households were found heavily burdened with debt repayment obligation, compared to their affluent counterparts.

Bank alone constituted above one-third of all loan incidence. All other institutional agencies were seen fast disappearing from the rural credit scenario. Informal sources constituted three-fifths of all loan incidence.

Extent of debt was found higher among the non-agricultural households than that of the agricultural households. This new trend appeared partly because of the sizeable amount of housing loans registered by the non-agricultural households, particularly by the salaried people.

It was an interesting finding that among the social groups, the incidence of poverty was highest (56.45%) among the SC households, while debt-incidence was the lowest(33.9%). The incidence of poverty was less pronounced among ST households (37.50%) and 'non-ST and non-SC' other households (41.0%). However, relatively much higher incidence of debt was recorded among these people (ST – 43.3% and general – 44.6%). This may help dispel wrong notions about the caste-class and debt-caste linkages in our society.

The volume of debt per household (Rs. 5416) and per indebted household (Rs. 12596) registered a substantial increase in recent times, even if we take into consideration the increase in price level and much higher incidence of debt.

Current Year Borrowings: Very interestingly, institutional loans constituted as high as 73.7 per cent in the total current year borrowings. Even more encouraging fact for the state was that KCCs constituted more than one-third of all institutional loans. Informal sources (including SHGs and village welfare societies) constituted slightly higher than one-quarter of the total loans. The most worrying feature was, however, the very high share of personal loans incurred by the well-to-do for consumer durables including house building which constituted 60 per cent of the total institutional loans during the current year. The other areas of concern were (i) not a single PMRY loan was reported in the current year, (ii) not a single loan was reported from cooperative banks, (iii) no loan was registered at 10 per cent or below interest rate, and (iv) the SGSY and SHG-bank linkages constituted merely 6.30 per cent of the total institutional loan. It appears that institutional loans are getting dry for the weaker section of the society. The composition of the current year borrowings confirms that banks have moved away from the productive sectors lending, which may act as a major stumbling block in healthy capital formation in rural areas in the near future.

Interest free loans constituted merely 5.48 per cent in total debt, although this group accounted for 19 per cent of all debt-incidence. The sharp fall in the share of interest free loans in Assam might have been resulted (at least partially) by the growth of SHGs in certain pockets where 'friends and relatives' participated in large numbers. A few SHGs were seen acting as MFIs which was responsible for higher percentage share of 'with interest' loans and drying up of the interest-free sources.

Above one-third of the indebted households were found shouldering either high interest burden or had to mortgage-out a piece of arable land.

In spite of the government's initiative to lower the interest burden, the rates of interest carried by the KCC loans (11 – 12 %), PMRY loans (14 %) and SHG loans (14.5 %, including 1% each charged by NGOs and SHGs for loan administration) were found quite high particularly when compared with the housing loans taken by the salaried persons. It appears that the interest burden of both institutional and non-institutional loans has increased considerably in the state in recent years.

A little less than one-fifth of the total incidence of loan was incurred for food consumption. In all, 50.97 per cent of the total incidence of loan were incurred for different purposes under household expenditure group.

The institutional sources constituted less than two-fifths of all loan incidence, but their share in outstanding debt was estimated at 66.73 per cent. Of the total bank loans, 64 per cent were extended against different government sponsored schemes, while 36 per cent were personal loans for house building and consumer durables.

A lion's share of the total debt was incurred against personal security. Collateral security was found less frequent (only because of its unavailability) even among the institutional loans. There was a good beginning of the savings backed credit business, which seems to be the best type of security from both ends. However, this category of loan has not yet constituted a substantial amount. In fact, in Assam, this culture has not developed in many villages yet. Thus, too much emphasis in this respect may also cause more unequal distribution of loans across the different economic classes, at least in the initial years. In some areas, 'mortgage of land' was found the only security against which moneylenders extended loans which raises questions about the effectiveness of the government developmental schemes in removing this social menace.

Of the total 16 sample villages, only in 4 villages moneylenders were found ineffective, or at best, their presence was very thin. In 8 remote villages, institutional loans constituted less than 44 per cent of the total debt, while the share of moneylenders was above 52 per cent. Friends and relatives constituted 2.55 per cent, while the rest credit agencies were insignificant. In sharp contrast, in 8 villages located near urban centres, nearly 77 per cent of all borrowings were made from institutional agencies, while the share of moneylenders was 10.42 per cent.

It is a matter of concern that above 80 per cent of the institutional loans were extended among the villages located near urban centre, while the corresponding share for the remote villages was hardly 20 per cent. Even in advantageous villages, the increasing tendency of the banks to extend credit for house building or consumer durables, may further dry up the critical 'productive component of loans' required by the weaker sections of the society in near future.

It is significant to note that landed households have greater access to institutional sources, whereas the landless labour households were more exposed to double exploitation as they take loans from shop-keepers and other informal sources (also found true in author's two earlier studies — 1997 and 2004). However, the gap between landless and landed households in the spheres of access to institutional sources has narrowed down with the faster growth of the non-farm sector and the formation of the self help groups in recent times.

Very interestingly, moneylenders and banks contributed moderate to high amount of loans to all income groups. This reflects the fact that institutional agencies are successful to reach out more or less to all the economic classes, although they are still lagging in making the credit evenly available, in time and in adequate amount.

Institutional loans constituted two-thirds of the total loan outstanding. However, nearly 40 per cent of such loans were accumulated as bad loans sanctioned against government sponsored schemes before 1997 and since then not a single instalment was repaid. The presence of such a large share of 'dead loans' had its negative effects on the rural economy in the region. It also gives wrong signal about the composition of the rural credit which needs immediate attention of the policy makers.

In Assam, more than 50 per cent of the villages remain cut off from almost all the marketing linkages at least for 4 – 5 months in a year, either due to floods or absence of useable approach road. This is one of the important reasons for which many economically weak beneficiary households have failed to honour their loan obligation, in spite of their sincerity and hard work. The final concurrent evaluation study on IRDP (July 1995 – June 1996) revealed that in Assam 52 per cent IRDP beneficiaries were affected by natural calamities against all India average of 10 per cent. The incidence of flood damage to the loan assets was the highest in Assam, compared to the rest of India. This was an important concern for which banks were very apprehensive about sanctioning loans to flood affected villages and its recovery simultaneously (Government of India, 1996).

During the first Parliamentary election of the new millennium, debt relief was in the election agenda in many states such as UP, Maharashtra, Andhra Pradesh, etc. No loan waiver declaration (promise) should be made by the government. In this respect our past experience is not good. One important option which deserves immediate attention is the better insurance coverage of the loan assets. This is particularly important for a state like Assam where flood is a regular feature.

For the flood affected poor people, those who are already in debt-trap, and where decade-old institutional loans were accumulating with every passing year, government should think of a quick solution with due weight to the fact that these people should not miss the access to institutional credit in near future. The government may assign NGOs / FMCs / PRIs (with adequate financial support) to assist in the recovery drive wherever possible and the rest amount may be waived but only through NGOs active involvement.

There is no denying the fact that 'dead loan' component which stems from poverty (/natural calamities led poverty of the loanees) needs write off by the banks or waived by the government. However, any public declaration in this regard (keeping an eye on the vote bank) may further accentuate the problem in near future. Thus, in the case of loan waiver, utmost caution needs to be adopted so that no wilful defaulters (even in disguise) got the space for free ride. The negative impact of loan waiver scheme will be felt much less in this case, while the genuine defaulters would feel much relieved if the entire process of debt waiver is implemented in a judicious (professional) way through NGOs.

The strategy may be adopted as follows: (i) Government may provide adequate funds to a few reputed NGOs (/FMCs on area basis). NGOs will first try to motivate the defaulter households to repay their loan obligation. This will give them better idea about the socio-economic compulsions (strong and weak points) of the loanees. (ii) NGOs will be in a much better position to screen out genuine defaulters from the list which also included many wilful defaulters. Wilful defaulters must be persisted with repayment of their dues – both principal and interest accrued. (iii) Genuine defaulters may be given second time loans through NGOs participation, for their economic uplift and may be insisted on clearing their past dues in easy instalments simultaneously. (iv) For those defaulter households who were not in a position to repay loans immediately even after allowing them second time loans (because their main or only earning member was sick or physically challenged, or where agricultural land has already transformed into a barren land due to heavy silt deposit), NGOs may facilitate the liquidation of old loans with government's full financial support, but only through the hands of the loanees (all borrowers should feel that bank loans must be paid at any cost). (v) Supervision of NGOs in credit delivery and recovery will improve. This may help both the borrowers and lenders by developing relationship banking, and (vi) Few SHGs/FMCs may be invited on experimental basis to perform the above functions. A fixed percentage of the total recovery amount may be given to the concerned agencies (NGOs/FMCs/SHGs) to meet their operational costs plus minimum incentives for their specialized work.

At the aggregate level, overdues as percentage of total outstanding debt constituted 29 per cent. Apparently, it looks surprising that productive purposes of loans accounted for high amount of overdues (47.74%), while the unproductive purposes together recorded merely 2.65 per cent of the respective total as overdues. Productive component of loan constituted a sizeable amount of directed loans from banks where default rate was found extremely high across the income groups, while unproductive loans were either personal loans from banks with the provision of payment of monthly loan instalment directly from the salary account of the borrowers or, taken for long term purpose from moneylenders against mortgage of land.

It is seen that among the bottom two asset holding groups, the overall level of overdues was much higher (60.74 % and 59.43 % respectively) than that of the highest two asset holding groups (12.74 % and 11.08 % respectively). However, the third highest asset holding group (also the second highest income group) with very high percentage share of productive loans of above 91 per cent had reported nearly 58 per cent of the total outstanding debt as overdues. It seems that the size of overdues against different purposes of loans depend more on habitual factors of the borrowers and less on the strengths of asset holding or income flow. Only in the case of a small section fall in the 'marginalised class', accumulating overdues stem from (extreme) poverty, flood ravages or recurrent floods led uncertainties about the continuity of the current economic activities and, above all, the absence of vital infrastructural linkages which turns the incremental income resulted in by the loan assets often insufficient to repay the loan after meeting the deficits in the family budget.

On the one hand, interest free sources and bank's concessional loans have dried up to a considerable extent. On the other, moneylenders and SHGs constituted a considerable amount of high interest loans. Even banks have extended credit in recent times at 12.5 per cent to 16 per cent rate of interest other than KCC loans. (In the late 2002, i.e., just a couple of months before the investigation, commercial banks have extended a direct loan for productive purpose at 16 per cent rate of interest. The bank also provided loans even at higher rate of interest of 18 per cent in the late 1998, a substantial amount of which remained as overdue). In addition, high proportion of loan was borrowed against mortgage of land which contains high hidden interest. It appears that during the liberalization of the economy, rural borrowings have become dearer and scarce for the underprivileged.

On the one hand, the traditional village institutions which had supported the weaker sections of the society in distress have been disappearing. On the other, those we had created in the post-independence era (credit, markets, extension, etc) have a historical bias against the deprived lots. All of these are collapsing anyway (Jha, 2003). This has given an opportunity to the private sector including moneylenders to expand their business in recent times. Here lies the need of new strategies and institutions like SHGs and ensuring harassment free, timely institutional credit to the unreach through credit cards, viz. KCCs, etc.

Yet, another interesting observation was that SHGs used to extend small loans to the members at 2 – 5 per cent monthly rate of interest for contingent needs and also to assist household industries among the group members. Quite a few SHGs extended loans to non-members but only at higher rate of interest, i.e., 5 – 10 per cent monthly rate of interest. The increasing tendency of some of the SHGs to provide high interest loan to outsiders has been instrumental in promoting a section of the SHGs to the club of moneylenders (minus any greed for land).

It is significant to note that during the past 3 years, 12 households (3 households in the current year) had borrowed money from moneylenders against mortgage of land. As reported by the households, the incidence of loan against mortgage of properties/land was much higher in the years prior to their membership with SHGs.

There is a clear indication that in the rural areas of Assam, the moneylender is regaining their lost ground slowly but steadily. It is partly because public sector banks have already started withdrawing from certain activities (including extension of small loans) particularly from rural lending in remote areas. The RRBs originally meant for rural lending (priority sector lending) have started to emphasise on lending to the salaried people for consumer loans. The cooperative credit infrastructure has been found to be miserably poor and almost on the verge of withering away.

During the past 3 years, the sample households borrowed Rs. 8,07,200 from the banks (/ institutional sources). In the total loan drawn from banks, the share of loans against KCCs constituted nearly 25 per cent. The loan under the SGSY scheme (SHG – Bank linkages) constituted less than 7 per cent. The housing loan (including major repairing) constituted above 49 per cent, while the other purposes including business loan, scooter loan, etc constituted above 19 per cent. Direct bank loans were given to the better-off people with the provision of compulsory realization of monthly instalment from salary (in the case of salaried people) or against savings certificates / insurance policies.

The increasing tendency of the bankers to extend bigger loans against good security on the one hand and the limited access of KCCs and SHGs in Assam on the other, will definitely add to the miseries of the already marginalized class.

Quite a few households who had borrowed IRDP loans were found in default. Misuse of loans, low amount of initial investment which failed to generate sufficient amount of incremental income, flood havoc, political interference led transformation of the image of these loans as grant, etc were responsible for putting at least some of these defaulter households at a disadvantage. Banks stopped extending loans to many villages by labelling them as 'defaulter village'. Off and on, loan compromise schemes were announced for easy repayment of old dues. However, in these cases of settlements, as said by the bank officials, the loanee households will not get any loans from banks in near future. The response to the scheme of repayment of old debt in easy instalments is, however, extremely poor.

It can be recalled here that the Committee to Review Arrangements for Institutional Credit for Agriculture and Rural Development (1979) cautioned that '.... Facile credit results not only in the locking up of funds and stagnation of lending agencies, but the borrowers also suffer in the process as a result of increased burden of unproductive debt which prevents them from borrowing again. The danger of credit becoming a burden, instead of an instrument for uplift, is greater in the case of loans to the vulnerable sections of the rural community'.

Many SHGs denied membership to defaulter persons thinking that it will reduce their chances of getting loans from banks. Similarly, quite a few households borrowed from the moneylenders against mortgage of land failed to release land for quite some times. It seems that both productive as well as unproductive loans were restricting the economic operations of a section of the weaker communities alike. Proper utilization of loan and repayment in time is very important which sometimes need counseling and managerial skill upgradation – the infrastructure of which is, at present, missing in the state of Assam. On the one hand, loans given against KCCs and SHGs have generated sufficient enthusiasm and entrepreneurial venture in some parts, while wrong application of the IRDP/SGSY schemes put some loanees at a disadvantage, on the other. It seems that the volume of debt, the share of productive debt in total debt, etc are important issues, but equally important issues are also the presence of other vital infrastructural linkages.

Under the IRDP scheme, subsidized micro credit for creation of critical minimum asset- base among the 'landless and other assetless' poor was tried for. But the programme could not achieve any noteworthy success due to lack of involvement of the local people with the scheme, lack of coordination between government agencies, partisan local political interests, wrong selection of economic activities/beneficiaries, high level of corruption at the implementation level and flood devastation. In this regard, SHG movement is a completely different approach towards poverty eradication/livelihood development. 'Being self supporting, self governing organization, they are devoid of bureaucratization and politicization'. SHG encourages most economic use of the group funds among the members. However, many of the SHG members were unskilled, illiterate, and placed in the remote villages without vital market linkages, and other capacity building exercises so as to derive maximum benefits in terms of generating productive employment, raising agricultural yield, and exploiting hidden opportunities in cottage and small industries in the rural areas.

In the flood affected areas of Assam, MFIs or SHGs to be successful, appropriate insurance coverage of loan assets including standing crops urgently needs to be evolved, the culture of which is, at present, missing in rural Assam. The adequate insurance services can also provide 'survival' security to a MFI (/SHG) as much as to its clients.

It was reported that a large number of potential borrowers have submitted proposals for loan. Quite a few 'direct loan' proposals remained unattended year after year only due to the fact that the applicants could not provide collateral security (in spite of the fact that they were ready to deposit documents of immovable property to the bank). A larger number of proposals for PMRY (DIC, etc) loans remained unfulfilled either due to government's resource crunch or bank's reluctance to comply with. The loan proposals varied from extension of small/medium tea gardens to fishery, agro-service centre, livestock, auto-rickshaw or to launching a small garments factory. Needless to say that the task before the bank is formidable and complex as it has to deal with two diverse challenges, viz addressing the basic problems of rural development and transforming some areas of agricultural sector globally competitive. Today, institutional credit agencies required to deal with two distinct clientele groups: credit needs of the millions of 'subsistence farmers and artisans and much higher volume of credit required by a small section for practicing capital intensive, export-oriented agriculture such as tea, coffee, oranges, ginger and spices. However, the twin problems of high transaction costs (particularly in the former case) and poor repayment performance would need to be tackled first, if a vibrant credit delivery system specifically designed to meet the development imperatives is to be evolved (Agarwal et al, 1997 and Majumdar, 1997).

It is unrealistic to think that the commercial banks can revitalize agricultural credit delivery without a completely revamped extension services system (Ghosh, 2005). In Assam, recovery ratio was found extremely poor against the directed loans. However, government machineries – politicians and bureaucrats — have not yet realized the serious consequences of unhealthy repayment culture in the state and consequently, bankers' reluctance to extend developmental/ productive loans in rural areas. Even the academicians of the region were seen holding seminars and conferences on the other related important issues like region's relatively low percentage share of agricultural credit and poor credit-deposit ratio, etc, but little attention was given to the mounting problem of overdues which has already pushed the cooperative sector almost in 'death bed'.

Academics, politicians, bank staff and NGOs (FMCs / Women organizations / PRIs, etc) must come forward in their capacities in a more integrated manner so as to create an atmosphere for relationship banking — to foster a better linkage between input and output markets in the state — without which no radical changes can be brought in the standard of living of the mass people.

In spite of bringing about some positive changes in the society, it can not be denied the fact that the SHG movement in the region by maintaining high interest culture of the informal sector has also made the moneylender's job easier and tolerable even to the eyes of the die-hard critics including NGOs in the region. Three crucial findings of the present study which need immediate corrective measures were: (i) resurgence of the 'land greedy' moneylenders, (ii) nearly reintroduction of the class banking in the rural credit market and (iii) The growth of SHGs has led to drying up of the interest free sources like 'friends and relatives', since groups were mostly formed by the closely related members (affinity group). The most worrying feature was, however, the 'informal group loans' which carried very high rate of interest.

•

References

1. Agarwal, K.P., Puhazhendhi, V and Satyasai, K J S (1997), 'Gearing Rural Credit for the Twenty-First Century', EPW, October 18-24.
2. Ghosh, D N (2005), 'A Policy Approach for Agricultural Lending' EPW, January 8.
3. Government of India (1996), 'Concurrent Evaluation of IRDP Report (1995-96), Ministry of Rural Development.
4. Jha, D, (2003), 'Policy Drift in Agriculture' EPW, November 22.
5. Majumdar, N.A. (1997), 'Overhauling the Somnolent Rural Credit System', EPW, October 18-24.
6. Purkayastha, G., (2004), 'Dimensions of Human Development and Rural Indebtedness in North East India', Anmol Publications Pvt. Ltd., New Delhi
7. Purkaystha, G. (1997), 'Rural Labour Indebtedness In Assam', Mohit Publications, New Delhi.
8. RBI (1981), Committee to Review Arrangements for Institutional Credit for Agriculture and Rural Development (1979), Bombay.

Index